4/July '08

DANCE
SASKATCHEWAN

SASKATCHEWAN
LOTTERIES

BOX 8789 SASKATOON, SASKATCHEWAN
CANADA S7K 6S6 PH. (306) 931-8480
TOLL FREE NUMBER: 1-800-667-8480

CLASS ACT

CLASS ACT

THE JAZZ LIFE OF CHOREOGRAPHER

Cholly Atkins

CHOLLY ATKINS
AND
JACQUI MALONE

COLUMBIA UNIVERSITY PRESS

NEW YORK

Columbia University Press
Publishers Since 1893
New York   Chichester, West Sussex

Library of Congress Cataloging-in-Publication Data
Atkins, Cholly.
    Class act : the jazz life of choreographer Cholly Atkins / Cholly
Atkins and Jacqui Malone.
        p.   cm.
    Includes bibliographical references (p.   ) and index.
    ISBN 0–231–12364–7 (cloth)
    1. Atkins, Cholly. 2. Choreographers—United States—Biography. 3.
Dancers—United States—Biography. 4. Jazz dance—United
States—History.   I. Malone, Jacqui. II. Title.
  GV1785.A84 A3 2001
  792.8'2'092—dc21

                                                    00–010606

Designed by Brady McNamara
Casebound editions of Columbia University Press books are
printed on permanent and durable acid-free paper.
Printed in the United States of America
c 10 9 8 7 6 5 4 3 2 1

2010-064

For Maye Atkinson

and
to the memory of

CHRISTINE ATKINSON
SPENCER ATKINSON
DOTTY SAULTERS

and

LILLIAN GORDON GREEN

Contents

Preface and Acknowledgments

After hours at the Mile High Tap Summit in Boulder, Colorado, in July 1987, tap dancer Dianne Walker and I were discussing *Over the Top to Bebop*, a documentary featuring the class act tap team Coles and Atkins. Dianne stunned me by asking if I knew that Cholly Atkins was the guy who coached the Motown groups.

Not only was I amazed to find out that a tap dancer had been the in-house choreographer at Motown but, given the overwhelming success of the company, I couldn't figure out why his role there was such a well-kept secret. I had come of age in the sixties listening to Motown groups and imitating their steps at house parties. I had read the liner notes to numerous Motown albums and seen all of the Temptations' and Supremes' television specials. I also had a copy of the documentary *Motown 25*. Cholly Atkins was not even mentioned in any of these obvious sources.

A few months after the festival, I enrolled in a wonderful graduate course called American Tap Dance, taught by dance historian and critic Sally Sommer. My term paper, "Let the Punishment Fit the Crime: The Vocal Choreography of Cholly Atkins," was a first attempt to analyze the impact of Cholly's work. The most informative material at that time was in Marshall and Jean Stearns's *Jazz Dance: The Story of American Vernacular Dance* and Nelson George's *Where Did Our Love Go?: The Rise and Fall of the Motown Sound*.

Those two sources helped me formulate the initial outline for the paper, but I also consulted numerous books on Motown, videos that featured Cholly's choreography, and documentaries that included interview footage with him. Still there remained many unanswered questions. I could not piece his career together in a way that helped me understand just how he created a new dance genre and how that form fit into the evolution of American vernacular dance.

It was clear that I needed to go directly to the source to pull everything together. Honi and Marion Coles, whom I'd already met, graciously arranged for me to talk with Cholly by phone in January 1988. A few months later, when he was visiting New York, they set up a second interview at their home in Queens. We hit it off right away.

Getting to know Cholly has been an incredible experience. He is a wise, warm, and very funny man, who is one of the most organized persons I've ever met. I was amazed to find that practically every newspaper article ever written about him was neatly placed in his closet along with dozens of photographs, flyers, and programs. Some of them dated back to the thirties.

When I first started researching Cholly's career in the late eighties, it was clear that his story was one that greatly needed to be told, not only because he is one of our unsung heroes but also because his life brings together so many art forms that define twentieth-century American culture: jazz dance, jazz music, rhythm and blues, musical theater, and rhythm tap.

At the time he was not interested in a book, so I asked if I could include a chapter about his career in *Steppin' on the Blues: The Visible Rhythms of African American Dance*, published in 1996. Subsequently, we taped several six-hour sessions about his life and views on dance. *Steppin' on the Blues* helped me formulate a historical framework for Cholly's contribution to American culture and enabled me to see him as essentially a *jazz* dance artist, whose training and early professional experiences placed him solidly within a jazz music context. By that time I'd thought a lot about the interrelatedness of dancers, musicians, and singers in African American culture.

In the meantime, between 1988 and 1994, Cholly and I worked together on a series of projects, including his press kit, grant proposals, workshops at several colleges and universities, and panel presentations at Lincoln Center and the Smithsonian Institution. I also traveled to Boulder, Colorado and Portland, Oregon to document his classes at tap festivals. Through the years we developed a wonderful friendship, out of which this book grew.

In the mid-nineties, with the support of a Ford Foundation grant, I traveled to several states to talk with people who had played instrumental roles in his career, and when those interviews were combined with previous ones, Ted Panken's excellent transcriptions yielded two thousand pages of material. A John Simon Guggenheim Fellowship and a Queens College Presidential Research Award made it possible for me to take time off from teaching to shape those pages into a narrative.

Cholly had made it clear right from the beginning that he wanted me not only to write the book but also to decide on the format. So the major question I had to confront then was how to shape that material into a story; how to render the story most appealingly, giving texture to the lived experience; and how to give it the density of historical accuracy.

Since my only writing experience had been as a historian, the idea of writing in another person's voice seemed impossible. So I began reading biographies and autobiographies in search of the best narrative style. After I'd combed through the transcriptions and other materials many times, it was clear that the story was begging to be told in Cholly's voice so that the reader would be able to hear him talking and to feel the full complexity of his nuanced responses to real people and events.

Class Act draws from many sources including interviews, books, articles, films, panel proceedings, and videos. It is not a memoir but a study of the cultural milieu through which Cholly moved. Although many of the sentences can be traced to transcriptions of his words, I also taught myself to write in his voice, blended my research and writings on American vernacular dance, and drew from my upbringing in African American culture, where I experienced the flavor and style of black American expression and heard the timbre of black American speech. This was not to falsify his story but to amplify it. As I completed the chapters, I read them to Cholly over the phone to make sure I was not misrepresenting the events of his life. Many people helped fill in pieces of this narrative, but Marion Coles and Leonard Reed played monumental roles in tying together loose ends and helping me to define a golden era in American culture.

I have tried to create a narrative that is personal and honest, yet valuable as a piece of dance literature that chronicles the career path of a jazz dance artist who comes of age in the early thirties, struggles through the divorce of jazz music and dance in the late forties and fifties, and rises to create a classic dance genre that has stood the test of time and influenced people all over the world.

I wish to extend warm thanks to the following people who graciously agreed to interviews: Marion Coles, Charles "Honi" Coles, Maye Atkinson, Evelyn Atkinson, Charles Atkinson II, Leonard Reed, Buster Brown, Jean Stearns, Bertye Lou Wood, Norma Miller, LeRoy Myers, Jimmy Peyton, Johnny Allen, Earl Carroll, Jan Corbett, Esther Gordy Edwards, Mary Wilson, Gladys Knight, Merald "Bubba" Knight, Melvin Franklin, Eddie Levert, Sammy Strain, Pete Moore, Harvey Fuqua, Walter Williams, Otis Williams, Richard Street, Ron Tyson, Melissa Hathaway, Martha Jordan, Pauline Jones, and LaVaughn Robinson.

Special thanks to colleagues and friends for their knowledge, support, and encouragement: C. Daniel Dawson, John F. Szwed, Karen Hewitt, Robert Farris Thompson, William Ferris, Deborah Willis, Erness Brody, Beverly Bruce, Isabelle Coles Dunbar, Janice Monsanto, Jill Williams, Leroy Williams, Hank Smith, Dianne Walker, Sally Sommer, Eleanor Harris, Brent Edwards, Barbara Reed, Susan Goldbetter, Steve Good, Donna Good, Vickie Powell, Judi Moore Latta, Joseph Latta, Delilah Jackson, Mary Gordon, Arthur Cash, Ernie Smith, LaVern Moore, Raki Jones, Charmaine Warren, Alverta Barksdale, Melba Huber, Jo Rowan, D'Lana Lockett, John Bedford, J. C. Sylvan, Nicole Stahlmann, and Jonathan Kahn. For their professionalism and kindness, I applaud Alan H. Goldberg and Carolyn Evans of Modernage Custom Imaging Labs. Others who helped in a variety of ways are Ted Panken, Joe Guercio, Jimmy Slyde, Phil Groia,

Richard Slotkin, Ronnell Bright, Sally Banes, Alice Atkinson, Chuckie Atkins, Deborah Kodish, Germaine Ingram, Claudette Robinson, Rob Gibson, Dan Morgenstern, Albert Murray, Louie Bellson, Marilyn LeVine, Jack Bradley, Al Greenberg, Hortense Allen Jordan, John Pearson Kelly, Harold Davis, Michael Cogswell, Peggy Schein, Jim Huffman, Karen Rosen, Chuck Stewart, Harry Weinger, Jane Goldberg, Ernest Brown, Frank Driggs, Jackie Alper, Wayne McWorter, Nancy Toff, Ralph Tavares, Mabel Lee, Lisa Kahane, Bernice Johnson, and Patricia Perrier.

To Queens College, which supported this project with a leave of absence and a Presidential Research Award; to administrators Allen Sessoms, Ray Erickson, and John Thorpe; and to my colleagues in the Department of Drama, Theater and Dance, I offer my thanks.

I extend my gratitude to the staffs of the Institute of Jazz Studies, the Schomburg Center for Research in Black Culture, the Buffalo and Erie County Historical Society, the Motown Archives, the Michael Ochs Archives, the African American Museum Project at the Smithsonian Institution, the Louis Armstrong Archives at Queens College, Jazz at Lincoln Center, and the Center for Jazz Studies at Columbia University.

For their generous support, I am pleased to acknowledge the Ford Foundation and the John Simon Guggenheim Foundation.

I am indebted to the O'Jays and the Manhattans, who welcomed me to several vocal choreography rehearsals. To Bubba Knight, who literally spent hours talking about Cholly's impact on the career of Gladys Knight and the Pips, I offer a huge thank you.

Many thanks to our editor, Jennifer Crewe; her assistant, Jennifer Barager; our manuscript editor, Leslie Kriesel; and the staff of Columbia University Press for their care, sensitivity, and exceptional professionalism. Working with them has been a tremendous pleasure for both of us.

Most special thanks to Andy Davis for his kindness, patience, good humor, and good work.

I am deeply grateful to Sheila Biddle, Roger Abrahams, Sali Ann Kriegsman, and Jim Bartow for their support and strong belief in this book. I also wish to thank my sisters, Barbara Halsey and Linda Malone-Colon; my wonderful parents, Maggie and Fred Malone, who supported me in countless ways; my sons, Douglass and Gabriel; and my partner and friend, Robert O'Meally, whose penetrating questions made this a better narrative.

I am profoundly grateful to Maye Atkinson and Leonard Reed, my wonderful friends and West Coast "correspondents," and to Marion Coles, my "New York research assistant and big sister," who told me to call her any time of the day or night for help. Their trust, support, and love have truly been phenomenal.

Finally, many thanks to my friend and coauthor, Cholly Atkins, for sharing his stories with me and now with our readers. Those conversations I will treasure always.

—*Jacqui Malone*

When I look back over seven decades in American show business, there are literally hundreds of people who have touched my life in a special way. First, to all of the dancers, musicians, singers, and producers in the world of jazz who shaped my training and gave me the inspiration to perform with class and style, I am deeply grateful. Several people were extraordinarily helpful to me during those early years: Bill Robinson, Leonard Reed, Honi Coles, Count Basie, Cab Calloway, Louis Armstrong, Lil Hardin, Billy Eckstine, Pete Nugent, the Mills Brothers, Sy Oliver, and Jimmy Crawford.

To all of my R & B clients, from the early fifties into the new millennium, a huge thank you for allowing me to "crack that whip," and for sharing many hours of creativity, warm exchange, laughter, and plain hard work. Your commitment to mastering the Cholly Atkins technique has made it possible to showcase my choreography all over the world. For that I am most appreciative.

The process of coaching and helping to produce shows for rhythm and blues artists has enabled me to collaborate with some of the best minds in the business. Among them are the late Maurice King, Gil Askey, Harvey Fuqua, Johnny Allen, Dennis Williams, Benjamin Wright,

Shelly Berger, Don Peake, and Billie Bullock. I salute you and thank you for our many successes through the years.

I extend my sincere appreciation to Sali Ann Kriegsman, Dianne Walker, and Joe Delaney for their support and to my brothers, the Copasetics, for a whole bunch of good times! Much gratitude to extended family members: Jacqui Malone, Bob O'Meally, and their two sons, Gabe and Doug; my goddaughter, Patricia Pennix, and her parents, Lucy and Buddy; my friends, Lou and Estella Ragland, Susan Martin, and Bob and Jeannie Johnston; and especially, my second family for more than fifty years, Honi Coles, Marion Edwards Coles, and Isabelle Coles Dunbar.

Finally, heartfelt thanks to my immediate family members who have showered me with love and support and helped make all things possible: Gloria Harrison, Delores Sherrod, Curtis Sherrod, Shawn Sherrod; Ron and Maria Atkinson; Chuckie and Alice Atkinson and their three daughters, Lauren, Lynette, and Erin; Hazel Willis, Cherry and Cindy Atkinson; my nephew and namesake, Charles Atkinson II; Evie Atkinson, Spencer Atkinson, and my dear mother, Christine Atkinson. To Sarge, my wife and number one press agent, who is always there to say, "You can do it," I am forever grateful.

—*Cholly Atkins*

Introduction

He can dance as well as those kids on Soul Train. . . . *I mean he was showing us how to moonwalk before Michael Jackson was doing it. And when you can be that age and outdance anybody . . . you're going to be around.* —RICHARD STREET

This is a book about one of America's most influential twentieth-century dance masters, Cholly Atkins. The broad spectrum of American dance figures includes very few artists who have had a comparable impact on the evolution of indigenous American dance forms and their dissemination to a worldwide audience.

From the 1920s through most of the 1940s, American tap dance in the jazz/rhythm tradition experienced its heyday. Suddenly in the late forties, the bottom dropped out for many rhythm tap dancers who had established successful careers in vaudeville, in musicals, and with big bands. By the sixties, even Marshall Stearns, the great champion and chronicler of American vernacular dance, wondered in what form classic jazz dance would survive.[1]

Although we know now that black vernacular dance evolves in a cyclical pattern, no one could have predicted in the sixties that dance movements from the twenties, thirties, and forties would live on through the nineties and beyond in many of the performance traditions that span African American culture. The lively existence of such black dancing vocal groups as the Temptations, the O'Jays, and Gladys Knight and the Pips has helped preserve and recycle much of the vocabulary of classic jazz dance, including some tap, and the man largely responsible for this particular cultural transference is Cholly Atkins. He is America's quintessential jazz dance artist.

Beginning in 1929, Cholly sharpened his skills as a jazz dancer and choreographer on the stages of traveling shows, nightclubs, and theaters throughout the country. His most enduring partnership was formed in the mid-forties with the high-speed rhythm tap dancer Charles "Honi" Coles. This class act, now one of the most celebrated tap dance teams of the twentieth century, toured with many bands including those of Count Basie, Louis Armstrong, Cab Calloway, and Billy Eckstine. Coles and Atkins worked together throughout the forties and fifties, until tap jobs became almost nonexistent.

During the lean years, Cholly was building a new kind of dance career with a new kind of dance form. As early as 1955, he periodically coached doo-wop groups, who were replacing variety shows at theaters around the country. With the apparent demise of tap dancing, Cholly easily made the transition from tap to rhythm and blues, and by 1965 he was staff choreographer at Motown Records. From this vantage point, he trained Motown's recording artists to perform choreographed visualizations of their music.

Cholly Atkins set the standard for presenting America's leading rhythm-and-blues singers and created a unique dance genre. Vocal choreography is a newly recognized movement form designed specifically for singers. It is professionally choreographed dance that takes into account such factors as breathing, pacing, the use of microphones, and a subtle and complex approach to music.

Thanks to his expertise and exposure, he helped to keep much American vernacular dance alive in the choreography of popular vocal groups. His superb "vocal choreography" might appear natural and effortless, but it is very difficult to execute. The body is always doing something that is rhythmically different from the voice.

Vocal choreography is characterized by precise visual polyrhythms. The movement is continuous: even when the backup singers are not in the mike area, they are still performing interesting steps derived from authentic jazz movements, especially black chorus line dancing of the twenties, thirties, and forties.

Sometimes his work includes actual tap moves, like cross steps, over the top, and trenches done in a jazz manner. Performances by Gladys Knight and the Pips, in particular, embody elements of tap's class act tradition, minus the taps: precision, detached coolness, elegance, flawless execution, and dignity. Many of the leaning pull-ups, casual slides, and gliding turns so characteristic of performances by Coles and Atkins appear over and over in the Pips' choreography.

The Atkins contribution to American culture has been extraordinarily significant. He made polished performers out of rock-and-roll singers who started with a hit single and raw ambition. And he taught them to *perform* their music, not by retelling a song's storyline in predictable pantomime, but by punctuating it with rhythmical dance steps, turns, and gestures drawn from the rich bedrock of American vernacular dance.

Thoroughly versed in twentieth-century African American dance forms, from social dances like the Charleston to street-corner (and then stage) sensations like rhythm tap, Cholly gave his singing groups a depth and appeal that was not always present in their tunes and lyrics. Without knowing it, popular groups of the sixties, seventies, eighties, and nineties were performing updated versions of dances of the forties, thirties, and twenties—classic jazz dances—and projecting them to a larger audience than ever before. Marshall and Jean Stearns noted, "In whatever shape and form his steps materialized on stage, they became immediately enshrined in the hearts of adoring teenage audiences. Thus these vernacular movements, simplified and reinterpreted, took on a new and widespread life."[2]

Television, the "ultimate drum," broadcast black American vernacular dances into American homes from coast to coast. At its peak in the sixties, Dick Clark's *American Bandstand*, with its rock-and-roll dance hall format that showcased singers as well as the latest dance crazes, was televised over 105 stations, reaching approximately 20 million teenagers.[3] In the seventies and eighties, *Soul Train*, with its similar format, joined *American Bandstand* in continuing to keep millions of American youths abreast of the latest dance steps performed both by singers and by the show's hired teenagers. Like the *Motor*

Town Revue, these television shows, very often presenting Cholly's work (and its imitations), have helped keep black vernacular dance alive and in front of a growing audience.

For over twenty years, black stars also have sung and performed his vocal choreography in international concerts and in films, spreading these dance steps to a worldwide audience. Meanwhile, back home, African Americans copied their idols' steps and "moves," adapting them for talent shows and house parties—reclaiming material that had come full circle back to its vernacular source.

Since his years at Motown, Cholly has won many awards for his contribution to the "class act" tradition in American tap dance, numerous gold records for vocal choreography, and a 1989 Tony Award for his choreography in the Broadway musical *Black and Blue*. In 1993, the National Endowment for the Arts recognized Cholly Atkins as a national treasure by awarding him a three-year Choreographers Fellowship, its most prestigious dance grant. During 1994, the Smithsonian Institution's Center for African American History and Culture sponsored a special tribute at the Hirshhorn Museum, "From Tap to R & B: Celebrating Choreographer Cholly Atkins." There he became the first recipient of the Elder Mentors Award. That same year he was inducted into the Alabama Jazz Hall of Fame.

At the Fifth Annual American Choreography Awards (formerly the Fosses) in Los Angeles, he was given the 1998 Innovator Award. Also in 1998, Cholly won the Heroes and Legends Pacesetter Award. During the spring of 1999, he traveled to Oklahoma City University to receive the "Living Treasure in American Dance" award from OCU's School of American Dance, the first dance program of its kind anywhere. Most recently he was selected as one of *America's Irreplaceable Dance Treasures: The First 100* by the Dance Heritage Coalition, an alliance of several national dance collections that are committed to documenting and preserving America's dance.

At eighty-seven, "Pop" Atkins, as he is affectionately called by his clients, continues to choreograph and stage acts for vocal groups and still says that he will dance "until he dies." Through his workshops at

American colleges, universities, and dance festivals, including Jacob's Pillow, he is enjoying a second career as educator and embracing the current generation of dance and music students. His legacy is one that bridges dance and musical genres and touches people of all ages. He is the ageless hoofer. This is his story.

NOTES

The epigraph for this introduction is from Danielle Masterson, "From the Roaring '20s to the Space Age," *Rhythm and Business* 1, no. 4 (June 1987): 36.

1. Marshall and Jean Stearns, *Jazz Dance: The Story of American Vernacular Dance* (New York: Macmillan, 1968), 358–362.

2. Ibid., 360.

3. Art Cromwell, *Watch Me Move!* (KCET, Los Angeles, 1986); Arnold Shaw, *The Rockin' 50's* (New York: Hawthorn, 1974; reprint, New York: Da Capo, 1987), 176.

CLASS ACT

GOING NORTH

One evening Maye and I were leaving the Apollo and ran into a friend of mine, Marghuerite Mays, the former wife of Willie Mays, the great ball player. She said, "Cholly, I have a group I want you to work with. I'm planning to make big stars out of them." I said, "Well, what do you want me to do?" She said, "They're opening here next week." "Next week?! You expect me to get them ready in a *week*?!"

Now, the Pips had just come up from Atlanta, so they didn't know about Coles and Atkins and they weren't familiar with my choreography for the groups. None of them had seen the Cadillacs, for example. But, Marghuerite really talked me up; told them how their act lacked class and how I was gonna take care of that. Then she brought them by the studio where I was rehearsing. Bubba said he saw me over there in the corner sweating and dancing and carrying on, and he said, "*This* is the guy who's gonna give us class?"

We started working that same day. I told Marghuerite, "Okay, you can leave now. I'll take it from here." I asked them to show me what they could do dancewise, which wasn't much. Then I said, "All right, put on your thinking caps. Do exactly as I tell you." But I was gentle with them. Step by step, I broke the material down, then we'd polish the whole phrase. They just mimicked everything I did and I could see immediately that they were sharp and eager to learn.

There was a mutual respect and a love that developed between us right away. They had that same kind of sophistication as the Cadillacs. Even if they tried to be funky, they did it in a sophisticated way. But there was a lot to tighten up in their act, because in addition to the choreography, they needed theatrical etiquette—the things that performers are supposed to know about presenting themselves to an audience.

Marghuerite rented a little studio for us to rehearse in each day and when our time ran out there, we would pack up and head on over to my place, move the rugs, push all the furniture back, and keep working. Man, we had scuff marks all over the floor. When it was time for Maye to come home from work, we'd be throwing the windows up and running around trying to put everything back in place. When she came in, the Pips were sitting there covered with sweat. The place smelled like a locker room. But Maye was so patient and supportive. She would put all the little knickknacks back in their right spots, then sit down and critique whatever new steps they had learned.

That week leading into the Apollo date I hardly got any sleep because we were working all day and into the night. Gil Askey was assisting me as musical coach. And it was like a nonstop thing. But when they hit that stage at the Apollo, those Pips were on the money. They were decked out in black tuxedos with shiny linings. Marghuerite had one of her gowns cut down for Gladys, so she was dressed to the nines, too.

"Giving Up" turned the place out. The guys were hitting everything right on the button. Gladys was strutting the stage, doing her thing, and the Pips were doing their little dancing on the side. At one point they sang, "Giving up!," there was a pause, then they unbuttoned those jackets, threw their arms up, and did a little hip thrust. That's all it took. When the girls saw that red lining, they went berserk! You could hardly hear the singing. From that moment, we never looked back! Gladys Knight and the Pips became my number one group.

I can't remember a period in my life when I didn't dance. As a matter of fact, I won a Charleston contest at a local theater when I was ten. Around 1923. The Charleston had become very popular and there were contests all over Buffalo. First prize was about five or ten dollars. There was some promoter who had a bunch of kids that would participate in these contests and everybody who could dance would try to make them all. You'd win some and lose some. Eventually I learned all those jazz dances! See, my mother was an excellent dancer. At one time she won a cup for ballroom dancing. I guess that's where I got it from.

Mama used to have me and my brother, Spencer, get up and dance to the Victrola when we were five and six years old. She'd wind up the gramophone, put those blues records on, and we'd dance for her friends. I'd be showing my little steps, carrying on like a yard dog. I didn't know what I was doing!

I was almost seven when I moved with my mother and brother to New York. By that time my parents, Christine Woods and Sylvan Atkinson, had broken up. Mama met him at a party in South Carolina, when he was there on some sort of construction job. She had grown up in Westminster, South Carolina. His folks were originally from Georgia, but at some point they all moved to Chicago. Not too long after they got married, my father landed a job in the steel plant down in Pratt City, Alabama, which is a suburb of Birmingham. That's where I was born, on September 30, 1913.

Why my parents left Alabama has never been made clear to me. Maybe the plant was laying off people. I guess mostly during those days, people would migrate to wherever the work was. Our family moved on to Atlanta, Georgia, and during that period my brother was born.

Since I was so young when my father was still around, I don't remember playing with him at all. In fact, I don't have any recollection of a father-and-son relationship. A few things that happened when I was four do stand out in my mind, because they were so strange. For instance, I only met a couple of relatives on my father's side of the family. Two light-skinned teenagers came to visit us when I was real small, before my father left.

But that was a short visit, and I don't recall anybody else. No other cousins, no grandmothers, no uncles or aunts. I know all of this hap-

pened around the beginning of World War I, because when I think
back on it, one of my mother's brothers went into the army and left
his motorcycle parked on our porch. Mama would let us climb up on
it and play.

My father's family was what they used to call "uppity"-type people,
pretty well-to-do. I don't know what they were into or whether they inherited their wealth or worked for it, but the breakup between my parents was basically a class issue. They were disappointed, I guess, that
my mama didn't measure up to their standards, and from what she told
me, they never wanted him to marry her and refused to accept her as
part of their family. I guess it was around 1917 when my father left Atlanta with my mother's brother, Uncle Joe, to find a job in the Chicago meat-packing business. But I have no memory of their departure.
Years later I learned from Mama that they couldn't get any work and
when he wanted to come back to us, his family insisted that he stay
there. Uncle Joe said he waited a few days for him because my father
really wanted to leave. They were planning to hobo back together.

My father pleaded with Uncle Joe to wait until he could make his
family understand, although I don't see what the big deal was. That
was never explained to me. All I know is that my uncle finally decided to go without him, because he figured he'd been putting it off long
enough and wanted to get back to his own family. He said my father
was running down the railroad tracks, crying and yelling, "Please
don't leave me! Don't go!"

I never heard from him again. Many years later one of my mother's brothers told her that he had died, but there was no word from his
relatives. I don't know what was happening back in those days as far as
broken families were concerned. It seems like people didn't think
about child support. They just accepted it and went on with their lives
as best they could. That's why I always admired my mother, because
she scuffled like crazy with the two of us, and we never got into any
major trouble.

All my life I've wondered what would make a father leave his two
young kids and never contact them. Maybe he saw me during one of
those times when I was working in Chicago. That I'll never know. But

even if he did, he might not have known who I was since I had changed my name from Charles Atkinson to Cholly Atkins. Eventually Mama found out that he had remarried and had two daughters. She used to tell me if I was dancing in Chicago, "Be careful fooling around down there, you might be making it with your own sister!" My mama was something else.

Our house in Atlanta was located just below the campus of AU, Atlanta University. We were set down in a little valley, like, and along the side of the campus is where Spencer and I used to play. That was right on our street. Mama would run around with me and my brother on the campus and during the summer she'd play catch with us out on the grass.

There was a lady down the block who kept us while my mother went to work for this white family. Mama cooked, cleaned, the whole bit, and always cooked enough to bring home for our supper—greens, sweet potatoes, macaroni and cheese, black-eyed peas and rice. See, white folks ate all that stuff, too, and loved it! Now, you talking 'bout good. Mama could burn! She would come in with the little shopping bags of food, and my brother and I couldn't wait for her to get it on the table.

The lady she worked for had a sister who lived right next door and she also had someone to come in and cook and clean. I can't remember the family's name, but the housekeeper was Ethel Moore. She and my mother became tight buddies. Ethel was married and also had two sons, who were about the same ages as me and Spencer. Eventually we moved to their neighborhood and her older son, Ivor, became my best friend. We called him Snook. Well, Ethel's brother and my mother got together, and they became an item, you see. I think he had part-ownership in some kind of shooting gallery.

Now these two sisters, who had the houses, decided to move to Buffalo with their relatives and they asked my mother and Ethel to go, too. They were very wealthy and made all the arrangements. So Ethel moved up first, found a house, then we moved. And later my mother's boyfriend joined us and he and Mama got married in Buffalo, where he started working for the Pullman Company.

I remember when we first went up north, we stayed in Ethel's house for a few days, then we moved in a place down the street. And right at that time, across the street from us, they were building a new public school, P.S. 75. I had gone to kindergarten and first grade in Atlanta, but I was skipped, so I started P.S. 75 as a third grader when I was seven. Spencer and my cousins, Snook and Jackie, went there, too.

We also lived close to Bond Bakery where Mama could get six loaves of yesterday's bread for a quarter. Six loaves! You could smell that bread for blocks and blocks and blocks. And at night they'd be baking, and you'd have your windows open and you'd smell that bread and have to get up. You just *had* to make a sandwich or something.

My brother and I would have long talks before we went to sleep. Maybe discuss our plans for the next day. There were a lot of things we'd do together as young kids . . . go to Sunday school or go roller skating. We'd both come home right after school, do our chores, and then go out to play. That was Mama's rule. So by the time she and my stepfather got home, everything would be cleaned up. No dirty dishes, no unmade beds, no dirt on the floor. We'd run that little jive sweeper across the floor or maybe go to the store to pick up some bread. A lot of the time I used to help Spencer with his homework.

Until I was about ten years old, we'd spend most summers with my mother's parents in Westminster, South Carolina. Mama would take us down by train, stay a day or two, then come back at the end of the summer and pick us up in time for school. When we got down to the Mason-Dixon line, we had to change trains and go to the "back of the bus," as they say. But at that age, the reason why was not that obvious to us. We really didn't understand what was happening, because our whole environment in Buffalo was integrated.

My brother and I used to have a lot of fun down there with Mama's sisters and brothers. There were three children still at home, who were pretty close to our ages, Katherine, David Lee, and Thomas Alan. So we played with them. And Mama's older sisters would visit from Charlotte. My grandparents had a great big farm with a lot of land, a big garden, and a couple of big shade trees that had sheds underneath. Maybe ten or twelve feet from the back of the trees was a little stream and springhouses where they used to keep the milk. It was real cool underneath those trees near that water.

My grandmother's name was Emma Woods. We called her Mama. In fact, that's what everybody called her. We called my grandfather Papa, like his children did. But everybody else addressed him as Reverend Woods. I don't recall what his first name was. I think it was a common name, like George or William or something like that.

Papa was a minister, a farmer, and a carpenter . . . all around. He could hardly handle all the work he was asked to do, just a jack-of-all-trades. I remember a couple of times we went down there when my grandfather was working on a project, maybe some masonry. He would take all four boys to help him carry the bricks and do other things. And we'd have our little lunch, just like he would have his lunch.

You know what he used to do? Now, he didn't have a horse, so he'd put us in front of this plow, and he had little harnesses for all of us, and we'd pull it for him. It wasn't like a big field plow, but one just for his garden. He grew tomatoes, corn. Oh, they had cabbages and everything you can imagine in that garden. A lot of the food that we had on our table was grown right there. The other farmers would come by and bring more vegetables over; Mama would give them a bushel basket full of pears or something. Later when I read in school how people used to trade off food, it reminded me of that happening in my family.

My grandmother was tough when it came to discipline. One thing she would not tolerate was running away when you were getting a whipping. She would throw things at me and I'd be flying through the backyard—ninety miles an hour. She didn't stand for no fooling around, but we still had a lot of fun. She baked loads of sweets . . . made preserves. Mama was real nice about baking cookies and all kinds of goodies for us.

One time my grandmother was trying to teach me how to wring a chicken's neck. She needed a couple to cook for dinner, but she wanted them killed a particular way. So she said, "If you don't learn how to do this right, I'm gonna give you a whipping."

My grandfather had heard the whole thing, so he came running over. "Now, don't whip him, because I know why he can't do that.

See, one time there was a bluebird up in that tree right over there and Charles hit that bird with his slingshot and killed it. So, I told him, 'Boy, you shouldn't have killed that bird. He's going to come back to haunt you. You'll be trying to sleep at night and that bird will be flying around over your head.' "

For a long time I was really ashamed of the fact that I had killed that bluebird. I didn't think I would hit it. But after he told the story to my grandmother, Papa said, "That's why he can't kill the chicken, because the chicken reminds him of the bird." So she never bothered me no more about that. Besides, David Lee was three years older and he didn't mind doing it.

Mama used to take in laundry for a couple of rich families. They would bring their clothes there, she would wash and iron them, and they'd come pick them up. She never worked outside of the house. First of all, she had too many kids. And it was a big house. Then, she also had the chores of any farmer's wife . . . churning the milk, cleaning up, washing our clothes and her own kids' clothes. They had one of them big pots in the backyard, and they'd put their laundry in there and boil the water. We used to help get the logs to put underneath the thing to heat it up. Then she'd be up all hours with the iron; one of those big irons that they put on top of the stove. Most of the time we were down there she'd just be ironing and cooking around the clock.

And they had food for days! At every meal, the table was covered with all kinds of things. We might have chicken and ham, sausage and eggs, fried potatoes, grits—that was breakfast. Sometimes we would have different kinds of fish for dinner. There were some friends of Papa's that used to go fishing a lot, and they'd give him part of what they caught every time. I remember they'd come by the house in their wagons: "Reverend Woods, we've got some fish here for you." And Mama would take them and clean them, get all the scales off, cut them up, or whatever they do. Put salt and seasonings on them and take them down to the springhouse. You'd see hams and hogs hanging up in there. It was cool and they never spoiled. The milk and the eggs and everything else was in there.

Some mornings we'd go swimming in the pond across the road. Papa didn't want us to because they had snakes, like water moccasins, in there. Still, every chance we got, we'd sneak across the road and jump in anyway. It was fun times. We looked forward to going down to South Carolina and I have real pleasant memories of the rural life because everything changed for us there. It was strictly city life when we went back to Buffalo. Most of the roads in Westminster weren't even paved. Only the downtown areas were asphalt. All the others were strictly dirt.

I don't know what happened to my mother's sisters and brothers. When I got in show business, I was away from home a lot, so I lost contact with her family. And my grandparents died pretty young. In their early sixties. I know my grandmother died when she was sixty-two. But once in a while one of my mother's brothers would come to Buffalo. When I'd get a letter or talk to Mama on the phone, she would tell me, "Uncle Joe was through here." And after a while, there was no contact at all with the relatives.

Buffalo was a real melting pot when I was growing up. There were a lot of immigrants from Russia, Poland, Hungary, Germany, Czechoslovakia—you name it. Many of the sanitation people were Hungarians or Yugoslavians and the policemen were mostly Irish or Italian. You didn't usually find too many blacks in those jobs. Certain kinds of occupations were monopolized by one or two ethnic groups because everybody in political positions looked out for their own kind. You never saw any blacks working the city maintenance jobs. At least, that's the way it seemed to me.

Our folks were usually hired as teachers, bellhops, porters, or domestic workers. The law didn't say things had to be this way. It all happened because of politics. There were no segregation laws, as such. If the Italians were controlling the streetcars, all the drivers were Italian. If the Polish were controlling the sanitation department, the garbage collectors were all Polish.

We always lived in mixed neighborhoods. They were primarily Jewish or Italian or black, but they were still mixed. I remember going to my good friend Tony Scalato's house. We'd get snowed in, so I would sleep over and his mother would cook all that good spaghetti and sauce. She made her own bread and everything. It seemed like we'd be eating all night long. And the same thing when he'd come to my house. We'd sleep on the floor and the whole bit. I didn't know too much about prejudice until I got in show business and started traveling.

My brother always remembered more details about our childhood than I did. Although we didn't hang together so much as we got older and my crowd wasn't his crowd, there was a real brotherly thing, a warm thing going on between us. Spencer was more like Jackie, Snook's brother. So they used to be buddies. But don't get me wrong, Spencer and I were always tight, even though most of the time I was running around with Snook. Back then the community center was the main hangout spot for teenagers. Snook and I spent a lot of time on the basketball court, swimming, or playing games like dominoes and checkers. Sometimes we watched little movies. Other times speakers from the community would be invited in to give us talks about "keeping our noses clean" and becoming good citizens.

The center was run by this heavyset black man, Mr. Newman. He was such a nice person. But after a while he started to lose weight, and then he passed away. They brought in a white guy to replace him and then none of the kids, not even the white ones, came around as much. There was nothing wrong with the new guy, but he just didn't have the same kind of personality as Mr. Newman. I guess I was about twelve when he died. We were all devastated because the kids really loved that man.

By that time Snook and I had transferred to P.S. 47, which was an industrial preparation school. In other words, we had shop work half the day and academics the other half, but you had to be interviewed and your marks had to be real high to get in. It went from grades seven to nine. There were about five junior high schools like that around the city and most of the kids that came out of them went to Tech High, which was primarily geared toward students who might not go on to college. The school would prepare them to work in the sheet metal business, electrical business, woodworking—all those kinds of fields.

Part of the reason Snook and I wanted to go there was because getting into P.S. 47 was kind of a prestigious thing, but the other reason was because it had the best sports teams. All the athletic guys wanted to go to that school, especially the kids who were into basketball. At that time, we used to shovel the snow off of the playground court. There would be no nets up there. And in our little mackinaw winter coats and galoshes, we would be out there shooting the basketball with gloves on. That's how much we were into it!

P.S. 47 had a championship basketball team. Snook and I played all three years and we were also on the football, baseball, and track teams. We were into everything! I held the junior high hundred-yard-dash record for two years. I forget how fast I was, 10.4 or something like that, but pretty good. I really didn't like football so much, but basketball, track, and baseball, I loved. I usually pitched or played first base, but Mr. Russo made everybody learn all the positions.

He was a Russian immigrant who taught physical education and coached most of the teams. I remember he had an accent . . . a very nice man, very wonderful. Everybody loved him because he was just great with kids. He would put on musicals in the auditorium once or twice a year. They were like little variety-type shows. We had scripts and everybody had to learn their lines—little animal stories and things of that nature. I remember singing "Way down upon the Swanee River, far, far away . . ."—all that Uncle Tom stuff.

Mr. Russo put together a little elementary soft-shoe for three of us guys. He also knew about the cakewalk, struts, acrobatics, and a little bit about tap. Nothing complicated. We did a soft-shoe with taps on . . . just TIK-A-TA, TAK-A-TEE, TIK-A-TAK-A-KOO, PAH—anybody could do it, you know! At the time, I thought he was a good tap dancer, but when I think back on it there was no flow. The sound would be there, but you had to look real hard for the feeling. That was the first time I was introduced to any type of choreography. Most of the moves that he taught us were done in a jazz vein because he was familiar with all the American dance crazes. Surprisingly, he'd learned them in Russia!

Music was an important part of our education, even though 47 was an industrial school. Everybody had to have an instrument assigned to them if they were musically inclined. My cousin Snook always wanted to play a violin, so that's what he picked. I wanted a saxophone, but by the time I got to the instrument room, they were all gone.

See, the instruments were donated to the public schools. There was only a limited amount and the most popular ones would go fast. After I couldn't get a saxophone, I decided I'd take a clarinet—and they were all gone. Only a tuba and trombone were left, so I wound up taking the trombone. In addition to that, I had sight-reading and voice classes. Those lessons in junior high were the real foundation of my musical knowledge, because you *had* to go to your music classes. Those teachers didn't stand for any foolishness.

When school was closed, Snook and I still played a lot of sports. At 75, right around the corner, at the back of the school, there were handball courts. We'd go over there and play all day—go home, and come right back—because it was only a half block from where we lived. Sometimes we'd go and play basketball for a while, then play some more handball. That's how we became double handball champs in junior high.

Every day, during the summer, we were out there at 75. We would take a little break to eat. I'd go over to his house or he'd come over to my house. Most of the time we'd fix lunch for ourselves. Our mothers would leave a big pot of food in the icebox already cooked when they went to work and we'd just have to warm it up.

Snook's mother was very religious, and he used to go to church with her all the time. My brother and I went on Sundays, but Snook would even go to church in the evenings—choir practice, and all that kind of stuff. His little girlfriend's father was the pastor of one of the big churches in Buffalo. Even then I noticed that he leaned toward religion because many of the mischievous things that kids were doing as teenagers, he'd have no part of.

For example, at that time the grocery stores put all their vegetables and fruits outside. This is when we were around thirteen. Kids would run by and steal apples and oranges or maybe some cabbages. But he and I never got involved in that, and the other guys used to get mad with us because we wouldn't participate. Snook eventually got his doctorate degree and became the pastor emeritus of the Walker Memorial Missionary Baptist Church in New York City. He was real active politically. In fact, Dr. Martin Luther King was one of his closest friends.

He and I had some real good times at 47. We remained ace-boon-coons all the way through school. Right up to when we were fourteen, chasing after the little chicks, we were just two peas in a pod. The only thing is, he wasn't really into dancing and I always loved it. Around that time, I started going to a lot of city-sponsored parties out in the park. Local bands played the most popular tunes and there would be a band shell, a swimming pool, and a whole bunch of kids . . . a big, big dance floor. People would bring food, and they'd sit around and eat; just enjoy themselves. The big dances were held primarily during the summertime and all ages would be there. Those were some real, real fine days. It wasn't like going to nightclubs or anything like that.

At that time teenagers could also go to the ballrooms to dance because they didn't serve alcohol. Prohibition laws were in effect. Generally the dances would be on the weekend. By the time I was fifteen, I was one of the most popular social dancers in Buffalo. There were three guys that all of the girls wanted to dance with. We'd be dressed to the nines and strutting around, trying to look cool. Some girls would just come right up to you: "Cholly, you gonna give me a dance tonight?" "Yeah, baby, you're on." "When?" "I'll let you know." Man, I thought I was on top of the world!

During my mid-teens, I always had some kind of job. After school I worked in barbershops, portering, cleaning up, and shining shoes. Basically, I was making more money than my stepfather because on the weekends, early Sunday morning, I'd go around and clean up three or four different barber shops, then go home and get dressed for Sunday school. The shops didn't have porters and after Saturday night the barbers were so worn out they'd just close up their place. I'd clean them up on Monday morning, too. When they opened, everything would be fresh. So I was a real little hustler and able to help my mother a lot.

One summer the chamber of commerce was providing jobs for school kids, and I was hired as a porter on the bus line between Buffalo and Albany. That was a big thing for me. They had a lot of jukeboxes around during those times, and when the bus would pull into rest stops, the people would put money in the jukebox, and I'd be standing there, just cutting up, doing some of my tricks. They said, "Come on, boy, let's see you do this." Now, you know I'm happy about that—I loved to put on a show. I'd be dancing and they'd throw me money! I said to myself, "Oh, this is good!"

So I told the bus driver about it, and he said, "Hey, man, we can set it up every time we get to a rest stop; you can make yourself a nice little piece of change like that." Boy, we had some fun! He started introducing me! And I'd come out and dance. He'd be there first, he'd shill—throw a quarter down. He told me, "Now just make sure I get my quarter back!"

One day a passenger on one of the buses saw me doing this little dance. He was in charge of personnel at Alhambra on the Lake, a big restaurant in Buffalo. He said, "Hey, can you sing?" And I told him, "Yeah, that's my forte; I'm really a singer." He said, "Well, they're hiring some kids for summer jobs at Alhambra on the Lake. Can I put your name on an application for singing waiter next season?" I said, "Definitely!"

One of the jobs that stands out in my mind was at I. Miller's Shoe Store, where I dyed shoes. The gentleman who ran the bootblack department taught me how to mix dyes, so my manual training at P.S. 47 came in real handy. I'd run like hell after school to get up there and I worked until nine o'clock at night.

In May of my tenth-grade year, I dropped out of school and began working at I. Miller's full time. The reason I didn't go back was because my stepfather had become very violent with my mother and finally my brother and I had to jump on him. He was a little puny-type guy, and I hated to do this because he was real good to us, always nice to me and my brother, but I wouldn't allow *nobody* to mess with my mother.

I had told him the next time he laid a hand on her I was going to jump on him and he said, "You wouldn't dare do that." I said, "Well, don't you ever hit my mother again." So when he got half-juiced and he came in and started banging on her, I lit into him, boy. My brother and I sacked him up pretty good, put him out of the house, threw all of his clothes in the backyard. Out of fear I almost killed him. My brother was the one who had to stop me because my feeling was that I had to really finish him off quick. I thought if I didn't get him knocked out, he might take control. I wasn't going to stand around and see him hurt her. But even after that I'm pretty sure they met other places.

At any rate, I didn't go back to school. I wanted to work steady and take care of her because around that time, she began to have trouble with her teeth. Now they call it pyorrhea. All that inflammation was running into her system, so she stayed sick all the time. Consequently, I never finished high school. But it didn't bother me too much, because I was doing pretty good. My stepfather had only been making about $21 a week, and I was making like $25 or $30—it depended on how much I hustled. We got along okay, though. My mother got better and the lady that she had cooked for in Atlanta left her a little something in her will.

The bootblack department at I. Miller's was real busy all the time and there were only three of us filling all those orders. But, basically I enjoyed working with my man Sam on the shoe-dyeing thing. He was a nice guy and he liked the way I handled my job. I learned a lot about matching colors there. Eventually the head guy, who was Italian, went out to California on vacation and wound up working for some relatives in the motion picture business. Whoever was in charge of hiring and firing got rid of all the personnel in that department.

So I just did odd jobs for a while, until one day early that summer, the personnel guy, from Alhambra on the Lake, showed up on our doorstep. He told me, "You don't even have to audition; I've got it fixed already." I said, "Shoot, I'm in real show business now!

THE RHYTHM PALS

Alhambra on the Lake was located right on Lake Erie and run by a corporation that owned a lot of downtown nightclubs. People would come there, hang out on the beach all day, then go up to the restaurant to eat. It served as a gathering place for families during the summer. All of the waiters and waitresses were teenagers right out of high school, kids who could either sing, dance, tumble, tell jokes, or do some kind of novelty act that would fit into a variety show. Usually a producer was hired to line up the acts for a thirty- or forty-minute evening production that began right after the customers finished eating. Nobody ordered anything while the performance was going on; they just sat and watched.

We did a pretty good job in those shows. Basically all of the kids had seen a lot of vaudeville before they were hired. By that time, acts had been coming into the Century Theater downtown, Shea's Buffalo, and the Lafayette Theater every week for quite a while. Even though Buffalo was not a great town for developing performers, a few came out of there and it wasn't so far from New York City. That helped. We had about four different chains of theaters and movie houses. Black people didn't have to go to the balcony and all that kind of crap, we sat anywhere we wanted. And no theaters were closed to blacks. So, I saw most of the top singers and dancers that came through.

All of us had to arrive at Alhambra before it opened to set up the place, so we would meet early in the day and go swimming, just hang out. Man, we had a ball out there on the lake! And got paid besides. You met a lot of kids. That's how I got to know my first partner, William Porter. We called him Red, because of his freckles and red hair. He was hired as a dancing waiter and, like I said before, I was a singing waiter, so we got to be real good friends, just hanging out together, going to dances, the whole shot.

Red had left Chicago, after his mother passed, to live with an uncle in Lackawanna, New York, which was a suburb of Buffalo. That's where the Bethlehem Steel plants were and a lot of blacks, including his uncle, got jobs in Lackawanna. We used to sneak in a place out there that had dancing and drinking. It was like a roadhouse. We'd dress adult and everything, and go in there looking for girls. Every time, somebody would spot us and tell the owner, "See those two over there, they're young kids; get 'em out of here!" Generally, we'd stay over because the only way to leave town was by bus, and after a certain hour it would stop running—so we'd have to sleep at his uncle's house.

Red was the one who suggested that we put a little act together. He said, "You can sing and I can dance." I told him, "Yeah, man, but I can do *some* of the dancing, too. Maybe you'll teach me a little tap dancing and we can put a little song together." Then I figured out that he was tone deaf, so that left the singing on my shoulders. The tap dancing came pretty easy to me because of my musical background, and I understood how to fit the dance and music together.

Well, we got hung up into this thing and started doing some appearances together. I was singing, "When It's Sleepy Time Down South"! We wore straw hats. He'd come on and do a little solo dancing, we'd do some Charleston stuff together, then it would be the big finish! We dressed real nice and wound up being a pretty good act, Billy and Charles, the Two Rhythm Pals. We started doing a lot of little club dates around Buffalo.

Eventually Red and I went to work in a place called the Vendome. It was a black-owned hotel, with a big club down on the ground floor. The Vendome was run by some of "the boys," big numbers people, who might have been associated with the white mob. The owner used to bring in big bands and acts, but like most clubs at that time, it had its own stock chorus line, which was used for all the productions. That's where we met a little girl who was a helluva tap dancer. Her name was Katherine Davis and she was in the chorus line.

Katherine had a beautiful shape and was real stylish. In no time, my partner had a thing going on with her. When we'd rehearse, she would be in there helping to teach me tap, because I needed all the coaching that I could get at that point. Katherine knew a whole lot of steps and she could take them apart and make them real clear. She also taught me how to make tap combinations. First you think of a rhythm, then you try to duplicate the rhythm in your feet. Katherine taught me all that kind of stuff.

Red could really dance, but he didn't know how to align the steps with the music. I could break down whatever they showed me and adjust it to musical bars. So that was my contribution to the group. I'd tell Red, "Don't do this five times; you do it four times." That cat said, "Well, what if I *feel* like doing it five times?" I looked at him. "*Feel?* Man, it doesn't fit into the music." Then I would show him and he understood it. He said, "Yeah, that works out much better!"

So the more creative I became, the more I was Red's teacher, rather than his student. But Katherine really taught both of us some very intricate things, like wing dancing. Around that time, Red and I saw the Chocolate Steppers at Shea's Buffalo with Cab Calloway. They did flash dancing, a girl and two guys. So we decided to put Katherine in our act and change the name to Billy, Charles, and Katherine. We became a big trio in Buffalo. People were even talking about taking us away.

Well, that didn't last long because Katherine became very ill and was hospitalized with tuberculosis. So we just went back to our original act. Then Red and I had a disagreement about a girl that both of us liked. She had a lot going for her but was kind of fast. Anyway, we had a major fight and he threw a milk bottle at me. It hit the wall and a piece bounced off and cut me in the face. Luckily, he and a couple of other guys in the neighborhood were able to rush me to the hospital because one of them was older than we were and had his father's little old Ford. The doctor wanted to know how it happened, so I told him we were playing and I fell against a piece of glass and cut myself. But that broke Red and me up for a minute.

Then a producer named Sammy Lewis came to town with one of those traveling shows and set up a little theater off in the neighborhood. Quite a few of the performers left the show in Buffalo, so he held an audition for new dancers. This was around 1929 or 1930. I heard about it and went over to talk to him. He said, "Yup, you look like you ought to be able to dance pretty good." So I signed up with Sammy Lewis's Revue. I was out on the road for about six months and I was having a *lark* out there. They had comedians, chorus girls, singers, and the whole nine yards.

The revue was traveling down through Ohio—not Cleveland, but Columbus, Dayton, Cincinnati. We played a lot of the smaller towns, like Medallion. Then into West Virginia and down to North Carolina. You'd go in and do a week in this town, a week in the next town, mostly black theaters. That's when I started really learning how to dance. I mean, real good, authentic tap dancing, you know, because we had a lot of old-timers on the show. Many of them had been carnival people, just old show business people in there.

They were great dancers who taught me a lot more about wings, and I wound up getting a good spot in the lineup. They called it more or less flash dancing then. I would watch other dancers real close and ask questions. And they were so good about helping you. They'd break it down, show me how to do it, and then I'd go and practice and practice until I got it. So when I came back home I was dancing like crazy!

Some of the comedians were good dancers, too. There must have been four or five of them in the show in different spots. They would do a whole lot of standard comedy situations. And even though you were a dancer you had to work in bits. These were short comedy presentations and you might have to play the straight man to a comedian. You learned how to do lines; things you didn't even know you could do. The guys would say, "You can do this man! Now, come on, this is the way you do it."

It was almost like a threat. But what a learning process! And if you were studious at all, you could get it. Later in my show business career, I saw some of these same bits at the Apollo, because they were such standard things. But all of the comedians added their own little touches. There were also a lot of good singers, male and female. They would sing these heavy things, like "Old Man River" and "St. Louis Blues." There were some singers with those big, heavy, good voices, not formally trained, but they had a wonderful quality. Now, I don't mean to say that you have to be formally trained to be a good singer. I'm just saying that they were being trained the same way I was—on the job!

The chorus line dancers were doing what we characterize now as authentic jazz. None of that modern jazz stuff. That came along later. It was pretty much the same type of moves that came out of street dancing. A lot of it had flash steps or expansive physical moves as opposed to close floor work. There was also what we called picture numbers or picture soft-shoe dancing, which had soft movements. The choreography was made up of traveling steps that led the dancers into various formations or figures, all performed to a flowing melody. There were a lot of arm movements and the costumes had a springlike look: light colors, soft flowing fabrics, and big hats.

There were also up-tempo numbers and a lot of tap. In fact, the basic dancing was tap. All of the chorus girls tap danced . . . some good, some not so good, but tap was the foundation of the chorus numbers. Since about four or five spots in the show required male and female dancers, you learned how to do certain things with the girls. My social dancing experience came in real handy; I was accustomed to partnering.

Working those shows was really like going to a university. If you went out with the Whitman Sisters, Irving C. Miller, or someone like Sammy Lewis, you'd hardly get any pay at all, but you learned like crazy. Because of segregation, you lived mostly in people's houses, occasionally a hotel, but the producers had a list of available houses for each town. And there was always somebody at one of the houses who would fix food for the whole cast. It might not be the house where you were living, because there were usually twenty-five to thirty people or more in the show, but the producers took care of the tab. They would also go to the drugstore and places like that and set up a deal with the owners. So we could go in, buy toothpaste, hair lotion, or whatever we needed every day. The store manager would just write it down, you'd sign your name, and the guys would go in there later and pay your bill. You'd get four or five dollars at the end of the week. If you were doing a lot in the show, you might get ten dollars. That was for your pocket, you know.

I remember there was a young boy like myself whose name was Chick Underdew. He was out of Columbus, Ohio. A good dancer, too; taught me a whole lot. We did a couple of things as a team in the show. Chick and I got stranded in Wilmington, North Carolina, because Sammy Lewis ran out of town with all the money and left everybody in the hotel.

I found out later that producers like Sammy had a tendency to run off if they didn't make a lot of money in a particular place, especially if they were near the end of a booking. So the people housing and feeding the cast would look up and the producer would be nowhere in sight. Somebody in the show would find out that the owner had left and all you could do was try to get out of there as fast as possible. Chick and I had to climb out of the window to leave the place. Thank God it was just the second floor! We tied sheets together, grabbed as many clothes as we could handle, and slid down!

Then we took off over to the freight yard and jumped in the first boxcar we saw. Had absolutely no idea where we were headed. There were so many guys in there already that the railroad officers ran us out at the first stop. So we landed in a coal car and wound up in Huntington, West Virginia. A couple of yard detectives, who made a living chasing hobos, ran us off the tracks.

Since we'd played that town before, we looked up some people we knew and they put us up for a few days and gave us some money and food. Finally they took us back to the tracks. It was the tail end of the winter, rainy and wet, so they handed us a couple of slickers to wear. One of them had worked on the railroad. He said, "Now you get on this train right here. This one is going to Ohio." So we struck off again, and sure enough, we got in the boxcar that evening, and the next morning we were in Columbus. Chick recognized the buildings and everything. He said, "Hey, this is it!" So we got off, and oh, we must have walked ten miles to get to his house.

We tried to find jobs as porters, janitors, or dishwashers; couldn't come up with a thing! This was during the Depression and it was hard on his family trying to feed another mouth, so I wrote to my mother and she sent me a Greyhound bus ticket. It was March in Buffalo, the snow was about so high. When I stepped off the bus, wearing that slicker and two sweaters, Mama just broke down and cried!

By that time, her health was better, she was working part time, and my stepfather was back on the scene. Everybody was so glad to see me. That week, my brother ran into Red and told him I was home, so he came by the house and said, "Hey, man, I sure missed you, boy. I'm sorry about the fight and everything. I mean, I really missed you, man. I been looking forward to our thing. Maybe we can get back together." I said, "Look, I ain't got no clothes or nothin' like that." So he said, "Well, you know we're about the same size, I'll let you have some of my things. I've been doing pretty good, and I found an agent. I'll hook you up with a couple of little dates, until you get yourself together."

In the neighborhood theaters on Tuesday or Wednesday nights there were variety shows and you could make ten or twelve dollars. So I did a couple of those and when he saw how I was dancing, he said, "Hey, man, we really got to get back together!" So we started getting nice little bookings around Buffalo and built our ourselves back up. That's when we became The Rhythm Pals.

Our act was so much stronger. We went out on the road around 1932 with a guy named Stringbeans Williams. He was a very, very popular comedian down south and also on the East Coast. When Stringbeans came through Buffalo with a show, he saw us doing a combination bottle dance. You put a bottle down and you dance around it. He signed us up, picked up a singer, and took us with his show all through New England . . . Boston; Providence; Worchester, Massachusetts; and somewhere in Connecticut. In the larger theater places, bigger acts or more well-known acts were sometimes added to the show. For example, the Will Mastin Trio joined one of these.

Will Mastin was an old vaudeville guy, a strut dancer with the straw hat and cane and so forth. A great salesman. I mean he could really do that stuff. Flash dancing was also one of his fortes, but he wasn't a real tap dancer. Sammy Davis Jr.'s father was a member of that trio. He did splits, cartwheels, and Russian steps, like kazotskys. There was another guy whose name was Monty. I can't recall his last name.

Little Sammy traveled with his father and had a part in the act. Not a big part. He was like whipped cream on the Jell-O. I first saw him when he was around seven years old, and even then he was cooking! There was a little piece of business set up to show him off after the trio finished most of the stuff they were doing. They staged the thing so that Monty was having a disagreement with Will and Sammy Sr. about some problem, then he says, "Well, if that's the way you guys feel about it, I quit!" Will said, "Naw, you can't quit." Monty told him, "Oh, yes I can. Watch me."

After he walked offstage, Sammy Sr. looked at Will and said, "Well, what are we gon' do now?" Will said, "Don't worry about it." He walked over to the wings and hollered, "Hey, stage manager, wake that big boy up out there sleeping by the radiator and send him in here." And whoever was watching Sammy would turn him loose and he ran out there in a full-dress suit, with a little top hat on; the cutest thing you've ever seen.

He'd do a little paddle and roll. Then when he got through doing his dance, he took his bow and the music struck up and the three of them got together and did their exit. By the time Monty left the group, Sammy was much older, so he took his place. That's when he played drums and everything. He could also play trumpet, sing, do imitations, and to top it off, he was an excellent tap dancer. Just a well-rounded entertainer.

After Stringbeans's show closed, Red and I went to Montreal and stayed up there a couple of months, then came back to Buffalo. During that time, I had my first experience choreographing chorus line routines. This was 1933. One day, the owner of the Moonglow, in Buffalo, just came up to me and said he'd like to put in about four girls and build a little show. I don't know why he was telling me. I guess he liked the way I danced. While he was talking to me, I said, "I can do that." He said, "Can you put the whole thing together?" I said, "Yeah, I can put it together." I hadn't ever done it before, but I just figured that I could. I certainly knew how to do all of those little things that the chorus lines were doing just from watching them.

See, the chorus line moves had been passed down through the traveling shows and they contributed to the thirties and forties chorus line steps . . . the arm movements, legs kicking, the strut, all of these moves that are typical of *us* (meaning blacks). Then there was the black bottom, Lindy, Charleston, and truckin.' All of the chorus line steps were cousins to the social dance steps.

I managed to put together a little soft-shoe for the chorus girls. I remember there was a girl who worked at Ann Montgomery's, a local nightclub. She was a seamstress and I got her to make these fabulous costumes. Oh, it was a heck of a show. Red and I were in it. And Billy Eckstine was in the show as a headliner. Outside of being a great singer, he had a wonderful personality and sense of humor. He was also very articulate and had a special way of talking to his audience. That's a quality that most entertainers must have—the ability to communicate closely with the audience, not just perform for them, but get into them and bring them into you. This made Billy much more than just a singer. He also played a trumpet and a valve trombone.

Billy was one of the most generous cats I've met. When he had his own band, in the forties and fifties, they appeared regularly at the Apollo. There used to be this Italian guy who sold hot dogs in the back of the theater; the best hot dogs in the world. And he was there summer and winter. Billy would go back there and ask the guy, "How many hot dogs you got?" Then he would buy him out completely and tell him to give them to the guys in the neighborhood. That's how he was, just a real good person. Through the years we became real close friends.

Back in '33, he had just come to Buffalo from Pittsburgh. Red and I put together a little soft-shoe thing to do with him because he always wanted to dance, you know. There was a traveling part where we went downstage and Billy had a way of flirting with the girls at the tables.

So, the first night, he got to looking at this little girl that was on the ringside. There were about three of them and he was watching this particular one and dancing up front. So Red and I moved back. Then all of a sudden he looked around, and he didn't see us, and he just went blank! He couldn't do nothing. We cracked up and everybody in the audience did, too. After that, he'd tell everybody, "Them dirty MFs; you don't know what they did to me." Boy, we laughed about that thing for a long time.

Eventually we went into the Vendome again, where they had big bands, like Jimmie Lunceford's. I had taught Red a ~hole lot of new steps and our act was really popping! Willie Bryant came through. He had a band at that time and we worked with him briefly. Then Louis Armstrong's second wife, Lil Hardin, came in. She had a very good band. A lot of musicians who were with her ended up with Louis and with Basie.

Lil was a piano player and seemed to be very much in charge, although in those days the band leaders didn't do much conducting or anything. They played an instrument and just blended in. This was the first time I'd worked with a female band leader. She had this singer Velma Middleton with her, who also danced and did splits. She eventually traveled with Louis's band.

Sometimes, when a band came to one of the theaters or clubs and there was somebody on the bill that they liked, the band leader might call the next theater booked and find out if supporting artists could be added to the show. This wasn't like traveling constantly with the band. These were just little brief things that happened.

During the thirties, big bands moved from playing in the pit to the stage and they were presented in variety shows as the main attraction in dance halls, theaters, and clubs throughout the country. The band leaders would hire dancers, singers, and comedians and play popular recordings between the different acts.

Anyway, Lil called someone in New York and asked if she could bring The Rhythm Pals with her. After we closed at the Vendome, she took the whole show to the Apollo Theater, and that was our very first venture to New York City. It was 1935, about a year after the Apollo had switched from being just a burlesque house. She had a caravan of Plymouth station wagons and the guys in the band drove the cars.

Red and I were doing a stair dance, which we had performed back at the Vendome. That was where Bill Robinson first saw us do it. He was in town appearing at Shea's Buffalo and dropped by the hotel one night to see the show. He came up, embraced us, and did a little bit on the stairs himself. So it was with his blessing that we kept this in our act, which was an honor for us, because he was very possessive about his stair dance. Now, when we took it to New York, everybody said, "Man, don't let Bill Robinson see you doing that dance." I said, "Well, he saw us in Buffalo, and he said it was okay with him." "Yeah, but you wasn't in New York! He might not want you to do it in New York!" Boy, we got a whole lot of mouth behind that, but we kept right on doing our dance.

We were pretty good at the Apollo, not great though. That's where Honi Coles first saw us dance. He used to say, "Well, one thing about Cholly and Red, they were dancing so fast, man, you couldn't tell what they were doing!" We had the fastest soft-shoe in the business! He used to ride us about our glittery shoes, "Yeah, man, you guys were strictly from Buffalo; good feet, but no conception." Boy, he kidded me for years about that, although there was nothing really that you could put your finger on to criticize. We were a midwestern-type dancing act and New York had a different style of dancing. Back then you were only exposed to the dancing where you lived, unless you saw a vaudeville dance act from out of town. If you got to see enough of those shows, you could tell when you saw an act what part of the country the dancers came from.

When a new show came into the Apollo, all the buck dancers would show up. That was an affectionate term used by black tap dancers. We'd run into each other on the street, "Hey, buck dancer!" Which meant you were a member of the club—the fraternity of real tap dancers. A long time ago buck dancing referred to flat-footed dancing that was close to the floor, but the expression had been passed down through the ages and meant different things at different times. By the time I came along the term "buck and wing" referred to a style of tap dancing that was a combination of wings and close-to-the-floor dancing, affectionately called hoofin'.

So, as I was saying, the buck dancers would all pile into the theater and sit on the front row for the opening show. The first two rows would be nothing but dancers—to check you out. Red and I were doing a combination of the stair dance and the bottle dance. We had painted champagne bottles with glue on them and we danced around the bottles and up the stairs like little hops. You'd just set them up and you'd kick over them, go around them. . . . We had seen somebody do it in a movie, so we expanded the routine. There was a song, "That old empty bottle, that old empty bottle. . . ." I don't remember the lyrics, but I'm sure it came out of a show. I was doing wings and Red was doing his rhythm.

After that engagement, we didn't know how to really operate in New York City, or even go downtown and get an agent, so we stayed there ten or twelve days just fooling around. We were living in a hotel called the Woodside. That's where all the big bands and all the big acts stayed, up on Seventh Avenue, at about 142nd Street or somewhere in that vicinity. In fact, that's where "Jumpin' at the Woodside" came from. The manager was real nice. He especially liked musicians and dancers. All performers, really. There were three or four floors and on each floor he'd set up a kitchen and the guys would put on those pots and share them; a real community type of setup.

We didn't have money to pay him at that time, but we had big theatrical trunks for our clothes, so he said, "Well, I'll let you take a few things out of your trunk, and we'll hold the rest until you get the money to pay us off. Then we'll send your trunks to you or you come back to New York and pick them up," which was real nice, in a sense. But we were young. You know what I mean? It was just clothes. I figured, "I'll buy me some new duds!" So it was back to Buffalo. Mama had to bail me out again.

When we got there, we cooked up some gigs in Toronto and did a couple of small hotels on Lake Ontario—resorts. Then we did a couple of road dates and came back to Buffalo. That's when I met

Leonard Reed, a producer, who had been Willie Bryant's dance partner. They were the guys that originated the shim sham shimmy.

Leonard had just closed a production in Baltimore called *Rhythm Bound*, and he came through Buffalo with six chorus girls from Chicago to appear at Ann Montgomery's nightclub, where Red and I were working. He had a line of girls that he used to take from city to city, and he'd put on the shows in different nightclubs. There was a string of small black nightclubs that ran through Buffalo, Cleveland, Pittsburgh, Cincinnati, St. Louis, Chicago, and Detroit. By the time you'd go around the horn, it was time to go around again! Then you'd put a whole new show together.

Leonard brought this Chicago chorus line in and they were a *powerhouse*! Great dancers, the Reedettes. One time they had a battle with the Apollo's line. I think it was drummed up by Ralph Cooper, the originator of *Amateur Night at the Apollo*. Ralph was an exceptionally creative and multitalented person . . . an actor, comic, band leader. And early in his career he was Eddie Rector's dance partner. It seems that Ralph talked Frank Schiffman, the owner of the Apollo, into having this contest, so he brought the Reedettes in for a week to challenge the Apollo dancers and those Chicago girls cut 'em down.

But getting back to the nightclub thing . . . Leonard liked our act, so around the spring of '35, we rode in his car all the way to Chicago to dance in a show he was producing at a nightclub called the Grand Terrace. This was one of the very prominent supper clubs that had nothing but black talent. The chorus line there was smoking! Lois Bright, who later joined the Miller Brothers and Lois, was one of the dancers. We became very good friends! In fact, Lois was like a sister to me. Another fabulous dancer in the line was Marie Bryant. She laid into whatever she did. Deenie Gordon, from Philadelphia, was there, too.

I had eyes for Catherine Williams, from Des Moines, Iowa, and Red was straight with a dancer named Doris. I can't remember her last name, but we called her Garbo, because she had that Garbo attitude, like the movie star. All of us used to have a lot of fun hanging out together.

Lois, Marie Bryant, and a whole bunch of those Chicago dancers had gone to the Mary Bruce Dancing School. There was another girl in Chicago named Ernestine Ford who did a tap dance on her toes. Such great talent came out of the Midwest. Marie Bryant had extraordinary physical projection, which is not easy to develop. Then there was a girl, captain of the Reedettes' line, Mary Stevens, an excellent dancer. Some dancers just stood out. You could look at every chorus line and see that certain ones had the potential to become stars. They'd always give you just a little something more than the other dancers.

Red and I were in Chicago for about a month or six weeks. One night we went out to the Club DeLisa and the producer there was looking for a substitute house singer. So we told him about Billy Eckstine, who was still in Buffalo. He said, "Can you get in touch with him?" We said, "Sure." They got ahold of Billy and he came to Chicago to sub for two weeks. At that time Earl Hines's band was playing at the Grand Terrace and something happened to the guy who was booked to sing with them. Earl was telling us about it at the Terrace, so we mentioned Billy. Then we said, "We can go out there to the Club DeLisa. He's pinch-hitting with Red Saunders's band." Earl said, "Let's go after our show tonight"—because they had real late shows at the DeLisa. We went out there, he heard Billy, and he said, "Yeah, man, I like him; let's go back and talk to him." So that's how Billy Eckstine got with Earl Hines, just through Bill Porter and myself. Billy always said so; he was always grateful.

Now, a lot of little funny things happened right here. You've got to follow me real close. During this time Ananias Berry, of the Berry Brothers, was leaving the group. They were a top-notch strut and cane act that also did acrobatics. James, Ananias, and Warren were actual blood brothers. Ananias had married Valaida Snow, who was from Chicago. Valaida was a great singer and trumpet player; she did imitations of Louis Armstrong and all that stuff, a wonderful singer. She wasn't noted for her dancing, but she definitely had some moves. Valaida was hired by Frank Sebastian to produce shows at Sebastian's Cotton Club in Culver City, California, so she came through Chicago with Ananias and stole five girls out of the chorus at the Grand Terrace to take to the West Coast. Some of those same girls I was telling you about.

When they got to California, Valaida said, "You know those two guys that were in the show with you in Chicago? Does anyone know how to get in touch with them?" And the girl I was messing around with said, "I do!" That was my first wife, Catherine. But we were just going together then, you know. Valaida told them that she would like to get us in Sebastian's Cotton Club.

In the meantime, Red and I had closed at the Grand Terrace with Leonard Reed and gone on to Pittsburgh to dance in Larry Steele's show before returning to Buffalo. So Valaida called us at home and asked how soon we could get out there. We said, "Well, we can leave tomorrow." She said, "Catherine is right here, and she'll tell you what the address is, and I'll make arrangements for you to have a room in one of those places that has kitchenettes." Valaida wired us two hundred dollars for expenses. We'd just bought a little '35 Ford, so we got ourselves packed up, got on the road, and shoot, we tore out! In about three and a half or four days we were there!

The show was a huge production that ran forever. It wasn't a one- or two-week deal. There was a big chorus line, showgirls, all black, with variety acts in between. Valaida liked a lot of good dancing and some of the original girls were good looking, but they couldn't cut the mustard, dancewise, so that's why she weeded them out and brought in the Chicago girls to spruce up the show. There were twelve girls in the line and a lot of wonderful performers.

I remember Rutledge and Taylor, two boys from Chicago, doing a one-man dance. We had the comics, Dudley Dixon and Eddie "Rochester" Anderson, who was later hired to do the *Jack Benny Show*. May Diggs was on the bill. She was an excellent dancer. 'Nias Berry had a big spot and he did a couple of things with Valaida. They were the two stars of the show.

Lois and I helped her come up with a lot of the steps for the choruses. Lois Bright was very adept and very ambitious. Excellent talent. We performed a couple of things together in the show. Everybody used to say that she moved just like me and they'd ask me if I taught her. I said, "No, I found her like that!" She was a natural. Had great body control and very fluid movement. Her whole body got into whatever she did. That's why they said she was a lot like me, because they accused me of having that same talent.

Lois and I got another chance to work together in California at a little club called the Cafe de Paris. The whole show was built around Lionel Hampton. He was playing the drums, vibraphone, and everything. I remember Benny Goodman and Teddy Wilson used to come in the club almost every night. That's when Hamp was really *Hamp*! All the things that he's doing now, he was doing back then. So you see how far ahead of the business he was.

The Cafe de Paris had an all-black show, and a local girl, Patsy Hunter, had been hired to put the chorus numbers together. She did most of the black gigs around town; very popular. Patsy was a good choreographer and a very lovely person, but she was having a lot of trouble handling the job, so she asked me if I was interested in taking over, because Red and I were working in the club at that time. I said, "Okay. I'll give it a shot." So Lois and I worked out the dances and that was the third time I got a chance to choreograph for a chorus line.

While I was working in California, Catherine and I got married. That was 1936. It was a rushed thing, you know. Her mother was coming to visit and we were living in the same apartment. See, when Red and I first moved out there, he and I were living together, then he moved to another section of the city with some girl, so Catherine gave up her apartment and moved in with me. Her mother, brother, and sister were coming from Des Moines, and it was a question of either moving or getting married. Catherine said, "Well, we've got to do something, because if my mother comes out here and we're *living* together, I don't know what she might do!"

Neither one of us felt like moving, so we hurried up and got married in time for Catherine to call home and give them the news before the visit. That put it on the safe side, you see. The landlady's uncle was a minister, so she got him to come over to the house and all of our friends showed up. We had the wedding right there in the living room. I was about twenty-three.

Being in California was so exciting because Hollywood musicals were a big thing then. We did movie shorts, tap soundtracks for some of the films, and we also worked as extras in dramatic pictures. Honi had a light-skinned cousin that rode regularly in the westerns, Bob Clark. He was a helluva horseman. Bobby Evans was another guy who did that. If you were light enough, you could get parts in the white westerns as extras. Bobby spent his whole life in those kinds of minor roles. But that happened to most of the blacks in Hollywood. You couldn't really get a featured role unless it was a black film, and those were few and far between.

Some of the brownskin dancers were used in movies like *Charge of the Light Brigade*. They made us up with beards and hats . . . put hair on our heads. They didn't even have wigs. They would paste little pieces of hair on to make us look like Mongolians. Honi used to joke about these films. He said they'd call Central Avenue: "We need six niggers in this picture. Get out the nigger-catcher! Let's group 'em up." Sometimes they'd call five hundred or six hundred people, and they'd only want ten or twenty.

I remember when we did *Old Man River*, they put cork on us for the levee scene. They had their favorite guys who showed up on a regular basis, so they'd say, "You guys don't mind putting cork on, do you?" "No, it's okay by us." See, we were getting $11.50 a day. That was a lot of money, then. At the time, we didn't necessarily consider it demeaning, it was just something that happened.

A lot of black guys did the soundtracks for white chorus-line dancers, who backed stars like Eleanor Powell, Ann Miller, and Fred Astaire. They had those big tap dance sequences with about forty background guys, mainly ballet dancers. They were doing the moves, but we were making the sounds! They couldn't tap a lick, not real rhythm tap.

Two of the movies we made the tracks for were the *Big Broadcast of 1938* and *Broadway Melody of 1938*. By the time we did those I had organized a group of sixteen excellent dancers who could respond to directions and didn't need eight years to learn a two-bar thing. Red was in that group; the Three Rockets; the High Hatters, a popular West Coast trio; Earl Robinson. Oh, we had some great dancers.

So we would go in, learn these tap routines from the choreographers, and make the soundtracks. When the movies came out, it looked like the white guys were tapping. Sometimes, the technicians couldn't quite get the sound and the movements synchronized, but only professionals noticed it. I had a lot of success with that, because eventually, instead of having open auditions, the studios would call me when they wanted tracks made.

I worked closely with Eleanor Powell for a while, doing her personal choreography. She had her own studio and staff out there on the lot. There were about five of us who put choreography together for her. Periodically, she'd come over and look at what we had done. Sometimes she'd say, "Do you think that's good for me?" And naturally, we said, "Yeah, it's great for you!" If she thought certain steps were too masculine, we'd leave them out.

One thing I was always noted for was my ability to do wings, so I used to try to interest her in doing them, but she never liked to. Actually, she did try, but they were difficult for her. Eleanor would set up private rehearsal periods when she'd pick from the things we worked out, to see how she could use them, then call in the dance director to figure out how they fit into the entire scene. Some of those things looked real difficult, but those people knew almost a year in advance what routines they needed, so they had plenty of time to learn them.

Red and I did little pickup jobs like that in the daytime and worked the clubs at night. But I learned a great deal from those experiences. Throughout my life, I've learned a lot from observation. And working in Hollywood was an important part of my education, since I was exposed to how all those big musicals were made. And dramatic pictures, too.

The guys used to call me a rehearsal freak. When I was working as an extra, I would get an apple, a sandwich, and a bottle of milk and go on my lunch hour. They had the commissaries staggered, because not all of the studios would close down at the same time. Every time we had a break, I'd grab my things and go to watch another shooting. Maybe *The Great Ziegfeld*, where the choreographers were working with chorus people. One time I got hooked up on *Green Pastures*—that wasn't a whole lot of dancing, but watching those guys move those people around, shoot . . . I was learning something every day!

In 1938, Valaida Snow's show finally came out of the Cotton Club. I don't remember if there was a fire or what, but Frank Sebastian was associated with the gangsters, so there's no telling what happened. Anyway, that was the end of that gig. We had been at Sebastian's for three years and a lot of good memories were created there. Sometimes Nat Cole was brought in to play for our rehearsals. He and his first wife, Nadine, finished a black road show out there around '37. I think it was a revival of *Shuffle Along*. She had danced in the show and he had been in the band. One of my buddies, Tyree Glenn, was in that band, too. We had a lot of fun with them, and since Nat had grown up in Chicago, he knew Valaida and all the girls already.

After Sebastian's, Red and I joined a show produced by Ralph Cooper. There was a string of white burlesque houses out on the West Coast that ran through San Diego, Los Angeles, San Francisco, Portland, and Seattle. Ralph convinced the owner of these theaters to put an all-black show in the Los Angeles house. He was duplicating Apollo presentations and setting them up like stock productions so they ran for a long time.

That show we did was a real good experience for me, because in addition to performing with Red, I staged and choreographed pieces for the chorus line and did a number with Louise Cook, who was an "exotic" dancer. This was a spooky type thing. They had a guy in there who did levitations. When he brought Louise up, I came on and we danced together, then he returned and she stretched out on this surface. I remember the lighting was real strange and dim and there was a lot of smoke swirling around her, then she completely disappeared.

Ralph eventually got some people out there interested in producing black westerns. All of the big studios had rental spaces and they would rent them to independent producers who wanted to do shows. At that time, Herb Jeffries was in California and as a result of those westerns, he became a big star because those movies were marketed to a lot of black theaters in the South.

Red and I had a pretty good run in that L.A. burlesque house, but as soon as the show closed, we decided to go back east. He was originally from Dumas, Arkansas, so he wanted to go back the southern route and eventually meet me in Buffalo. Catherine and I drove the northern route because we were planning to go to Des Moines, see her folks, then stop over in Chicago for a short visit.

As usual, the clubs in Chi-town were jumping! One night we went out to the Grand Terrace. This was the new Grand Terrace, but they still had big shows. I'll always remember that night, because it was my first opportunity to officially meet Honi Coles! Earl Hines's band was on the stand. The comedian Dusty Fletcher was there. Bert Howell and Honi were in the lineup. Their thing was basically a comedy act. Honi played straight man to Bert, then Bert sang and Honi did his solo dance spot.

They had a nice act, but I was really knocked out by the kind of things Honi was doing with his feet. After the show, Catherine and I went backstage and I introduced myself to him, because his dancing was just fascinating. Although he had seen our act in 1935, I don't think he remembered me. We chatted for a while and I told him I'd probably be coming to New York soon.

Red and I finally met up in Buffalo and worked in and out of there for about a year. I remember we played the Pythian Supper Club in Pittsburgh, then we did a couple of things with Ziggy Johnson, a very popular producer of floor shows. When we finished the Plantation in St. Louis, Ziggy took us on with him to Dave's Cafe in Chicago. I guess we were pretty much traveling around the horn, as usual. During that time, Red looked up an old girlfriend in Rochester, which was about forty miles away, so he was running up there whenever we had a dry spell. Then they got married.

I don't exactly remember how it happened, but Catherine was hired, along with some of the Chicago girls, to work in the chorus line at the Apollo Theater, and around the same time Red's wife inherited two beauty shops in Long Island. Soon, both of them were making plans to move, so Red and I started packing our bags, too!

When we arrived in New York, Catherine and I got a room right next to our good friend Lois Bright, at 2040 Seventh Avenue. Man, that place was jumping! Dizzy Gillespie, Chu Berry, all the great musicians lived there. Dancers like Chuck and Chuckles were there. I would run into Cook and Brown. The Mills Brothers were up in there.

Everybody you could think of lived in that building. And everybody in show business stopped by there. It was an international house! You could hear sounds in there at all hours of the morning or night . . . people running up and down the stairs! It was a crazy place, but we loved it. A lot of great friendships came out of 2040.

After being there a couple of days, I ran into Honi on the elevator and reminded him that we'd met in Chicago. Gradually we found ourselves developing a real friendship. He had just started going out with Marion. Her last name was Edwards then. Maggie is what I always called her. She was in the same Apollo chorus line with Catherine. Honi and I would go over to the theater to meet them after their rehearsals and just hang out.

Things didn't work out too well in New York for The Rhythm Pals. Red and I tried to get some bookings for two solid weeks. Nothing happened. Then he came over to the house one day and told me he was giving up show business because his wife had these beauty parlors and she needed help managing them. I could understand his position, but, boy, it left me high and dry, because I was never really a solo dancer. Never developed that. I could do my spot, but I mean, to go out and dance forever by myself, I definitely wasn't into that!

3

CHOLLY AND DOTTY

Around the time that Red stopped dancing, Honi and his partner, Bert Howell, broke up, so all we were doing that summer was playing softball over at Mt. Morris Park and hanging backstage at the Apollo or on 126th Street. Everybody would sit out there and run their mouths for hours. Danny Miller, Little Joe, Bubba Gaines . . . all the hoofers would show up, and a lot of the guys who had acts, like Brother Ford and LeRoy Myers. Whoever was in town and wasn't doin' nothin', you know.

There was a bar on Eighth Avenue and 126th Street called the Braddock, right beside the Braddock Hotel. You could find all the musicians, chorus girls, buck dancers, and everybody in there. People would even run over between shows to catch the action, but nobody was doing a whole lot of drinking, we were just having a good ol' time. The jukebox was poppin', playing everybody's tunes, cats were singing . . . I remember when Coleman Hawkins's "Body and Soul" came out. It was a big record at that time. Now, Coleman Hawkins was one of the greatest tenor saxophone players who ever lived! So everybody was learning Coleman's solo and we'd be gathered around the jukebox, just cutting up. It was a house-rocking thing. All the chorus girls, everybody knew how to sing that solo.

Right next door to the Braddock was the *Amsterdam News*. Reporters would come over and write a big article about some act like Cook and Brown. Guys would be just stylin', taking pictures, then buying a whole lot of papers. Man, you talkin' 'bout some good times! The Braddock was *it*!

Even though Red and I couldn't stay together, I was having a ball in New York. Honi basically took me under his wing and introduced me to all of his friends, all the dancers, musicians, and producers— because he knew just about everybody. He said, "Hey, man, I'm going to show you how this is done. I'm going to show you how to go downtown and see agents . . . all that stuff." And every now and then he'd get on my case: "Man, you don't do that kind of thing in New York; I know you *from* Buffalo, but you ain't in Buffalo now."

After a while, I started to pick up little odd jobs here and there. One of those times when I was lying around, starving to death, Maggie lined something up for me at the Apollo with the producer, Leonard Harper. She told him, "Why don't you get Cholly Atkins to do a couple of chorus line numbers for this show?"

At that time the Apollo had chorus girls and chorus boys. The guys called themselves the Linen Club Boys. Mr. Harper asked me to do a special number to a tune called "Every Tub," with the headliner, Count Basie's band. You talking 'bout swinging! All the dancers loved to work with Basie because his music was very earthy and had so much feeling. And see, Basie got a big kick out of the whole thing because he loved dancers, especially tap dancers. He couldn't do a whole lot of dancing himself, but he'd sit down and play that piano, though, and direct that band.

Working with him was just as much fun for the choreographer as for the dancers, and "Every Tub" was a great selection for the Apollo's chorus lines. I just loved putting the thing together. I studied that tune, then went into rehearsal full steam. Gave them a whole lot of authentic jazz movements. It was a smash hit! Every time they performed the number, it stopped the show cold because there was a happy marriage between what the music was saying and what the dancers were doing.

The guys were decked out in zoot suits and the girls wore little short flapperlike dresses. I mean it killed that show. I had to go back in there and put a tag on it so they could come out and do a little more. And naturally, I didn't want to repeat the last eight bars—I wanted to put my print on it. So I did something different. Wanted to come back and add some, but the producer said, "No way, the show's got to go home."

That was the first piece I choreographed at the Apollo. Then Mr. Harper got to the place where he'd just call me up, "I'd like you to come do a number for me, man." These were spot assignments. I'd go in there and he'd give me forty or fifty dollars for one piece, which was a lot of money at that time. Besides, I liked what I was doing.

When it came to creating dances, chorus lines were basically my first love, because at that time there was nothing else for me to chore-ograph—other than pieces for myself. All the acts were doing their own choreography. Sometimes a friend might say, "Hey, man, put this step right." But that didn't happen too often because most dancers did-n't think about getting help choreographically.

Vocal choreography, or what I did later with the singing groups, is based primarily on black chorus-line dancing. See, the big thing that I passed on to the Temptations and all the groups I work with now is precision based on jazz. I use all of the moves that the chorus girls used back in the twenties, thirties, and forties. That's really the foun-dation of my choreography.

Early in my career, I didn't have a reservoir of movements that I could use, because I was still learning and I had to really work hard at putting things together. I knew that I had a flair for swing dancing or flash dancing . . . authentic jazz is what I would really call it. Just the things that black dancers did to jazz music. I was trying to create a happy marriage between the rhythmic pattern of the move and the rhythmic pattern of the music—just put the music with the dance steps and have it all make sense. So I really studied how the chorus dancers were moving.

See, chorus-line dancing is much more important than people re-alize. Those dancers were the backbone of the shows around that time. There wouldn't hardly be much show without the chorus line because in addition to closing and opening the production and tying things together in between, they did comedy bits with the comedians, and some of the really excellent dancers were selected to do specific spots in the show.

Most chorus lines had some outstanding personalities, really energetic dancers, who could project. And the producers used them as soubrettes, if they could also sing. You might say a soubrette was really a glorified chorus girl who was multitalented and had a good physique. Producers would build production numbers around them or pair them up with a male dancer for a special number in the show. This gave extra-talented girls opportunities to develop into solo artists. Then there was another thing that used to happen with chorus lines. There was always some vivacious person with a lot of flair, who was used to tag the choruses. When the girls would go off, they'd put her on the end, and she'd carry on like a yard dog! And the audience would just yell. I think Florence Mills was one of these type of performers who developed into a great personality.

There were so many excellent dancers in the choruses. Some could dance better than the featured acts but never got a chance to go beyond the line. Well . . . it's like a football team. All the guys in there that are pushing, being knocked around, and opening holes for the big stars to run through, never get any recognition. In the chorus lines the same thing happened. Come to think of it, that's the way I felt out in Hollywood. I used to sit up and look at guys who were making big money, like Johnny Downs. He was a young featured player who tried to move like Donald O'Connor. Although Johnny's dancing was pretty elementary, he got all the breaks, which was typical of Hollywood. I knew I could outdance him and a lot of them guys, but I wasn't getting the opportunity! Those producers were more concerned with how you looked than how you danced. I remember when Katherine Dunham took her company to Hollywood, they tried to get her to fire some of the women and find dancers with lighter skin. That's just the way it was.

Between those little spot assignments at the Apollo, I was still searching for a steady gig. One night when I was lying in bed at 2040, Honi came running downstairs to my room with a new plan. "I don't know how you're going to feel about this, Chazz, but word just came out that one of the Cotton Club Boys in the *Hot Mikado* might get fired and they'll need another dancer. You want to check it out?" At first I was a little reluctant because being a chorus boy was considered a step down from having your own act and I was hoping for something that would help me move up. Then I thought, for a moment, "What the hell, I'm not doing anything else. I can at least go out there and look at the thing."

A swing version of *The Mikado* was running in Flushing Meadows, Queens, at the 1939 World's Fair, and the chorus boys from the Cotton Club were doubling there and at the downtown nightclub. It seemed that Bill Robinson, the star of the show, was not pleased with one of the dancers, so they were looking for someone to replace this guy.

I spoke with Chink Lee, captain of the Cotton Club Boys, and he arranged for me to go out to Queens and watch the show for a couple of nights. Then Honi and I talked it over again. He said, "These guys are not the greatest dancers in the world, but they get a lot of gigs, and it will keep you busy until you find something else that you want to do." That's pretty much the way I was thinking about it, too, so I decided I'd definitely give it a shot.

After all, it was a stable job and would at least put some bread on the table. I went in, rehearsed with them a couple of days, tried on the new costumes and everything. That's all it took. The steps that they were doing were simple; it was just a question of remembering the sequences. The next thing I knew, I was in the show. Then I learned the choreography that the guys were doing at the Cotton Club.

Remember, I had met Bill Robinson before in Buffalo, so he said, "I know you, boy. You and your partner did a stair dance, and you apologized to me for not getting my permission and I appreciated that. I remember you." Then he said to the Cotton Club artists, "You guys gonna have to dance to keep up with this boy!"

Bill Robinson was very stern about things that happened when you were on stage with him. We all called him Uncle Bo and everybody understood the type of person he was. So we stayed on our toes. The last thirty minutes of the show, the whole cast was up there. We had huge costumes, very heavy, and you couldn't be fidgeting around and doing a lot of moving. The lights were hot. People were sweating and in certain spots we had to just stand still and respond to him. He would be telling jokes to the audience and we could laugh, but we couldn't move, so a lot of dancers dreaded this part. For me it was a real lesson and not a chore at all. I was studying what he was doing, dancewise, and how he was handling the audience.

Uncle Bo really knew how to mesmerize people with his feet. Being on stage with him was like going to school every night, because he had so much style and finesse. And you just can't imagine how many different ways he could engage an audience. That was one of the greatest experiences of my career. In fact, I often think about how much I learned from watching the master work. Years later, when I was choreographing a dance in honor of him with some of the buck dancers, I could contribute a lot because I knew exactly how he moved.

The *Hot Mikado* had a huge cast and it was very well produced—no question about that. A number of Whitey's Lindy Hoppers were in that show. I had already met some of them in California, when they were shooting *Day at the Races*, in 1937, so I was real glad to see Norma Miller and Willamae Ricker, two of my close buddies. Leon James was in that show, too. During the *Mikado*, I became friends with the whole group. We couldn't get together as often as we wanted because everybody lived in Manhattan, and car pools were set up to take us back and forth. You couldn't go when *you* wanted to; you had to go when the car was leaving. Once in a while we'd all meet in one place, get some food and a drink or two, but later when we took the show on the road, we got to hang out and have a lot of fun together.

The Lindy Hoppers had some real wonderful spots in the *Hot Mikado*. We did one number with them called "Three Little Maids." Dressed in yellow tights and light green jackets, the Cotton Club Boys played the wandering minstrel band. Our dances were all tap routines—different wardrobes, different sets, different music, but all tap. Although the musical arrangements were fabulous, the choreography was pretty elementary.

We finished our engagement at the World's Fair during the latter part of September '39. I think I was there for just a couple of months.

Then the show we were in at the Cotton Club changed and the *Mikado* was getting ready to tour. So we were out on the road with Uncle Bo at least until the beginning of 1940.

I could see that the Cotton Club Boys had a lot of real talent mixed up in there, so early on I started planting the seeds that would change them into a real act. Let's face it, there were not too many Broadway shows that black dancers could get into, so I was starting to think about how we could prepare ourselves for other performance options, like appearances with jazz bands.

I said to the guys, "Look, we could be great and we could get a lot of work, but we're going to have to do more interesting things." Periodically, I would hold rehearsal sessions when we went into a city for two or three weeks during the *Hot Mikado* tour. These were not mandatory all the time, but we did a lot of rehearsing, getting things in shape to build a better act. So they were aware of what my intention was, and they were very much for it. Especially Louie Brown, because he really wanted to learn how to tap dance. We used to hang out together a lot.

The cast traveled by train, mainly through northern cities, playing legitimate theaters in Detroit, Omaha, Nebraska . . . Kansas City. After a few months, Michael Todd, the producer, decided that he was going to lay the show off for a while. Uncle Bo said, "If you're going to do that, why don't you just go ahead and close the show?" So that's what he did.

We came on back into New York, went immediately into rehearsal, and I started choreographing for the Cotton Club Boys. I had the crew build three boats for that set, and placed two guys on each one, dressed in sailor outfits. They'd jump from one boat to the other, real production stuff. We were back to appearing at the Cotton Club, and Cab Calloway's band was in there, so I asked Cab to come up and look at us one day. He said, "Hey, I'm getting ready to go on tour; I'd like for you guys to go with me."

I said, "Great. I want to choreograph a number with you dancing and with us dancing behind you—put that in the show." Cab said, "Yeah, why don't you go on and do that and let me know when you need me at the rehearsal." I was really getting excited then because I'd never done a big ensemble number with a star like Cab Calloway up front. He would be doing his own moves, but the Cotton Club Boys would be the frame around the picture. I told him, "I'll call you back and consult, so you won't be confined. You'll be free to do whatever you want to do, and we'll be doing the moves behind you. You pick the tune, let me know what it is, and I'll work it out." Later, our spot with Cab became a big feature on the tour.

I drilled those guys night and day! We had access to the rehearsal hall under the Apollo, and whenever it wasn't in use, we were there. The Cotton Club Boys came out doing a fantastic act. We opened with a regular vocal type thing, canes and straw hats. It was a sort of strutty dance to a show tune, but I can't remember the name. This was sixty years ago!

Right after that, two of us did a little legomania for about two and a half choruses. That involved a lot of kicks and twisting of the legs from the knee and the ankle, real eccentric types of moves. Rubber-legs Williams and Dynamite Hooker were both great exponents of legomania. I really liked doing that stuff, the kicks and all. When we finished our two choruses, the other guys came back and we did our regular little soft-shoe to "Puttin' on the top hat, puttin' on the dance shoes." We also did a lot of in-and-outs, with two guys going this way, two guys backing up—a lot of picture moves, but intact.

After that we did what we call a challenge right into an up-tempo number. I was the last one to dance because my pace was bright, almost like a double time, which threw the tempo way up, so we'd go into something similar to the b.s. chorus, then over the top, through the trenches and a half-time cakewalk exit. A big strut thing. It was great!

During that tour, the act was in its infancy and if we had stayed together, we could have taken everybody in the group to a new level, because many of the guys had hidden talents. For example, Louie Brown eventually did a comedy act with Moke, of Moke and Poke. Poke passed, so Louie replaced him and they became Moke and Doke. The longer we were together, the easier it was to recognize those special talents, pull them out, and cultivate them. All that takes time.

Back then, big bands were the new attraction, and that's who a lot of dance acts worked for. Vaudeville had declined, and most bands traveled with four or five acts. We went with Cab all across the country for about six or eight weeks, from New York to California and back.

When the tour ended, we started doing a lot of "'round the world" dates with other big bands, like Andy Kirk and Lucky Millinder. This included black theaters in Baltimore, Washington, New York, and Philadelphia. Then the guys began to have internal problems—families. A couple of them wanted to stay close to home; they didn't want to travel. Jules Adgers wanted to move out to California with his girl. He thought he might get a chance to work in the movies because he was real fair and looked like George Raft. So we had to find somebody to replace him. Then Louie Brown got an opportunity to work as a liquor salesman, so he left. To make matters worse, bookings started to get a little lean, so the Cotton Club Boys just broke up. But it was great while it lasted!

Honi and I were still living in 2040. He was out of work again, too, so it was back to the drawing board. We were going to shows together and just hanging out in pool rooms when he got a call from a friend in Philadelphia, a tailor. Eddie Lieberman was his name and he was producing a revue in Atlantic City, at a club called the Paradise. He asked Honi if he was interested in directing and choreographing a show at the club.

So Honi said, "Yeah, I'll do it and I'll get Cholly Atkins to help me because he's been doing a lot of work with chorus lines." Well, the guy didn't know me from a hole in the wall, but if Honi said I was okay, it was fine with him. Lieberman had known Dotty Saulters as a child star and was handling some of her dates, so he wanted Honi to include her in the show.

Dotty was a dancer and singer from Philadelphia. I didn't know her well, but I had met her when she was making a movie in California. A comedian by the name of Nicodemus ran a center out there where black singers, dancers, actors, and everybody hung out. It had a restaurant, rehearsal studios, and all sorts of facilities for relaxation. In '38, Dotty was there at a birthday party for Herb Jeffries, the singing cowboy (in black movies), who was becoming a popular jazz singer. Dotty was chaperoned by her mother.

I hadn't seen her since then, but Honi and I were happy to have her come on board, because she was real talented and had a bubbly personality. The shows ran from the beginning of the summer until about the first of October, so we were looking forward to a good, long stretch. After that, all the big shows and everything closed down in Atlantic City.

We began rehearsals at the Paradise in the summer of 1941. By the way, we had a great line in that show, excellent dancers, very pretty girls. My wife, Catherine, was one of them. Honi and I started putting this thing together with a substantial budget, because the guys opening the club were connected with "the boys," therefore money was no object. He had a spot in the show as a solo artist, but I didn't have a partner then, so he said, "In the big production soft-shoe, let's start it off with the chorus line, and have Dotty sing a song in the beginning of it, then you come back and do a little soft-shoe with her." (He was trying to get me in the show.) "Then we'll bring the chorus back in. They dance, and you and Dotty will be down front."

It sounded like a good idea to me. I told him, "Yeah, that's fine." Now, my wife is checking all of this out and I don't know how she's feeling about the plan, but I decided to go along with it. Then there was a kink in another spot and Honi said, "Why don't you rehearse something with Dotty in there. You ought to do a little dance or something. Fix the continuity, so we won't have two singers back to back." Dotty was for that, too, so I said, "Okay, Coles, you got it."

Well, that was basically the beginning of Cholly and Dotty, because those spots became nice little tidbits in the show. All the newspapers gave the cast rave reviews, but the funny thing was that they kept mentioning "the most delightful musical comedy act of Cholly and Dotty." The critics were already calling us an act and we were just dancing together because Honi thought it was a good idea.

For a while there, everybody was talking about our revue. Larry Steele had a production over at Club Harlem, which was the most popular spot in Atlantic City, so he sent some representatives over to see what we were doing. We had Pigmeat Markham, Velma Middleton, Bardu Ali, Tondelayo and Lopez . . . oh, it was fantastic. We just sent those people right back into rehearsal. The next day they started making a lot of changes in their show.

We ran for the whole summer season and when we got down to the beginning of September, the members of the cast started wondering what was going to come along for the fall. Cab's office called Honi about going on tour with his band as a solo, so he was in good shape. About the middle of September, the Mills Brothers came in to see the show and asked me if Dotty and I could open for them in a Detroit club called the Plantation, at the Norwood Hotel. I said, "Well, let me talk to Dotty and her mother, because Mrs. Saulters makes all the decisions and she always travels with her." So I talked with them about money and they accepted the offer. I figured it was just another date. We hadn't even thought about becoming an act, yet.

In those days you'd go on one of those jobs and they would last for at least a month. It wasn't like a one-nighter or even a one-week thing. When Dotty and I went on the road with the Mills Brothers, it wasn't necessarily the best thing for my marriage, but she was exceptionally talented and people seemed to think that we had a great future together, as dancers. See, a lot of those kids coming out of Philadelphia could really sing and tap. Dotty was a child prodigy and had already been in the movie 52ND *Street*, with Cook and Brown. But her mother was handling her and Mrs. Saulters was a wonderful mother but she didn't have the necessary skills to be a successful manager. There's a difference between handling a child's affairs and actually knowing how to negotiate a deal without losing it. It was a shame because Dotty really had the potential to become a big star.

Around the same time that we left for Detroit, my wife went back to Chicago because the chorus lines were being taken out of the Apollo and there wasn't a lot of work available. Then the Midwest became our home base again. Catherine couldn't find many chorus line jobs there either so she started working as a secretary. Naturally, with me being away a lot, we began to just pull apart. She said she was sick of show business, she was going to seek a career elsewhere, and thought

I should do the same. I said, "What?!" No way was I going to even *think* about that! I wasn't prepared to do nothin' and I was just starting to get my feet wet in the business.

Well, we just drifted apart. I'd come into Chicago and she was distant. She had been hearing these rumors about me and Dotty. And, of course, she felt if I was going to do an act with a girl, it should have been her. But, hey, it's a crazy business and these things happen. I loved Catherine, but our lives were different; our social lives and everything. She realized that the life I wanted was not the life for her, so she decided to go back to Des Moines and finish her education.

Dotty and I stayed with the Mills Brothers for about six weeks. Then I met Rollo Vest, a booking agent around Detroit, and he offered to get us a lot of work there, so we made him our temporary agent. All of the neighborhoods in Detroit had a thousand little clubs that put small shows in on the weekends. The pay wasn't as good as the Plantation money, but it was good work, so we stayed there for about six months.

Then my friend Leonard Reed contacted Rollo to see if we could replace another girl-and-boy act, Chilton and Thomas, at the Grand Terrace in Chicago. Carol Chilton and Maceo Thomas were a very popular husband-and-wife ballroom team that played mainly white circuits. They were leaving the show to do something in California. So, Dotty and I packed up and took off for Chicago.

The Grand Terrace was operated by a fellow named Ed Fox, who worked for Memi Capone, Al Capone's brother. This was at Thirty-fifth and Calumet. Leonard was holding his rehearsals there during the afternoons and friends of the artists could sit in and watch. But there were so many people coming in and out—girlfriends and boyfriends—that Ed Fox said, "No more! Don't let no more people in during the rehearsals." He told the stage manager, "I don't give a damn who comes here. After we start, no one comes in that door!"

So Dotty and I got into town on the four o'clock train and headed on down to the theater. The guy at the door said, "No, I can't let you in. Ed Fox told me not to let nobody in." After a while, we could see that guy wasn't changing his mind, so we went back to the hotel. That night, when the club opened up, we went on down there, not knowing what to expect. Leonard said, "Where the hell have you been?" I said, "That stupid man on the door wouldn't let us in." Well, Ed Fox had a fit. He said, "You dumb son of a bitch! I didn't mean *nobody* when I said nobody!"

During that period Earl Hines and Fletcher Henderson were alternating dates at the Grand Terrace, and after our show ended, Earl was going out, so his manager, Joe Glaser, was on the scene, and he had checked out our act. Now he was also Louis Armstrong's manager, and he asked if we wanted to go on some dates with Louis's band in three weeks. We knew we were big time then. We went back to Detroit, played a few of those little neighborhood clubs, then went on tour with Louis Armstrong!

That was great because in addition to being an artist of the first order, Louie treated everybody like they were part of his family. He was always a lot of fun. We'd have sessions between the shows, when we'd sit up and "gumbeat," talk about our road experiences and all that kind of stuff. Louie was not like a boss. You could see right away that he and his musicians were buddies. Generally, you didn't go to him with problems, anyway. You'd see his road manager, who was a very nice guy.

Louie made his audience feel like they were a part of his show. He'd get involved with them: "Yeah, man. You know what I mean, Joe? You been there." He'd be talking to the audience and everybody felt that he was talking directly to them! He was not only a great musician and singer, but a great personality, like Bill Robinson.

I'd come of age listening to Louie's music and watching him perform because he came to Buffalo quite often. At that time we had big dance halls and all the big bands came through—Jimmie Lunceford, Louis Armstrong, Cab Calloway. They'd come to the dance halls for weekend appearances and everybody would flock there. Louie was always one of the favorites.

I'll never forget our first tour with him, because we were performing at a theater in Kansas City, Missouri, when Pearl Harbor was bombed in 1941. Boy, that was a shakeup! By then, our act was really starting to develop and we just got job after job. We'd dressed it up quite a bit. After our opening, we did a real jazz dance. Then Dotty went into a vocal spot. We did a couple of tunes in there and the second tune set up her solo dance. Then I came in back of that and did my solo dance, almost like the same ending that Honi and I developed later. After my solo, which was up-tempo with a lot of wings, we did some big kicks and some Lindy hop things with over-the-back moves, for the big finish.

Like Basie, Louie had a special fondness for dance acts. He'd even strut a little bit on stage, himself. After our first appearances with the band, he'd tell Joe Glaser, "Hey, man, see if you can get Cholly and Dotty to come out with us on this next gig. I like them kids." Joe would call up, "Hey, Chazz, Louie wants you and Dotty to come out and play a few dates with him. What do you think?" I'd say, "Well, can we get a little more money?" Joe said, "It ain't about money, it's about how many weeks he can give you." I said, "Okay, man, you got me. We'll make it." But see, generally if you mentioned a raise beforehand, there would be a little bit more money in your pay envelope, because Joe was that kind of guy.

There was a general pattern when you were going around the horn. Many big bands carried a boy-and-girl team, a comedy dancing act, and usually a couple of vocalists. And there were a few popular vocal groups who traveled with bands, like the Palmer Brothers. When we left Louie, we went back to do some more little dates at those neighborhood clubs that I mentioned before. They'd have just a trio of musicians and they would bring a singer and a dancing act in. Since we had both things in our act, a lot of those places would just hire us and pay us a little bit more money.

By this time, Leonard was back in Detroit getting ready to produce a show at Broad's Club Zombie, and he put Dotty and me in the line-up. He had rented a house for himself and some of the dancers. I moved in and that's when Leonard and I became real close friends. He started to include me in the production end of things.

We were doing stock in this club and the way Leonard had it set up, we changed the shows every month but kept the same people—

the same singers, the same dancers, the same chorus girls—just different costumes and numbers. This is when I started really getting into producing. I'd had a taste of it before, but not on such a major scale. Leonard had a great reputation in show business and was well established as a producer. He had years of experience under his belt.

I find that a lot of the things I got from him have been helpful to me in aligning shows for the vocal groups, because he showed me a psychological approach to figuring out how numbers should follow one another. I learned how important alignment is because shows are knitted together much better if you give a lot of thought to setting up psychological tie-ins. What I'm referring to is the way you make transitions from one act to another. Whatever you say to the audience between the acts either has to refer to what just ended or what is about to come on. You also have to take the acts you're working with and spot them properly in order to have good continuity. All those things I picked up from Leonard. Maybe a little of it I was aware of already, but I'd never had the chance to practice it like I did with him.

He was such a great person to work with. We never had any arguments . . . never really had a disagreement, because Leonard was the type of person who would ask you if you could do something, and if you said yes, he'd leave you alone and let you work it out, so I learned a whole lot assisting him at Broad's. The only time he ever interfered was when I first started teaching the chorus line some steps. He said, "Cholly, keep it simple. Don't be doing tricks that they can't do, because we don't have that much time. Teach the girls a step they can do now, not four days from now."

But that was real helpful to me because sometimes I could get a little complicated. I know that's what the Apollo's line used to say. But Leonard taught me how to expedite time and still make the dancers look good. I had a nice long run with him at the Zombie and I'll always be grateful for the time we spent together in Detroit.

When his show closed up, it was back to Chicago. Ziggy Johnson had a production on the South Side at Dave's Cafe. We stayed there for several months, then Rollo booked us on a Canadian tour. We

went to Toronto, Winnipeg, Calgary, and all the way over to the West
Coast, Vancouver (these are all little nightclubs); then down to Seat-
tle, Washington. We left Seattle and went to Portland, Oregon, then
from Portland back to Chicago to the same club that had been
Dave's. Now it was called the Rhumboogie and was owned by Joe
Louis's half-brother.

We worked there for about two months, at least, and while we were
there Cab came to the Chicago Theater downtown with his unit. Now
this is a funny piece of business right here! See, all of the bands, Andy
Kirk, Count Basie, everybody had softball teams. And the clubs in all
the different cities had squads, too. So whenever a new band came
into town, it would make arrangements to challenge local teams, like
on a Sunday morning. In Chicago, they'd get a reservation in Washington Park, where these games drew big crowds.

I was pitching for the Rhumboogie team. Remember, Honi is still
traveling with Cab, so he's on the opposing team. Just before the game
started, he came over and said, "Look, when Cab comes to bat, whatever you do, don't strike him out!" He knew I had a good fast ball because back in Atlantic City, when we had the team at the Paradise, I
was the pitcher, Honi was the third baseman, Brownie played second
base, and Cookie was in the outfield. Besides, Honi and I had played
softball together for a thousand years!

He said, "I know you're going to be throwing that little funny ball
up there. His head's gonna be bad and he ain't hardly gonna be able
to *see* the ball. I'm trying to get you this gig and if you strike him out
and embarrass him in front of all these people out here, he ain't never
gonna hire you!"

I went up there and I started lobbing the ball up to the plate, and
he was still striking at it and missing. He'd swing at the ball before it
even got up there! So I finally made up my mind, I'm not going to lob
this ball up; I'm just going to take everything I can off the ball and go
ahead and throw it up there—and pray! So I just guided it up to the
plate and sure enough, he hit the sucker past third base. Honi gave me
the sign. The next time Cab came up, I threw him the same kind of
pitch and he got a piece of it again, so that saved me!

Cab had an excellent adagio act in his show, Anise and Aland. They did an act similar to ballroom dancing, but with a lot of lifts and poses. In the fall of '42, Aland was inducted into the army and Anise began doing a solo spot in the show. Then Honi spoke to Cab about bringing Dotty and me into the show, so we started making the rounds with the Calloway band.

Dotty and I were smoking in Cab's revue, getting all kinds of great notices. We had become very close, but I was more or less a big brother for her. At least that's the way I thought she viewed me because I was nine years older and just coming out of a marriage. Besides I was a swinger! I wasn't even thinking about getting tied down to anybody. One day while we were playing a theater in Omaha, Nebraska, I was downstairs with one of the trumpet players trying to scare up a crap game between shows. Honi came to the steps and called me, "Hey, Chazz, come here. I want to talk to you for a minute." He'd just finished a conversation with Dotty, so he knew I had heard from Catherine's lawyer and a divorce was in process.

Now he's gonna play Cupid. "Look, man, you know how Dotty feels about you, right?" I said, "What you mean, man?" "The girl's in love with you. You ought to be able to see that, Mo." (That's what we called each other sometimes—short for Moses.) I told him, "Hooking up with your partner might be the best way to blow your act." "Well, you must have some kind of feelings for her, because you treat her like she belongs to you, and you don't want nobody messin' with her. You're working like a dog to build this act, so you'd better put some insurance on it and lock her up!"

Even though I hadn't been consciously thinking about Dotty in a romantic way, it wasn't too hard for me to start because I was attracted to her. Dotty and I were soul mates. Both of us loved show business and like I said before, she was just so full of life and loved to laugh. We'd always had a lot of fun on the road, but it was strictly platonic. Coles really opened my eyes to the situation, which was a good thing. About four months later, Dotty and I started rooming together. Finally, it got to the point where we were with each other all the time.

There was a very good singing group with Cab's revue called the Palmer Brothers, who did background vocals, close harmony. They had excellent voices. Something happened with their manager and they put a notice in, so there was suddenly a hole in the lineup. Honi went to Cab and said, "Look, why can't we have a shot at singing the background material?" Cab said, "Who is *we*?" "Well, me and Cholly and Dotty. We got a whole lot of friends in New York; we can get another girl there."

He finally went for it, but he wanted to bring in a singer that he knew from New Jersey, Frances Brock. In two weeks, we'd learned all of the vocals that the Palmer Brothers had done. We weren't as good as they were, but we were good enough! So, in addition to our separate acts, we did background vocals with Cab and when he had bookings in dance halls, where just the band played, we'd go along as singers.

During that period, the war effort wasn't letting up and the draft board started searching for Honi. Every time they'd get an address on him, we'd be moving to the next town. They finally tracked him down in April of '43. We were in Detroit and he opened the door to his dressing room, and there they were, *in body*. "Mr. Coles, we understand from New York that you've been a problem; you've been avoiding us. So we're going to have to do something about that! You're up here for a week?" Poor Honi, he's standing looking pitiful, "Yes, sir." "On Monday morning, report for your first examination. We'll make it early enough, so you can get back to the theater on time." They had it all arranged!

This cat went down there, man, they examined him and took his buns. He looked down at the report, and there it was in bold letters, "ACCEPTED!" They gave him thirty days in back of that. Honi said it was one of the saddest days of his life. We left the theater in Detroit and went straight into the Sherman Hotel in Chicago. Now we've got thirty days to replace him in the vocal group. So he suggested we bring in his brother, Baby Coles, who could halfway sing, but Baby was a street guy, a pool shark. We couldn't think of no buck dancer who could sing at that point, so Cab brought in Baby, because, you know, Cab was very fond of Honi and inclined to accommodate him.

We were in the Sherman for a whole month, and boy, that last night everybody was crying; we sure hated to see Honi go. About two weeks later, we were doing a dance date in St. Louis. We're standing up on the bandstand, singing like crazy, and I saw this cat coming down there with his army suit on, no mustache, hair cut short. I recognized the shape of that head! I said, "Damn, that sure looks like Honi." We're still singing away and this cat's coming on down the aisle.

All of a sudden, Cab stopped the band. "Ladies and gentlemen, one of our former partners and one of America's greatest dancers just walked in the hall. He's just been inducted into the service and we'd like to have all of you say hello to him." Cab brought him up on the stage. Oh, it was a big, big thing. Everybody was hugging and kissing and carrying on. It was just a great night!

He was stationed at Jefferson Barracks near St. Louis and had to be back before sunup. So we had a big party at the Deluxe Restaurant, a black-owned place that was famous for its breakfast menu. Cab made reservations for the whole band, everybody! And we partied until it was time for Honi to split.

It was just a thrill to see him. I think Honi had a little dab of ROTC in high school. He had become a drill master in just two weeks. Being a dancer and everything, he learned the close-order drill that quick. His camp had an induction center and none of those guys in there knew anything about marching, so his job was to get them in shape for that drill. It was so much like dancing, you know.

Pretty soon Baby decided that he was sick of singing; he wanted to make some pool tournaments, so Cab replaced him. We phoned Honi to let him know what happened. Periodically Cab would hook up calls from his dressing room to keep in touch with Honi. Every now and then I'd holler at him, "Hey, Mo, how you doin'? When you counting on breaking out of that place?" He said, "Man, when you coming in here?" I told him, "Naw, man, I'm sick. They ain't gonna take me, because you wouldn't want *me* protecting you or your family." Mo said, "You got a point there."

A few months later we were playing the Park-Sheraton in New York. That's when I went down to the mailbox in 2040 and there was this big message: "Greetings! We are trying to reach you, sir. Please report to the draft board immediately." They caught me while I was right in New York! It was September 1943.

Well, this letter was all I needed! I was already worried about my divorce and trying to keep everything straight with Dotty. And also, Cab's band was getting ready to go into the Apollo after we closed at the Sheraton. Since I had always suffered from gastritis, I figured that might save me. So this musician told me, "Look, man, just before you go down there, eat a little piece of soap. Complain about your stomach, and when they check it out, there will be like a little bubble in there and they'll think you've got ulcers and won't take you." I ate this little piece of soap, and I was sick as a dog!

So when I reported to the draft board, I took some medical forms documenting my stomach complaints. At the end of the examination, the guy said, "Look, under normal conditions I would reject you, but I've turned away so many people today, I'm going to just sign you up, and when you get in, they'll just put you out. If you continue to have problems with your stomach, they'll have no choice." I said, "Oh, man! Why the hell did I have to pick *this* guy!"

Dizzy Gillespie was in there that same day, at the very same time, and he was butt naked. He had taken off his clothes for the exam, so he was sitting there playing his trumpet, frothing at the mouth. The examiner said, "Get him out of here!"

Dizzy was still living in 2040, too. When I got back to the building, he said, "Man, I got out of it, man. How'd you make out?" I said, "They took my butt, man. I'm doomed." My report day was October 4. I'll never forget it.

We finished our run at the Apollo and I had a couple of weeks before my induction date, so we partied and carried on. Cab said, "You don't have to worry about Dotty, man. I'm going to keep her as my band vocalist." That's the kind of person Cab was, and I loved him for that.

4

STRUTTIN' FOR UNCLE SAM

Marching around in an army uniform was the last thing I wanted to be doing in 1943. But since there was no way to get out of this military business, I decided to just make the best of it. When we arrived at Fort Dix, the officers lined us up, gave us our khakis and barracks passes, and started making assignments. Now, usually at an induction center, you hardly know anybody, because people are sent there from all over the country. But as soon as I arrived, I ran into an old friend, Rudy Traylor, who was an excellent musician, a drummer. Rudy had been in the reserves and when the war started, he was inducted immediately and made a sergeant. I had seen him in his uniform at the Apollo and a lot of other places where Dotty and I were working.

Anyway, I got my assignment, located my building, and went in. Each of the barracks had two levels and held about twenty or thirty soldiers. At the end of each level there were little rooms called noncoms. I put my bags down, walked to the back of the barracks, and there was Rudy standing by the door. He looked over there and saw me and he just cracked up. He said, "Man, I don't believe this!" It turned out he was the sergeant in charge of my barracks and he made a point of giving me one of those noncoms, which was real nice, because they allowed you to have a little more privacy.

Next, we went through the inductee's schedule: line up for this, line up for that. Then I happened to meet John Hammond, who had just come down to Dix, too. He was a great impresario of jazz as well as a social activist. At the time, I didn't have a major book on him, but I was aware of his association with jazz music, so I was elated to meet him. John was planning to do a Columbus Day program for the officers and asked it I was interested in helping. I said, "Great! I'd be tickled to death to do it." I'm thinking, "Well, this army crap might not be so bad after all."

A few days later we started planning the show together. At that time the military was segregated, so John had to get permission to recruit guys from both the black and white recreation centers. He'd been doing that kind of thing for years. Since there were a lot of show business people at Dix from Philadelphia and New York, we had a big pool of artists to work with. Charlie Fuqua, of the Ink Spots, was there; a guy named Jack Leonard, who had been a vocalist with the Dorseys; Dan Minor, a trombonist from Count Basie's band; the pianist Bobby Tucker, who later played for Billie Holiday . . . oh, so many talented guys.

We worked hard on this thing and lined up a pretty good program that went over real well with the officers. The colonel of the post got up, congratulated all of us. John thanked everybody connected with the production and gave me a lot of credit for the structure and alignment of the show. The next day the colonel sent for me. "I understand from John Hammond that you made a major contribution to yesterday's show, so I just want to thank you again and also let you know that I'm one of Cab Calloway's biggest fans." We chatted about Cab for a minute; then he told me that I would be rewarded for my work. So I thanked him and left. I didn't give what he'd said much thought after that.

Three weeks later, they had to move everybody out of Fort Dix and make room for new inductees, so they sent the old guys to camps all over the country for basic training. As the orders came down, the guys would line up in the company street to receive their assignments. Rudy Traylor had the list for our barracks. When your name was called off, you were supposed to step out from the line, and he would tell you where to fall in. That is, which group you were with. Rudy said, "Private Charles Atkinson . . . Camp Shanks!" I thought, "Damn, that's a shitty name! Camp *Shanks*. Okay, man, here it goes. All right."

There were ten guys in our group and one of us had to be in charge of getting everybody else to Camp Shanks. But, see, nobody wanted to police these cats, so everybody was looking straight ahead, not blinking an eye, hoping they wouldn't be selected. Then I saw Rudy heading my way. He said, "You're the lucky brother, Cholly." I looked at him like he'd lost his mind. He said, "You're going to *Shanks*, man!" I said, "Man, where the hell is Shanks?" He said, "Twenty miles upstate from New York." I said, "Are you crazy?" He said, "Naw. You go in. You take these niggers with you. You're attached to the 375th U.S. Army Band. By the time you check in and get your barracks assignment, get your off-post pass . . . you can go on into New York tonight — be back in the morning, six o'clock." I said, "Man, you must be kidding!" He said, "I'm serious, baby. You got it made. Outside of that, you're in charge of these cats. Don't let nobody goof off, now. If one of them jumps the train, you gonna be in big trouble."

The military didn't let us stay on the train going into New York. Instead, we were told to get off in Newark, and trucks would be sent down to pick us up. It was my job to keep all those turkeys together for two hours in the train station, so there was more than enough time to lose somebody. I had Charlie Fuqua and Dan Minor with me.

Soon as we got to Newark, some of the guys started riding me, "Come on, man, let us go over to the city for a hot minute and we'll make sure we get back in time to meet the truck." I said, "No *way*, baby. You staying right here!" See, seven of them were from New York and the other two were saxophone players from Philly. They sent those trucks down, I turned them over to the sergeant, and I was home free! As soon as we got to Shanks, they took us over to the band barracks.

What they'd do at Fort Dix is this . . . they would look at your M.O., which is sort of like your history, things you've done in your life, what type of work, whether you're a plumber, an electrician, a baker, candlestick maker — whatever. When they looked at my M.O., they noticed that I had studied trombone and had a musical background, so that's why they attached me to the band. They ignored the dancing end of it altogether. They were trying to build those bands at Shanks.

We had an old army sergeant who was in charge of the military band, but Sy Oliver was directing the dance band at that point. There were a lot of jazz musicians stationed at Shanks, but I was still in the dark about it. Now, when I walked in the barracks, the first person I saw was the house drummer from the Apollo Theater. Next I ran into a saxophone player I knew, who had the same first and last names, William Williams. Then around the corner comes Buck Clayton. I couldn't believe it. I said, "Hey, baby!" Buck said, "Come on, man, I got my car up here. You want to ride back to the city with me?" I said, "Yeah, as soon as we sign in." I hadn't seen Sy Oliver yet. He was down in the PX drinking beer.

Then Mercer Ellington came by, saw me, and fell out on the floor! He said, "Man, how they let *you* in this man's army? They ain't supposed to be lettin' cats in here like you. Now I know we gon' lose the war!" It was like old home week! Half the guys there I knew. I wasn't even aware that some of them were in the service.

Mercer walked over to the PX and told Sy we were there. See, I really got to know Sy early in my career because Jimmie Lunceford's band used to come through Buffalo a lot and we got to be buddies. So Sy comes strutting back to the barracks . . . big old grin on his face. Came in there, "How'd *you* get here, man? This is for musicians." I told him, "I'm a trombone player." Well, he cracked up for real, then. "Man, get out of here!" I said, "Look at my M.O. It's 442." Sy fell out! When he finally stopped laughing, he said, "I got a little jug in my room, man. Come on over and have a taste." So he and Buck, Charlie, Dan Minor, and I went on over and chewed the fat for a while.

Sy had only been there for about a week, but right away he had started putting things together. He went down to the office and picked up musical scores; all of the arrangements that he had done for Tommy Dorsey. Shoot, he whipped those guys into shape fast, boy. He had the best band in that section because some of the greatest black musicians in the country were stationed at Camp Shanks.

Finally, Sy had to figure out what to do with me. He couldn't put me in the band playing trombone because I hadn't picked up an instrument since junior high school. So he made me the band's vocalist. I learned all of the top-forty tunes and I sang a lot of his things, "There, I've Said It Again" and "I'll Be Seeing You," and oh, I can't think of half of them. But I was doing all the vocals.

Remember, that's how I got in show business, as a singer. But it's like anything else. You get into dancing and you're not concentrating on singing, so you don't use your pipes, which is necessary. I wasn't no Billy Eckstine, but I never sang out of key and I had a pleasant-enough voice and a good concept.

One of the places I sang was at the recreation hall in the evenings between eight and eleven. Two or three times a week they would serve beer and other refreshments and guys could bring in visitors to dance, usually young ladies who worked in personnel on the base. Now, some of those soldiers would sneak out behind the recreation building with their dates, but the MPs didn't bother them as long as everybody was off the post by a certain time; they were really more concerned about making sure none of the chicks wound up in the barracks.

Before Sy got there, the white band had been getting all of the gigs at the officers' club, which was all white. But our band was swinging so hard that it got to the place where the colonel was requesting the black band all the time. Since there was no black officers' club to play for, we were always available.

You talking about some upset cats, those white musicians were "drugged," because you got special privileges when you played for officers. You could go home after you finished and you weren't due back until noon the next day. So the guys would jump into their cars and scoot on into the city by one in the morning. There were always rides, but you had to be on your P's and Q's because if you weren't back at the car on time, they would leave you. And if you came back to camp late, you would be AWOL, so everybody had to be real disciplined. It didn't matter how bad your head was, you had to get *up* and get *back*.

During that time, I used to see Dotty often because I still had my place in 2040 and she had moved in with me before I was drafted. Since

Cab's headquarters were in New York, Dotty would be home whenever the band wasn't on the road. And if they were booked in some place like the Zanzibar downtown, the gig might last for three weeks.

When I came into Manhattan, she and I would go to the movies, maybe out to dinner or to a show. She loved to ride them crazy ol' things at the amusement parks, but they were never my cup of tea. That was the kid in her because being a child star, Dotty didn't really have a lot of opportunities to do that stuff very much when she was growing up. I had messed around with carnivals and the whole shot, and I pretty much liked the chance games—knocking down pins and so forth. But them zippidy-doo-dah rides . . . I just couldn't make them. I'd say, "You got it, baby!" And she'd go right on by herself.

So you see, I was running in and out of Manhattan quite a bit. Some of the guys would go into the city and return late on the bus. Instead of coming through the gate, they would go down this little road and come through the hole in the fence, to get around the MPs. See, we had clipped places in the fence about thirty yards from our barracks where you could pull the wires out, go through, then set the wires back in, so the MPs couldn't see the cuts.

The old sergeant we had at Shanks taught me how to be a drum major. We had all the manuals, and I'd read up on it and . . . hell, I didn't have to learn about formations and all that kind of stuff, because I had been doing that all my show business career. Plus, I definitely knew how to strut!

Whenever the colonel sent down orders for a retreat, they'd bring the band on the field in front of the officers' quarters in the evening and we would do drills; then the guys would play while the flag was lowered. Sometimes the colonel or one of the aides would speak to the soldiers who were being processed. Then the trumpet section would play taps and I would give the signal with the baton to start the march. When the baton pointed out, the guys would step off on the next count at a forty-five degree angle. Then I'd be just stepping, keeping the time going!

A couple of times I got called on getting a little fancy. It had to be strictly military, no frills. But you know how a dancer will do; you try to get a little *body* into it. See, I have a tendency to follow the beat of the music. You're not supposed to be doing that. You're supposed to be just keeping that time. But I was gonna live it up a little bit. One of the officers would say, "Uh, that drum major you got over there, he's got a jazz thing going there. Get ahold of him and jack him up!"

Sy and those other cats were digging this—it knocked them out. "Pops, you were struttin'!" "Cholly, you was really struttin' out there, baby!" And the next thing you knew there was a notice sent down to the band leader: "Tell that drum major to cool it!" But those musicians in the band had problems, too. They'd be bending them notes in their marches. Shoot, you know how we'll do. They would play "Hooray for the Red, White and Blue" and jazz it all up. I'd say, "Hey, man, what were you *playing*?" Sy would be on their case, too. "You got to stick to the script, man." It would be hard for them cats to do it, because then it became a chore.

We spent a lot of time with all of those musicians who were out of big bands, because it was a whole new ball game to walk and play. Especially in time. They know about time when they're playing, but marching . . . a lot of them didn't have rhythm, when it came to the physical end of it. They would start messing up the music and not coming up right, stumbling, and getting on the wrong foot. And they had a lot to watch, because I'd blow the whistle and give them a signal, then when I'd bring my baton down for the band to stop, niggers would keep marching. They'd complain, "Aw, man, I was looking at the music."

They had those little staffs up there on their instruments. "I was starting to look over at that doggone staff, man, and I didn't see you bring that thing down. You got to bring it down *louder*." I said, "Louder?!" "Or sump'n, man; blow the whistle or sump'n." Those cats would march right up the back of the guys in front of them! So it took a lot of training, because they were not military musicians. And really, on a post like Shanks, most of the tunes they played were not military music.

I think in many cases, the officers running the camp understood this. They had read your M.O. and they knew you were out of Duke

Ellington's band, out of Basie's band, Charlie Barnet's band, Cal- loway's band. So there wasn't a great deal of emphasis on military stuff. A lot of the basic-training camps had reveille, taps every day, and they had all sorts of things for the military band, but because of the special nature of this camp, the scheduling and everything was fouled up to make adjustments for what we had to do on a daily basis.

See, Camp Shanks was a point of embarkation and debarkation, so things would happen spontaneously that had to be dealt with right away. For example, if some ships came in from Europe with casual- ties, they couldn't all get into the docks at the same time. So, per- formers like myself might be sent out to entertain the guys while they were waiting to get into the hospitals. Schedules changed daily to ac- commodate those kinds of dilemmas.

While I was at Shanks, I was in a show with Ethel Merman and I reminded her that we had been in a movie together back in '36, *Strike Me Pink*. So she introduced me to her husband, Colonel Levitt, who was stationed in Washington and was in charge of all five New York installations. They had been in the wings digging me because I was on the bill in front of her, doing a tap routine.

In a couple of days, Colonel Riley, who was in charge at Shanks, called me into his office and said, "I've got some good news for you!" Colonel Levitt had arranged for me to be frozen in the New York area for the duration of my stay in the army. Anyway, I pretty much had it made in the shade after that. Maybe Ethel got him when they were in the sack and said, "I want you to do something for me, baby." I always wondered just how the thing went down.

We stayed on at Shanks until they decided to close the camp. The quota for foot soldiers and so forth was basically filled, so they picked the cream of the crop from the two bands, sent that group on to Camp Kilmer, and the other musicians were sent overseas. By then we were corporals, classified as T-5s. Sy became a master sergeant, technician second grade, T-2. Guys in that grade had more responsibilities, pa- pers and all that kind of crap, and they had to be at the base a lot. Most of us were tickled to death to be T-5s, so we could make our little runs to the city as often as possible.

When I moved to Kilmer, my bunk was right between Jimmy Craw-ford, who was Lunceford's drummer, and this tenor saxophone player, Bo McCain. He never really made it big, but he could *blow* . . . just an excellent musician. Jimmy was a great drummer. A great person, too. So full of life. Never down. He and Bo were just so uplifting and I was lucky to be bunking with them.

Those two guys would ride me, "Man, you got all the chicks. You got to lighten up, Cholly." See, Buck Clayton, Skinny Brown, and I used to party together a lot. Skinny was a tenor saxophonist from New Jersey, and he knew all them little towns around New Brunswick; knew all the chicks and everything, so we used to hang with him. Boy, did we have some sport then. We would be partying like crazy!

Well, nobody knew if the whole thing was going to change and you'd be on the boat going overseas and *never* come back. So shoot, you'd be living it up. One girl named Etta, that I knew in 2040, had a family right outside of New Brunswick, and she had some pretty sis-ters. The way I remember the thing, I'd be kissing one and thinking about the other; get their names all mixed up. Every time I saw Etta in New York, she'd say, "Boy, you're some low son-of-a-gun!"

When I went to Kilmer, I was still a drum major, but I had other jobs, too. In special service, like that, you do a lot of things. For ex-ample, Charlie Fuqua became a drummer. Now Charlie was a little guy; ordinarily played the guitar, but in the military band he was car-rying that big old bass drum. Sy tried to get me to do it. I just looked at that thing. I said, "No way, man!" So he finally put me on the cym-bals. Shoot! I didn't even have to read. I knew all those little crazy sounds and places where you're supposed to hit the cymbals.

Like Shanks, Camp Kilmer was a port of embarkation and debarka-tion. So the soldiers that were going to Europe all came through the East Coast debarkation. They would bring the ships into the New York Harbor and within ten days, they were shipping those guys out. That's when we would go down to the pier and play for them while they board-ed the ship. And our band would be trucking on up the gangplank, swinging the "St. Louis Blues," good black music, you know what I mean? And the whites would be doing the same thing. The total personnel of each band was thirty-one musicians, and Sy made those arrangements for the full military band. So they would be poppin', baby, those thirty-one pieces, and I'd be banging those cymbals.

Jimmy Crawford set up a hi-hat type thing for me, because on occasion I became a drummer. They'd break the band up into little units of five or six and send them into mess halls and places where the soldiers were congregated, so they would have some music when they first came into camp off the boats. We would have a guitar player, bass player, two horns, and the drums. My drum set consisted of a snare, a couple of cymbals on the bass drum, a tall cymbal for me to play with the sticks, and a sock cymbal that I played with my foot. Jimmy rigged all that up for me. Yeah, those are memories, boy. Good to be thinking about those things.

In our barracks there were always two old army guys in charge and they were a great help to those of us who weren't military-minded. We didn't know regulations and all that kind of thing and they would keep you abreast and remind you to stick as close to the rules as possible. Sergeant Scott made all of the schedules and gave out all of the passes.

He was married, with four kids, and I would check out with him when I had a gig in the city on the weekend. I'd go into New York, take off my army clothes, put on my civvies, and go do a thing with Chuckles of Chuck and Chuckles, or go somewhere and do a dance single in a club and make two or three hundred dollars. Then I'd come back and give Sarge fifty. If I didn't have a job when the weekend rolled around, he'd say, "Man, ain't you got no gig this week?"

I loved dancing with Chuckles because that would be a big fat piece of change. I would go back and give Sergeant Scott a hundred dollars, man, and he'd even shine my shoes for me! A hundred dollars meant a lot to a family of six at that time.

All the acts working during the war were making big money, because so few were available. Since Chuckles wasn't able to do a single, I'd go and work with him or anybody else that needed a partner. At that time Chuck was in the hospital. Chuckles and I did an ad-lib act. He did comedy; little funny steps. I didn't try to imitate Chuck, but I would do some things that he and Chuckles had done together . . . jazz things, like the Suzie-Q and all that kind of b.s.—applejack. Comical steps. Then we did a few jokes and I would do my single, which was my own dance. The most important thing was to have two people because everybody expected that.

Well, the sergeant pretty much helped us avoid trouble with the other officers. The only thing I had difficulty with was my dressing habits. I didn't like the regulation clothes that they issued because I preferred my things to be kind of smooth. So some of us would go to the army and navy store and buy officers' outfits, like pants and jackets, and have the T-5 insignia put on them. We would be sharp, baby, because those officers' slacks had sheens to them, you know what I mean? And good cuts! We weren't supposed to do any of that stuff, but we got away with it. Most of the cats that bought officers' clothes were pretty smart dressers in civilian life, so they wanted to be like that in the army. We were making enough cash to still look sharp, so why not? And we knew if we wore smart-looking things, we could catch the eyes of the girls.

We'd also get flyers' caps and that's where the officers would really get on your case, because we'd take out the metal bands, like they did, then we could really style. When the guys caught you without the bands in your cap, they didn't arrest you, they'd just get on you and bug you. We'd play along, "Okay, man. Okay, Sarge." He'd say, "Don't appease me. Just the next time I catch you out here. . . . Matter of fact, you better go home now and get the thing and put it in your cap. If I run into you out here again, I'm going to put you in the brig." "Okay, man, I'm late." "Well, I'm still talking to you." "Ah, okay." So he'd stare at you for a little while. "All right, soldier, just observe what I'm telling you. Don't you get caught out here no more without that frame in that cap. As a matter of fact, take it off! Don't put it on no more until you get that band in." Just harassing you.

Those guys were sitting around in their little jeeps and ain't nothing happening, so they would create their own little excitement by bothering you. They'd tell you, "Don't wear that uniform no more. Take them stripes off and put them on your regulations." I was thinking, "Shee-it, not as much money as I paid for *this*." You'd get away from him, go somewhere else, and run into another one . . . he'd tell you the same thing. I'd get away and keep on stepping. Smooth, baby, and sharp.

After I was at Camp Kilmer for about eight or nine months, I was assigned to a job as a dance consultant on Forty-sixth Street, right downtown in Manhattan. The Army Department had taken over a whole building between Sixth and Seventh Avenues and set up a floor where soldiers with theater experience formatted amateur shows. We figured out everything from portable lighting straight through to performance and wrote it up in book form for camps that didn't have entertainment. I'd go in at nine, have an hour-and-a-half lunch break, then at 4:30 we started looking at the clock. Five, we were out of there!

Since we only went in Monday through Friday, I was performing around the city every weekend and hooking up with Dotty as much as possible. When she was on the road, we dropped notes and cards to each other on a regular basis. And occasionally, if I had three days off, I'd meet Cab's band somewhere like Chicago and stage a number for him or choreograph a little something for his chorus line. I ended up spending a whole lot of time with Dotty while I was in the service and we fell very deeply in love.

The guys at Kilmer used to say that I wrote pretty good lyrics, so Buck Clayton asked me to give him something that he could set to music. It was called, "Can't We Try Again?," a sort of love ballad; a very pretty tune. Buck made a big band arrangement of it for Cab, and Dotty sang it while she was still touring with the band. They were supposed to record it, but that never really happened, although it was published by Mills Music.

Sy Oliver and I did several songs together at Kilmer, too. One of them, "Baby, Are You Kidding," was recorded by the Delta Rhythm Boys on Decca Records, and Nat Cole recorded another one, "She's My Buddy's Chick." I still get a few royalties, every now and then, on an annual basis. Over the years the check would go from maybe $1,000 to $500. Now the money has dwindled down and most of the royalties are from foreign rights, but that's pretty good for an old man!

Captain Sachs was a white saxophone player at camp who hung out in the black barracks all the time with Sy's band. He was a jazz enthusiast and his wife loved tap dancing. I think she had been a dancer. Well, every summer we had productions and all of the top brass outfits would attend. I'd go on stage and do my little tap dancing, the singers would be doing their thing, the whole shot. These were complete shows. Captain Sachs's wife saw me dancing and had him set up a little place in the headquarters outside of his office so that I could give her some tap lessons.

Well, I was always complaining about stomach problems. Remember, that's what the examiner at the draft board had told me to do, "Go in and just keep complaining, man, and eventually they'll put you out." So that's what I did, even when I was drinking whiskey like it was going out of style. I'd go over to the health center and they would give me this old chalky stuff. . . . I'd take it back to the barracks and throw it in the toilet. Go back the next morning, same thing. See, every time you went over, they'd put it in your medical records.

Now, this next piece of the story is all politics. Mrs. Sachs's brother was in charge of the medics. He was Captain Rosen. And evidently she felt sorry for me and asked her brother if he could help me out. So every now and then, he would put me in the hospital for three weeks. When you went in like that the Red Cross would pull together all the sick guys who were able to move around, put them on a bus, and take them into New York City to see plays. Sometimes whole bunches of us would go to a big restaurant and have steaks and everything. And the Red Cross would pay. So those three weeks were like a vacation! You would have no duties, no going to the piers, none of that.

Now we're well into 1945 and soon the war is going to be over. A lot of guys were getting out on points. They were counting those things up, "Well, man, I'll be leaving here pretty soon." Some of those cats had been in the army a lot longer than I had, so I was in bad shape, pointwise.

Then Captain Rosen got an order from Washington stipulating that anybody who had been complaining about certain ailments could get a medical discharge. So he called me. "Hey, man, come over here. I want to talk to you." I went on over to the hospital and he said, "I'm going to bring you in here for two weeks, get you a medical discharge, and get you out of here." He said, "Go over and pack your things." I walked on back over to the barracks, grinning. I said. "Yeah, man, you cats talking 'bout your points and all that crap. I'll see you in New York. I'll be in the Apple waiting when you get there, baby!"

I packed up my duffel bags and went back to the hospital. Some days I'd go over to the barracks, visit with the guys and rub it in. They'd say, "Man, you *got* to be the luckiest nigger in the world!" They were all getting out, eventually, you know, but it was a process. They didn't let everyone out at once.

During that two-week period something real nice happened. Ethel Waters came down to Kilmer to visit me in the hospital. She was a big star at that time and all the guys were excited, especially Captain Sachs. He was telling the whole camp, "Guess who's over at the hospital visiting Corporal Atkinson? Ethel Waters!" The guys said, "What?!" Oh, boy, the nurses (they were mostly male) and everybody came running over. Darn near the whole time she was there, all she was doing was signing autographs. But it was just so nice of her to take the time out. She would do things like that, you see.

Anyway, my two weeks were finally up. I got my medical discharge with a 30 percent disability pension. About every six months they'd send you a notice and you would have to go in for a checkup. Finally the doctor said, "I wish my duodenal tract was working as well as yours." I knew what that meant. So I thanked him and left. By the time they cut off my money, Honi and I were well into Coles and Atkins.

He'd had a pretty rough time in the service. Honi was transferred from Jefferson Barracks in St. Louis to Greensboro, North Carolina, and ran into all kinds of difficulties there. He had a real cracker in charge of the post, who made it extra hard for the black GIs. The chefs were telling him, "Hey, man, them guys over there in the white section are eating good chop-steak and they're sending the bad cuts of beef and shit over here." In addition to a lot of other problems, the

Cholly Atkins (1914)

Cholly *(left)* and brother Spencer (1917)

Cholly's mother, Christine Woods
Atkinson (c. 1934)

Cholly's father, Charles Sylvan Atkinson
(c. 1915)

Junior high basketball team at Public School 47 (1926); Cholly is in back row, second from left; Ivor Moore is in back row, third from left; Mr. Russo is in second row, center

The Chocolate Steppers (c. 1930s)

Bill "Bojangles" Robinson (1935)

The Rhythm Pals in performance with singer, June Richmond, and the Les Hite Band (1936); *standing, from left*: Cholly Atkins, Les Hite, William Porter, June Richmond

The Rhythm Pals (1937); *from left*: William Porter and Cholly Atkins

Dancing the cakewalk in the Hollywood film, *San Francisco* (1936); Cholly is sixth from right   Courtesy of Delilah Jackson

Cholly performs in musical short (1937)   Cholly Atkins Collection

Apollo Theater (c. 1939); *front row, from left:* Lois Bright, Jackie Bass, Bernice Johnson, Catherine Atkinson, unidentified   <small>Courtesy of Ronnell Bright</small>

Hot Mikado (1939); *from left:* Chink Lee, Eddie Morton, Cholly Atkins
<small>Cholly Atkins Collection</small>

Apollo Theater (c. 1940); *front row, from left:* unidentified, Bernice Johnson, Lois Bright, Marion Coles   COURTESY OF MARION COLES

Cotton Club Boys in Chicago (1940); *from left:* Jules Adjers, Louie Brown, Freddy Heron, Chink Lee, Eddie Morton, Cholly Atkins   CHOLLY ATKINS COLLECTION

Rhumboogie chorus line (c. 1940); *from left:* Baby Simmons, Catherine Atkinson, Claudia Oliver, Pudgy Radford, Margie Tubbs, Blanche Shavers, Kathleen Dade, Harriet Hickerson   CHOLLY ATKINS COLLECTION

Cholly Atkins *(left)* and Dotty Saulters on stage with Cab Calloway (1943)
CHOLLY ATKINS COLLECTION

Cholly Atkins and Dotty Saulters with the Cab Calloway Revue (1943)

Cholly Atkins in performance at Camp Kilmer, New Jersey (1944)

Relaxing at a Chicago club (1947); *from left*:
Cholly Atkins, Slappy White, Frank Wess,
Billy Eckstine, Pete Nugent, Honi Coles

375th Army Service Forces Band, Camp
Shanks (1944); Cholly served as drum major
(standing, far left)

Coles and Atkins with Ziggy Johnson and his chorus line at the Rhumboogie in Chicago (1947); *front row, from left*: unidentified, Willa Mae Perkins, Pudgy Radford; *second row, from left*: Lorraine Knight, Ernestine Moore, Honi Coles, Claudia Oliver, Cholly Atkins, Jeri Steinberg, Greta Starks; *back, center*: Ziggy Johnson

Los Angeles after-hours club (1947); *front table, clockwise, from left*: Cholly, Honi, unidentified, Alice Key, Pete Nugent; Billie Holiday is seated at back table, center left

The classiest of class acts, Coles and Atkins, on stage (1948)

Count Basie Band (1939);
front, far left: Count Basie;
back row, from left: Dan Minor,
Dicky Wells, Benny Morton,
Harry "Sweets" Edison; *center*:
Jo Jones on drums; *saxophonists,
from left*: Herschel Evans,
Earle Warren, Jack Washington;
Freddie Green on guitar

Coles and Atkins take to the air in Broadway's *Gentlemen Prefer Blondes* (1949)

Gotham Golfers (1948); Cholly is seventh from left; Honi Coles is third
from left CHOLLY ATKINS COLLECTION

Copasetics and friends (c. 1950s); *from left, seated:* Henry Fenner, Cholly Atkins,
Ernest Brown, Honi Coles, Jean World, Libby Spencer, unidentified, Lorraine
Gillespie, Edna James, Lucille Preston, Harry "Sweets" Edison; *from left, standing,
front row:* James Walker, Curley Hamner, Cookie Cook, LeRoy Myers, unidentified,
Jesse Bridges; *standing, from left, back row:* Luther Preston and Francis Goldberg

The swinging Copasetics in
performance (1950s); *from left*:
Cholly Atkins, Louie Brown,
John Thomas, Honi Coles,
Phace Roberts, Pete Nugent,
LeRoy Myers

Copasetics' showcase, "On the Riviera" (1961); *from left*: Honi Coles, Marion Coles, Cholly Atkins, Dotty Saulters

Short subject comedy sketch (1953); *from left*: Willie Bryant, Leonard Reed, Cholly Atkins, Honi Coles

MPs would always give Honi and the cats a hard time when they went into one of the local towns.

As Honi tells it, the inspector general was coming to camp and Honi was selected by the black GIs to be the spokesperson. He ran down their problems and the very next day, this old captain called him in. "Sergeant Coles, I take it you don't like the way I'm operating this camp." Honi said, "Sir, I'm not concerned about the way you're running the whole camp, I'm just worried about the way you're treating the people in my section of the camp." "Well, what's the problem? We treat them like they're accustomed to being treated."

Honi said, "That is the problem, sir. The concept of custom is what we're complaining about. We'll be dying for our country like everybody else and we're treated like second-class citizens." The captain said, "I don't make the rules, Sergeant. I just see that they're carried out, because that's my job." So they talked the whole thing through. He issued Honi a three-day pass, so of course he left thinking he had the captain right where he wanted him.

When Honi came back and looked up on the assignment board, he had been demoted from a drill sergeant to a truck driver! He was processed right away to go overseas; they gave him ten shots in one day! They got that cat out of there fast. About two weeks before all this happened, he and Maggie had gotten married in Greensboro. She told me that after she came back to New York, there was no word from Honi for three months. Then this letter came from Karachi, India!

Honi and I used to write all the time. He loved to tell this story: "Here I am over here in India in all this heat and malaria and everything and I get a letter from Cholly saying how rough it was where he was!" He'd say, "Man, I'd cuss you out, call you all kinds of dirty names; telling me how rough it is at Camp Kilmer, forty miles from New York City." Later I'd say, "Well, I was just doing that, man, out of sympathy, to make you think that it wasn't so nice where I was either." He'd say, "Well, it didn't work!" He loved to tell that story to everybody . . . old ham Coles.

COLES AND ATKINS

While I was at Camp Kilmer, Honi and I had corresponded about doing something together when and if we got out of the scrap. So as soon as he was discharged in November of '45, we started making plans. My divorce from Catherine came through in the early part of '44 and I married Dotty on September 2, 1944, in Wilmington, Delaware, just outside of Philadelphia. Her father made all the arrangements. By that time she was well established as Cab's vocalist, which eliminated any idea of putting our act back together and opened the door for me to hook up with Honi.

Our original plan was to start a dancing school. Then we realized that setting up a business took a lot more money than either of us had. So we decided to throw a few things together, do an act for a while, then start the school. First we considered adding another person. Honi said, "Well, the only problem with doing a trio is that we'll be locked into so many things, whereas if we just have a duo we can develop all the variety ideas that we've talked about." So that's the route we took.

Rehearsals for Coles and Atkins really started in the beginning of '46. We worked on our act through the spring of that year, then went up to Buffalo and stayed with my folks for a week while we played around in a little old club to get a feel for the material. Then we came back to New York and opened at the Apollo. We didn't even have to audition!

Jack Schiffman, the owner's son, had already seen Honi perform as a soloist with the Three Giants of Rhythm. So he knew he was top drawer, and he had seen me dance at the Apollo with Dotty. Jack just went ahead, booked us, and we never looked back. After the act was so successful, we forgot about the school!

During the forties and fifties, Honi and I worked with several agents, but we were basically handled by Joe Glaser. Remember, he's the guy who hired Dotty and me to travel with Louis Armstrong. He took care of bookings for many well-known bands. And occasionally when Joe's other clients had dates, we were automatically put on the bill. Honi and I were really fortunate to have our act requested by a lot of band leaders.

Right after Coles and Atkins was formed, we did some dates with bands at different theaters—the Royal in Baltimore; the Howard in Washington, D.C.; the Earle in Philadelphia; and the Regal in Chicago. Once you finished at the theaters, you'd usually do a couple of nightclubs. We played a smart little Italian supper club in Baltimore called the Chanticleer. We were on a bill with Dean Martin, who was the headliner, and Jerry Lewis, who did a comedy act as a single. Jerry was such a flop, they were going to can him, but his agent asked Dean to give him a hand and play straight man to help him go over for that engagement. At the time, Dean was strictly a balladeer. From the Chanticleer, he was going into the Five Hundred in Atlantic City, and he had so much fun fooling around with Jerry that he took him along and that was the beginning of their team.

One of our favorite bands was Andy Kirk and the Mighty Clouds of Joy, an excellent group of musicians, out of the Midwest—through Kansas City, I believe. Mary Lou Williams was the piano player and her former husband, John Williams, played the saxophone. Andy was a real fine band leader and the thing that stands out in my mind is how good he was to Billie Holiday.

She did about eight dates with us. Bobby Tucker was her pianist. He eventually became Billy Eckstine's pianist, arranger, and sometimes conductor. Billie was notoriously late and Andy would move her around in the show and juggle the acts until she got there. Sometimes she would be in the theater and still late, but he was always extremely kind to her.

For a while there, every Christmas week, Joe Glaser had Andy's band booked at the Royal Theater in Baltimore, and he would offer us the date. Now, if there's any place you don't want to be at Christmastime, it's Baltimore. We'd think about it, then tell him, "Naw, man, we're not going back this Christmas." But the bookings would get real slow around that time of the year and nothing else would come up, so before you knew it, *bang*, you'd be doing it again. Because our families would need the money for Christmas.

We'd call Joe back, "Hey, Mr. Glaser, can we still get that Baltimore gig?" He'd say, "Yeah, I figured you were going to do it. I've already set it up." Honi and I used to laugh about that thing because first of all, if we had to work and be away from our families at Christmas, we definitely didn't want to go to the Royal.

It had the worst floor in the world and you'd get through your whole act and hear one single clap. But you were lucky if you didn't get booed off the stage. Once we worked there with Cab Calloway, and Cab finished his number and threw his hair down—you know how he used to do—and that head just hung there. No applause whatsoever. None! Not one person. Now, you know Cab didn't want to come up out of *that* bow! Man, you talking about a rough audience. The Royal was just one of those theaters.

Working with Louis Armstrong was so much fun. We used to hang out with him a lot. In between shows, we would sit around his dressing room, tell jokes, laugh, like we did when Dotty and I were traveling with him. He used to come up with stories about the acts he'd hired and things that happened on different tours. Louie was such a wonderful man. He didn't mind people who had habits as long as you could control them, didn't mess with his show, didn't miss no rehearsals, and when you got on stage you knew what to do and did it.

Charlie Barnet was another guy we had some good times with. There were about three black musicians in his band, but the fact that it was mostly white never came up. I always admired him for giving Lena Horne her first big break as a band vocalist. Charlie's favorite dancer was Bunny Briggs. That's who he liked to take on the road, but Honi and I did a theater date with him right in New York. See, at that time variety shows were presented in theaters along with movies and they used to keep the acts in until the film changed. Since this was a top picture, we stayed in the Strand Theater for about six weeks.

I remember only one time we had any kind of problem with him. To give you a little background, Honi was always coming up with some kind of new idea for our act. We'd rehearse a step over and over, put it in the choreography, and we'd be doing the hell out of that thing, then here comes Coles, "Chazz, I think I've got an idea." I'd say, "Again?"

This particular night with Charlie's band, we had gone to great lengths to get the music and everything just right, and the first show was a big success. Second show, Honi went over to him, "Hey, Charlie, instead of playing, *yot dot dee dee dot*, play it, *yot dot dah dah dot.*" So he went along with it. Third show Honi went back again. "Hey, Charlie, instead of playing, *yot dot dah dah dot*, play, *yot dee dot dee dot.*" He said, "Listen, if you come back here one more time, you gon' need a job!"

In the latter part of '46, we played the El Grotto in Chicago at Sixty-fourth and South Cottage Grove Avenue. This was a swank club that was opened in the Pershing Hotel by a couple of black guys. Ziggy Johnson had the chorus line in there. Maggie's cousin, Pauline Jones, was in that group. While we were there, Dotty came out to visit for three or four days and we learned that Cab was thinking about breaking up his big band. I believe she worked with him for about three or four more months after that.

When the El Grotto run ended, Ziggy asked if we wanted to go with him to the Plantation. So we packed up and left with him for St. Louis, took care of that gig, then made our way back to New York. That's when we hooked up with Count Basie for a tour out to the West Coast following a northern route and came back with Eckstine's band on a southern route. That was in '47.

Now we enjoyed working with all of the bands, but we had more fun with Basie than we had all the rest of our *lives*. Basie loved to take

people out there that *he* liked. That was real important to him. I remember on one tour, Pete Nugent was doing a single, the Two
Zephyrs were on the bill, and Coles and Atkins. Naturally, he had his
singers, too.

We traveled all over the country and since Basie was so popular,
there would be parties everywhere we went. But he was the kind of
guy who didn't want to go to anything unless the whole band was invited, his whole show. But half the time the guys didn't really want to
party. They would just hang out together, go to a bar or something.
When you're on the road like that, parties eventually get to be a drag
because you wind up with a whole bunch of crazy people you don't
know and don't want to know. Besides, for us, the best times were right
on stage with the band.

Once when we were on tour, Basie's birthday rolled around and
everybody chipped in and bought him a fabulous, expensive golf set,
with about four dozen top-of-the-line balls. Now, Basie never played
golf in his life, but he admired those clubs. He'd have the valet lug this
set around everywhere we went. Then he'd take it and set it up in his
dressing room, because people would come in to visit and see his clubs.

There were about three of us in the show that played golf together
all the time: Honi, myself, and Freddie Green. I can't exactly remember what started this, but something happened, and Honi and Freddie
stole all of Basie's brand new balls, then told him that I did it. The
next show, we went on, and we were dancing to a real pretty up-tempo
tune called "Sylvia." When it got to my solo, Basie played "Turkey in
the Straw." I backed up, "Basie, what are you doing to me?" He said,
"You dance to what I play. This is my choice. And I'm gonna keep
playing it until I get my golf balls back."

But he would do these things. We had that pretty soft-shoe, "Taking a Chance on Love." One show he told the saxophone players to
change the arrangement so they'd sound like Guy Lombardo. Basie
was having a ball! He would do just crazy things and have everybody
on the bandstand cracking up.

I remember, we were in Omaha, Nebraska, doing about five shows,
and Pete Nugent went out of the theater to get something to eat. The

show changed on the half hour, and when it started, Basie didn't realize Pete was out in the street. But the valet knew, so he had told Honi and me to get ready. The curtain opened and Basie said, "Here's one of the greatest tap dancers in the country, ladies and gentlemen, Public Tapper No. 1, Mr. Pete Nugent," and went right into Pete's music. So Honi went on, and after he did a chorus and a half, I went on. We were trading back and forth, trying to figure out what to do to Pete's music.

Now, in the meantime, Pete is on his way back to the theater, and he comes into the alley and up to the stage door, which is open. First he hears his music, he listens again, then he hears some taps. He says, "It couldn't be the food I ate. I'm on and I don't know how I'm doing!" Then he walks up to the wings and sees us out there scuffling with his music. So, when the next spot came up, Pete had to go on, and Basie announced Coles and Atkins and started playing all of our tunes. That included our soft-shoe, Honi's solo, then my solo, so the tempo kept changing. Poor Pete was out there struggling with our music for twelve minutes.

Basie had more songs for tap dancers than anybody. All the dance acts, chorus girls, and everybody loved to work with him. You couldn't listen to Basie's music and not pat your feet. He was out of this world. And the guys in the band would get just as carried away with the music as the dancers. They'd make up words to some of the riffs and sing along when we were on stage. Basie would say, "Keep that in!" You might be doing a traveling step, like walking, and the guys would sing right along with the rhythm of the music, "Where you going, Mr. Coles?" Man, Honi and I had so much fun with those cats.

A guy out of Philadelphia, Chappie Willet, arranged the music for our whole act. We had some real pretty melodic saxophone passages, and Basie's band just loved to get to a certain part. There would be no brass in there, nothing but rhythm and the saxophones. And the cats would start singing. Basie would say, "Hey, man, you all supposed to enjoy playing it, but you're not supposed to overshadow the man's taps." So he told the sound people to cut off all the saxophonists' mikes when we got to that part. I used to get on Marshall Royal. I said, "Marshall, you leading this thing, man." He said, "I'm loving it more than them cats!" So you couldn't get mad with the musicians because they weren't doing it to upstage you, they were just enjoying the music. That's the only problem we ever had with the band.

We worked with a lot of drummers. I mean big, big drummers, like Cozy Cole, but the one we loved the most was Jo Jones. He had so much respect for dancers and just the right feel for accompanying tap. Jo understood that it was his job to provide musical support for the acts on the bill and he'd stay right up underneath us. Wouldn't try to overplay it. Sonny Payne did the same thing. He found little rhythms in there like a crazy wing I used to do: HIPPYHIPPY-HIPPYHIPPY-STUR, STUR'A'DA'BOP. And every time Sonny would lay on it, he'd do that STUR'A thing with me.

Buddy Rich was like that, too. He'd try to lay the rhythmic patterns you were doing in places that would accentuate the steps. Louie Bellson was another one that was real fine. He was fascinated with the different rhythms that we would create, especially during Honi's solo because his steps were so complicated that if the drummer got too fancy, the whole band could fall apart and the musicians wouldn't know where to come back to.

But some of the drummers felt that they should interpret the music. They'd say, "Hey, man, I'm out there playing. I've got to play something for myself." I said, "Yeah, man, but you dropping bombs in the middle of my pretty step. All I want is some time there, HA-CH'BAM, HA-CH'BAM, HA-CH'BAM."

Art Blakey always gave us a hard time. He was with the Billy Eckstine band. Boy, we hated working with him. This guy had absolutely no respect for dancers. He'd say, "I'm not playing like that, man. I have to play what *I* want to play." So we would tell B, and B would tell him, "Look, man, you do that in our numbers, but don't be messing up the cats' act. These guys won't want to work with us." Blakey would say, "Well, we don't need them."

Honi and I tried to develop systems to get that type of drummer to cool it. You'd wave your hands, "down, down," and some would want to get louder because they didn't care about singers or dancers. But truthfully, they needed us as much as we needed them, because during that era, nobody wanted to just sit and listen to sixty or ninety minutes of arrangements with no diversion, especially if they were in a theater and couldn't get up and dance. But making everybody understand that we had to cooperate could be pretty difficult at times.

Finally, I'd tell Honi, "Don't mess with the musicians. Back up to the band leader and say, 'Bring them down,' because they work for him. If you ask them to do it, they'll say, 'Oh, nigger, go on and dance. We're playing the music. You just dance.' " But you couldn't go jumping on those guys, because then they'd never do what you wanted and you always catch more flies with sugar than that other stuff. But, truthfully, those types of guys were few and far between. The vast majority of the musicians were very, very good people to work with and extraordinarily talented.

Cab finally decided to break up his big band in 1947, so Dotty went out on her own as a soloist. I remember when I came back from the tour with Basie, she was working in Manhattan at the Savannah Club and the Baby Grand, the place that Nipsey Russell came out of. She was also singing at the 845 in the Bronx and doing a lot of little clubs down in Philly.

During the summer of '47, Honi and I went on the road with the Ink Spots' revue, which was top-notch. Johnny Otis was the band leader—an adorable person. He was a West Coast musician. The Ink Spots had June Richmond, an excellent singer, Coles and Atkins, and the Two Zephyrs. They did a slow-motion acrobatic dance, using jazz movements. In one routine, they enacted a slow-motion razor fight. Slappy White was Little Zeph's partner because Big Zeph had passed away by that time.

Since several of the guys took their wives along, we had a long fleet of cars. Dotty went just to be with me . . . I was glad! Bill Kenny, one of the Ink Spots, had a big Cadillac, and Charlie Fuqua had a huge Buick. We were riding in style—out to Chicago, Minneapolis, Winnipeg, darn near the same route that Dotty and I took when we went out with the Mills Brothers back in '41. We did some location jobs, like in Kansas City. That was when you stayed for a while instead of just a one-night thing.

Dotty was a great cook and she would fry up a bunch of chickens, make sweet potatoes, greens, potato salad. The guys would be eating for days. See, the band always traveled with a portable electric kitchen. I remember one time she was cooking some onions and steak backstage in the theater and the smell was so good, half the audience was turning around trying to figure out where it was coming from.

The same year that Cab broke up his big band, Sugar Ray Robinson, the great boxer, opened a cafe called Sugar Ray's, on Seventh Avenue, right down from 2040. All the buck dancers used to hang out at that joint; we were all Sugar Ray fans. Everybody in show business stopped by—musicians, singers, actors. We had a ball up in there! All the fighters, like Joe Louis, would drop in. Honi and I knew most of those guys because way back in '39 and right through the forties, the buck dancers would meet in front of the Theresa Hotel and chew the fat, especially when we didn't have gigs.

We'd stand up under the Theresa's marquee and b.s. for hours. Talk about the chicks and flirt with the ones walking up and down the street. Willie Bryant and Ralph Cooper were out there. The band leaders appearing at the Apollo would pass through—Duke, Basie, Earl Hines. They all stayed at the Theresa. That was just a popular spot. Chock Full o' Nuts was right on the corner. I'd tell Honi, "Looka here, man, my navel is talking to my backbone, let's go in there and get some grub." So we'd buy soup or doughnuts, come back out and "gumbeat" some more. Then pick up the morning edition of the *New York News*, which came out at 10:30 in the evening, and go on back to 2040. We even did that in the wintertime. It was like a ritual!

Sometimes when we were standing out there, one of the cats would say, "Come on, man, I'll buy you a little taste." So we'd hang out at the bar in the hotel for a while. Theresa's was one of the hot spots in Harlem. All the celebrities would be in there. Joe Louis had some suites on the top floor, so fighters were in and out regularly. On the way outside we'd see some of the fighters in the lobby and stop to b.s. with them for a spell. Sugar Ray was there a lot.

Ray was a good dancer. When he stopped boxing and went into show business, Pete Nugent was one of his tap teachers. Henry LeTang, too. There was one section in his act that featured rope slapping, which is what he did when he was training as a boxer—slap time with the rope and dance to the beat. He never liked the idea of jumping rope. In his book, Ray talks about the importance of rhythm and balance. Both of those things you get from studying tap.

He was also an avid golfer. Honi and I were invited to join Ray's club, the Gotham Golfers, one of the few black golf clubs on the East Coast. He started with about five guys from Jersey. We hooked up sometime in the late forties and played all over New York. Ray would call up one of the golf courses and make reservations for nine or ten people, and the owners would roll out the red carpet for him. Other times we'd play in threesomes or foursomes. On weekends there would be a bunch of us. Earle Warren, from Basie's band, was in the club, too.

If Joe Louis was in town, he'd join us and lose a bucket of money on the golf course. He was a real good-natured guy, a lot of fun. Joe and Leonard Reed had a comedy act together for many years. That's when Leonard taught him a few dance steps. Seems like boxing and dancing are first cousins.

In the summer of 1948, Joe Glaser had us booked for a July appearance in a primarily all-British show at a variety theater in London. And we were all set to go to Europe, when Honi injured his ankle trying to get out of the way of a rolling air compression barrel. He was crossing at 116th and Eighth Avenue and this huge thing was dislodged onto the street. Honi jumped over a rail, down into a basement entrance, and landed on his heel. So everything had to be put on hold until he recovered.

Finally, we left New York in August, on the *Queen Mary*. This ship was just like a moving city. It had every conceivable form of recreation and the seas were very calm during the whole trip. We always dressed for dinner, which was elegantly served, and there was usually a display telling you what was happening on each deck that night, like parties or first-run movies. I remember we saw *The Red Shoes* while we were going over.

The last night before the ship docked was called Captain's Night, and Honi and I did a little performance, a shortened version of our act which was a brief thing, but very well received. There were no other black dance acts on there. As a matter of fact the only other black person in the show was the internationally famous concert singer Todd Duncan. He was going over on a concert tour of several Western European countries before taking off for Russia.

Todd was an extremely interesting man, very down-to-earth and well educated. We talked with him about his gospel background and the fact that he had gone into European classical music. It was fascinating to see how much he knew about jazz and about tap dancers. He knew all of the jazz musicians. That took me completely by surprise because normally you figured, "He's in another whole phase of the music business, from an artistic standpoint. We're over here. He's over there. He doesn't know what's happening over here, man." But that was absolutely not the case. We spent a lot of time talking with him during those four days.

The London rooming house we were scheduled to stay in was pretty bad, so we ended up living in the home of a friend that we knew from New York, Mabel Lee. She was a fabulous dancer from Atlanta that I'd met when I was working with Cab. Back then Mabel was in the chorus line, but even before Honi and I went to Europe, she'd become a solo artist. I think she first went to England to star in a show at the London Palladium called *Here, There, and Everywhere.*

Mabel was a wonderful performer. She could really bring the house down! Still can from what I hear. She was cute as a button, nice little shape, and could definitely sell a song like you wouldn't believe. Not every dancer is a performer, you know, but Mabel had it all. Both Honi and I felt very close to her and it was a nice feeling to go abroad and have someone there who would welcome us into their home like she did.

In fact, staying there was really one of the highlights of our trip; had our own rooms and everything. Most of the time, though, we'd eat out at those little West Indian places, unless an executive from some big restaurant came to see the show and invited us to dinner. Those were the only occasions when we'd have steak because the food situation was terrible in England. Their belt was still tight from the war and everything was rationed: gas, cigarettes, meat, whiskey. Dotty and Maggie would send us those great big boxes of food through the mail. So we were better off than most folks, especially people in rural areas.

After we finished our run in London, Joe Glaser's contact there arranged for us to play some small theaters in the provinces like Manchester, Dover, Bristol, and Blackpool. Now, that was definitely not a welcome addition to our trip. I mean, you talking about some bad stages. All of them were raked—they were on an incline with the front of the stage lower than the back. So you had to struggle to keep from sliding forward while you were tapping.

The other problem was getting our taps caught in those tin-can tops that were nailed to the floor. Most of the stages were made of soft wood that had knots and when those knots fell out, the stagehands would take the tops of cans and nail them over the holes. So the nails would eventually work their way up and pull your taps loose.

We were working with little four- or five-piece pit bands. The British musicians were not bad, they were just old and couldn't half see the notes. The drummers were basically the problem. Trying to keep the bass drum going with very fast tempos and remembering the tempos from one show to another were problems for them. We had the feeling that they were possibly guys who had, at some point, been first-class musicians but had retired in the smaller communities.

One time Honi and I had to follow a donkey act. They had these animals that could do all sorts of things—bang on drums—all kinds of novelty tricks. Naturally these donkeys would wait until they got on stage to do their business. Then here we come—there's no time to sweep the floors—and we had to be dancing around all of this mess! A lot of times, you couldn't miss it; make a mistake and step right in that crap.

And the weather didn't help the situation one bit. All of England stayed damp and rainy. You were always cold. We had to wear sweaters, slickers, and jackets, even in August. On one trip Honi and I stayed in an old castle in Manchester that had been converted into a hotel. It was called a family house and heated solely with fireplaces. Boy, I would be trying to stoke up those fires; and since the chimney mechanisms were faulty, the smoke would be coming back in and we'd be coughing and carrying on. This was not a real happy period, although the credits served us well when we came back to the States. I guess the best thing about those gigs was getting paid and going back to London, where we could at least have some fun sightseeing or partying with the cast of the Katherine Dunham Dance Company.

They opened at London's Prince of Wales Theater on June 2, 1948, for an extended engagement, and the company manager had rented a big house right there in the city for the whole cast. Most of the black theatrical people in London were in contact with one another and that house became our main hangout. Since Dunham and her husband, John Pratt, were housed in a different place, we didn't see much of them, but we became pretty close to several people in the cast, especially Eartha Kitt, one of the chorus kids. She had a spot in the show where she hit a high C while doing a cartwheel— broke up the house every time! Eartha was thinking of leaving the company at that time, so she had long conversations with us about pursuing a solo career. Eventually the company finished up in London and went on to perform in Paris. Honi and I really hated to see them leave, because we had developed a lot of friendships during that period.

Another highlight of our stay in London was a television appearance on the show of a very popular English comic. The name of it was something like *On the Town*. Dunham had already been featured and June Richmond, too. That was our very first television appearance. I'm not even sure if they had televisions in the States then. Maybe rich people had them, but I don't think they were widely marketed.

We had hoped that the London engagement would lead to other European bookings, but many of those countries were recovering from the war and jobs were hard to come by. Finally, it was time for us to head back to the States. We returned home on a small Dutch ship that was a luxury liner but much smaller than the one we took over. We spent most of the trip in the cabin lying down because the weather was terrible—we were seasick every morning for seven days. Man, I was glad to get back to Harlem. But most of all, I was happy to be back with Dotty. Part of the time we were away, she'd been out on the road with a band led by Roy Eldridge, one of our greatest trumpeters. Singing gigs were even more scarce, but she managed to get jobs at small clubs around the city. And she was still running down to Philly from time to time.

Before the trip to England, Dotty and I had moved out of 2040 and into a rooming house over on Morningside Drive. We had a one-bedroom with a small anteroom. Honi and Maggie were also living in Harlem then, but after we returned from Europe, they moved out to Queens and two months later we did, too.

Although the property uptown was becoming pretty run-down, I guess the real reason we left Harlem was to be near them. Also, Dotty and I wanted to buy new furniture and live in a real apartment with more space. For Maggie and Honi, who had a child, our neighborhood in Queens was so much better because of the yards and schools.

It was the same area where Louis Armstrong lived and we used to go over and visit, sit up there and do the same thing we did in the dressing room—chew the fat, talk about agents and everything. There were quite a few artists in East Elmhurst. Harry Belafonte lived right down the street from us. He and Sidney Poitier had a barbecue place on Northern Boulevard. Ella Fitzgerald was over on Ditmars Boulevard, a few blocks away, and Willie Bryant lived in that same area on Butler Street. Those were real beautiful homes up in there. Sometimes at night Dotty and I would play pinochle with Ella and her husband, Ray Brown, the extraordinary bass player.

At one point we were having trouble with the landlord and considered going back to the city, but wound up moving into a place owned by Peg Leg Bates's relatives. He and his wife, Alice, lived out there, and she told us about a vacancy. When we checked it out, the apartment was just two blocks from Honi's and within walking distance of Leonard Reed's place, so we jumped on that deal right away.

Dizzy Gillespie and Bill Kenny also lived in that area, as well as Anna Mae Winburn, who directed the International Sweethearts of Rhythm, an all-female jazz band. The atmosphere in that section of the Island was real pleasant. Milt Hinton, a great bass player, and tenor saxophonist Budd Johnson lived with their wives a little farther out, around Jamaica.

I remember some black disc jockeys opened a nice little bar-club with entertainment that would seat about seventy-five people—they had blues and everything. That's where Billy Eckstine and I used to hang out together. If we were on our way home, we might stop in and have a little taste, and generally we'd see somebody from the gang.

Other times we would run into each other in the grocery stores or banks and try to arrange some kind of get-together, like a Sunday afternoon barbeque. But those kinds of occasions were rare, because most of us were road people. You'd hit the road and when you finally got back home, you were so worn out, you'd just want to shack up. Then by the time you got yourself together, it was time to go back out again. Still, it was always nice to run into each other in the supermarkets or restaurants and talk for a hot minute.

In 1949, our agent suggested that we audition for a Broadway show called *Gentlemen Prefer Blondes*, starring Carol Channing. Now, we liked the idea of being in a Broadway show together, but we hated auditions. We told him, "Man, we don't do auditions! You have to wait forever, you're packed in there like cattle with a thousand other acts, and generally you don't even get chosen." Honi and I had decided early on that we didn't want to put ourselves in that kind of position too often. But Joe Glaser thought we had a better than 50 percent chance of getting the part and he just kept insisting. So, reluctantly, we packed up our stuff and headed on downtown.

Sure enough, there were a lot of other acts there. We told the guy, "Just get us on and get us off." We did our opening song, then the soft-shoe, and from the soft-shoe we did a little challenge and ended with our closing number. Honi and I were packing up to get out of there when the assistant choreographer came backstage. "Let's see that soft-shoe again." Agnes de Mille, the show's choreographer, was sitting in the audience. After we finished, the same assistant said, "If you guys can sing a little louder, you've got this job." Boy, you could hear us for miles!

The contract was signed and we started rehearsals. Day after day, we went in there and just sat around. This went on for about two or three weeks. Agnes de Mille was buzzing through, but she'd pass right by us. So finally, Jule Styne, the musical composer, came in and said, "How are you guys coming along?" We said, "Coming along? We haven't done a damn thing." He said, "Come with me." And he took us upstairs to a piano and played the tune we were supposed to sing and dance to, called "Mamie Is Mimi." Then he said, "Look, you guys get a piano player and put some material together; I'll see that he's paid for. You know this song; put an entrance and a dance to it."

So the long and short of it is, we put our swing dance to that song and then one day in rehearsal, Agnes de Mille saw it and said, "Well, yes, this is great. We'll stick Anita Alvarez right in the center." That was her ballerina, but she didn't even choreograph Anita's part. Honi and I did that! And got absolutely no credit even though it was ours.

She adapted the whole thing to our opening dance. But to tell the truth, Honi and I were kind of glad because God knows I can't imagine what we would have done if Agnes had choreographed the number. The down side was that later on, we had to get permission from her to do our own choreography on television!

Gentlemen Prefer Blondes opened at the Ziegfeld Theater on December 8, 1949, and our dance became the biggest hit in the show. In the last eight bars, Honi and I are pursuing Anita. Here we are in immaculate white tails, and Anita is fleeing and we're reaching out for her. The minute we're offstage, I come right back on, then Honi comes right back on, then Anita. I grab her by the left hand and spin her into Honi and he spins her away from me and she goes immediately into a deep plié all the way down to the floor. And I guarantee you when she came out of that plié she was six feet off the floor. And while she's in the air Honi's swinging her. We stopped the show every night!

The orchestra's conductor, Milton Rosenstock, was so relieved to get away from that stuff he had been playing. We came from each wing and when we hit our introduction, Milton would holler at us, "Come on!" It was the way we'd strut-step coming down those boards all the way to the footlights. The people in the theater felt like we were coming right on out into the audience. We'd stop, jump into a stride pose with both feet apart and hold it, you know, just stylin.' Then we'd take our hats off and go into the vocals. Milton just loved it. He said he waited for that spot each night and he needed it like the alcoholic needs a drink!

We were the only black artists in the whole show. It kind of reminded me of the time I went to see Arthur Mitchell with the New York City Ballet. They were performing out on the Island and the theater was away from you—there was water between the stage and the audience. And when the curtain first opened, you saw about thirty dancers all dressed in white and this one little dark face moving in the crowd.

In *Gentlemen Prefer Blondes*, our dance took place in a French nightclub setting. The stage was loaded with the rest of the cast, then we came on, the only spooks in the joint! After the little opening, we went into the vocal, then the dance with Anita. There was so much excitement when we hit, nothing in the show could follow it. That should have been the finale. But there were about eighteen minutes of dialogue in front of it, which was the opening of the second act, and everybody was getting up and going outside to the bar because it was very dull. But our entrance really gave the whole thing a big lift. That's one of the reasons we got such rave reviews from the critics.

While we were on Broadway, a guy named Jack Entrada contacted us about doing an audition at the Copa, a club in midtown. They were looking for somebody to open for Frank Sinatra. So he said, "I just want you to do three minutes, Just BOOM-BOOM-BOOM, BANG-BANG-BANG." They were looking for the acts that you could just wind up like a machine, you know. Honi said, "I think you better find yourself another act. We don't do that."

Boy, that thing ticked us off! We rarely made those kind of compromises, because we were no slam-bang act just to warm up for Sinatra or Como or all those people. Besides, Honi and I had been getting a lot of press; we were in everybody's column. Some guy had advised us to spruce up our PR. He said, "Give these guys a hundred dollars a week man, and you'll be in Winchell, Dorothy Kilgallen, everybody." Those writers were manufacturing stories. They said we had a golf net in our dressing room and all kinds of things. We'd see people in our neighborhood and they'd say, "I didn't know you guys did that?" We said, "Did what?" "Well, I read in so-and-so's column. . . ." So here we were in the newspaper every day and this Entrada guy was trying to get us to open for somebody else. But, that's the way it was, especially for black artists.

During our run with *Blondes*, Dotty stopped working because she had a miscarriage. Dr. Hogan said her condition was weak from being on the road so much. That was a real heartbreaker, one of the saddest periods in her life, because more than anything she wanted to become a mother. I mean, naturally, I wanted a son or daughter, too, but it meant a heck of a lot more to her. She had such a wonderful way with kids and all of her friends had children. We were both very close to Isabelle, Honi and Maggie's daughter.

After Dotty got herself together, she decided to stop singing for a while and take a job at Gertz Department Store in Queens. Maggie was already working there, so she helped her get hired as a salesperson. One of the nice things about that job was the annual Christmas show put on by the employees. Dotty was in charge of some of the productions. She'd also star in them. They had programs printed and the whole shot. Local papers would write them up, too. I remember Maggie being listed as the choreographer and once Buck Clayton was in the band. The cashiers, managers, and all the staff would bring their families to see the shows every year.

There were also small seasonal shows to stimulate interest in the clothes and get people to buy more. Dotty developed several friendships at Gertz's and when I was on the road, she would play cards with some of the girls in the evening or scoot on over to the city. They had a lot of fun hanging out together.

In late 1949, Bill "Bojangles" Robinson died. All of the buck dancers in my generation really admired him because he had crystal-clear taps and superb showmanship. When he passed, a few of the New York tap dancers started a club as a tribute to Uncle Bo and named themselves the Copasetics, after one of his pet sayings. You'd ask him how things were, and he'd answer, "Copasetic. Everything's copasetic," which meant everything's fine.

The idea for the club originated with Lucille Preston, who was married to Luther "Slim" Preston. They had a dance act called Slim and Sweets and both of them were good friends with a lot of the dancers and musicians at 2040. One afternoon, LeRoy Myers, Charles "Cookie" Cook, and James "Chuckles" Walker decided to stop by Slim and Sweets's on their way from Uncle Bo's wake.

LeRoy told me they were all sitting around talking and Sweets said, "You guys are so close, why don't you get together and form some kind of club." So those four dancers—LeRoy, Slim, Cookie, and Chuckles—decided to set up a fraternity in honor of Bill Robinson. But the idea was not to set up a club just for dancers. They wanted to get a group of guys together who liked one another and could work together well. The four original members decided who would be invited to join. Honi and I became members along with Billy Strayhorn, Phace Roberts, Milton Larkin, Francis Goldberg, Billy Eckstine, John E. Thomas, Pete Nugent, Ernest Brown, Louie Brown, Peg Leg Bates, Frank Goldberg, Eddie West, Emory Evans, Elmer Waters, Roy Branker, Paul Black, and Chink Collins.

Strayhorn became our most beloved president. He was voted in about a year after joining and when he died in '67, we retired that office in his honor and made Honi chairman of the board. Stray was real close to a bunch of us. Even before the Copasetics was established, LeRoy, Honi, Pete, and I used to socialize with him quite a bit. It never mattered to us that Stray was gay because we had other friends who were, too. It was just no big deal. As a matter of fact, it never really came up. Duke's band would be playing somewhere and all of us would meet there, then afterward, go to some place like Wells for food and drinks. A lot of the time we stayed out so long, we'd end up having breakfast and watching the sun come up!

The Copasetics' meetings were pretty much regular club-type stuff, but they were very well conducted, especially after we started forming committees to handle everything. Then the whole group had to go along with whatever decisions were made by the committees. At first we had to get out a lot of the kinks. For example, somebody would ask, "Now, what was that we said we were gonna do last week?" "I don't know. Didn't it go in the minutes?" "No, I didn't put that down." "Well, looks like you won't be secretary long!" Later, when I became the recording secretary, I had to really stay on my toes, because there were a lot of sharp, creative minds in there.

Sometimes we had little arguments, especially when shows were being planned. But that was to be expected in a group of artists. Also, we had a lot of strong-minded, opinionated people like my partner, Honi Coles! The only person that would really set him down was Strayhorn. They were real tight. Stray would say, "Just a minute, Mr. Coles. Just a minute. You're out of order!" It wouldn't pay for me to say nothing. I'd just look at him, you know. I would walk around and give him that look, then walk away shaking my head. Mo was something else! We had a lot of fun and everybody's heart was there.

At some meetings there were open discussion periods and each person would come up with an idea about what the club should do. We ran it like Congress, you know. "Ah, Mister Speaker, may I have the floor?" Man, the guys would just fall out laughing at some of the suggestions. A cat would come up with some real off-the-wall idea like going to the park to feed the pigeons. Crazy things. And the guys would crack on him, "Hey, pigeon feeder!" Cookie would come up with something like that. He'd say, "I don't know. I'm just humane, man. I think about them poor pigeons out there. They don't have nothin' to eat." Somebody said, "Yeah, well, when I see one I think about throwing it in a pot to make some stew!" It was really a pleasure to attend club meetings. Afterward, we'd go somewhere together, like Showman's in Harlem, and turn the place out. That little bar is still a regular hangout for the buck dancers.

So many wonderful things happened with the Copasetics. The events were top-notch. Most of our affairs were named after trips, like cruises or safaris, things of that sort. Every September we had a big production and it usually revolved around that same kind of theme. I remember one show we had in '61, called "On the Riviera." Honi was the producer; Pete and I did the choreography; and Strayhorn and Roy Branker wrote the lyrics and music. Most of the acts in the shows were done by members of the club. Eddie Green did a take-off on the twist, in drag. Cook and Brown danced. Honi and I formed a little quartet with Dotty and Maggie and sang a few songs. They were members of our sister club, the Copeds.

"On the Riviera" was held at the Riviera Terrace Room, located at Fifty-second Street and Broadway. About two thousand people came. The audience looked like "Who's Who" in black show business: Lena Horne, Dick Gregory, Dinah Washington, Dorothy Donegan, Clarence Robinson. I mean, everybody was there. People in New York waited for those shows to come around every year. Occasionally Duke Ellington attended, or Billie Holiday. I remember once Ethel Waters was our honored guest. We had George Kirby several times because he requested it. Dizzy Gillespie also asked to perform. That happened with a lot of artists; they just loved to be associated with the club.

Milton Larkin was the musical conductor for all of the shows and that band would be smoking! The musicians got scale, but really, they wanted to play the gig, just to come up there and party, to be a part of it. Milton got Harry "Sweets" Edison from the Basie band; Johnny Hodges, out of Duke's band. Snooky Young was in there. . . . I can't remember half the guys. But Milt would have a hell of a band.

And I staged all kinds of swinging jazz and tap numbers. Once our guest artists were an African dance company that was very popular at that time, Olatunji's group. There were skits in the programs and we had social dancing after the show, because most of the affairs were cabaret style. Usually the places we rented had a stage and a large enough area just below it for dancing. Lights or anything else we needed to rig up were brought in. We had our own tech crews from the Apollo. It seemed like people were always glad to help out the Copasetics!

But the shows really were excellent. And the tickets went like hot cakes. LeRoy used to sell a bunch of them. Sometimes we'd give a few to our friends, then cover the cost ourselves. But we always made much more money than the nut—what it cost to put the show on—and there was always a nice taste left to go in the treasury. The Copasetics started out mainly as a social club, then later on we started giving money to charity and sometimes we'd do benefits for special causes.

They're only a handful of us left, maybe five or six. Slim Preston was the first member to pass. He had been having problems for a while when we found out that he really had cancer. Sweets told us that it was just a matter of time. The doctors had sent him home to die. Finally, Honi called me one day and said, "It looks like Slim is about to go out of here." I had a little Plymouth car, so I picked him up and we went over there and sat in the room. Slim was out of it when we got there, but we stayed by his bed to the very end.

There were a bunch of people in show business that for some unknown reason felt they didn't need insurance. "We're going to enjoy our money while we're still here," they'd say. Slim was like that and he hadn't been working in quite a while. Consequently, his AGVA [American Guild of Variety Artists] union dues had elapsed. The morning after he passed, Honi and I got up at five or six o'clock and went down to the AGVA office. We were waiting at the door when it opened. The lady there was a very kind person and knew Slim, so we told her what had happened and she let us pay his back dues. That way his burial expenses would be taken care of. But that's the only insurance he had.

Everybody in the Copasetics donated a little something, although nobody had a whole lot of money, especially the dancers. But we gave what we could, which came to around three hundred dollars. Then Stray added another four or five hundred and Billy Eckstine took it up to about a thousand. Slim's death hit the club pretty hard, especially since he was the first one to go. Many years later when Honi developed cancer and I was by his bedside, I thought back to the time when he and I sat together and watched Slim take his last breath.

6

THE END OF OUR ROAD

*G*entlemen *Prefer Blondes* stayed on Broadway for about two years; then we took it on the road until the beginning of 1952. It's a funny thing about being in a Broadway show, especially if you're a variety act. All the agents basically write you off, because you're not available. It's the same story when you go to Europe for a long time. Agents get in a pattern with the people they're representing; they know where to place you and how to set up an ongoing itinerary. But, when you move out of that scope, it takes a long time to get back in the pocket.

That's what happened to us when we came out of *Gentlemen Prefer Blondes*, although that wasn't the whole story. Any white act coming out of a big Broadway show would have become instant stars, but we had been in American show business long enough to understand why that wasn't happening for us. Even with all the publicity Coles and Atkins had gotten in the past two years, we were right back in the same position, constantly looking for work.

In '53 we had a few summer-stock dates in Texas, *Girl Crazy* and *Kiss Me, Kate*. Those kinds of shows usually provided about two weeks of work, a week of rehearsal and a week of performance. But that's the year we really started to feel the crunch. So much change was taking place in show business. We had definitely seen it coming in the late forties, even though it was a very gradual thing. The chorus lines had started to fade. Then the entertainment tax that was put on clubs helped close them down.

Every club had maybe a line of girls, a band, a lead male singer, a lead female singer, and a dancing act. But the city administration put a tax on that. Only the big hotels could handle the increase because they'd tack it onto rooms and restaurant checks. The clubs couldn't afford to pay the different types of performers and the taxes, so a lot of the owners said, "To hell with it." They began hiring just musicians. In the early fifties many of the big bands had become little bands; six and seven pieces. Imagine Calloway in front of seven pieces shaking his head, after having an eighteen-piece band.

At the Apollo Theater, variety was definitely on its way out by then. Vocal groups were taking over. The disc jockeys started bringing the shows in and they became the headliners and the ones who hired the recording artists. The deejays would get them for a song and dance because they'd promise to play their records on the radio, and then too, many of the groups' managers worked hand-in-hand with the disc jockeys.

By that time, Honi and I were looking for jobs in *Cashbox* instead of *Variety*, and truthfully most tap dancers were starving to death. You couldn't get enough gigs! The only available ones were little scratch dates in third-market cities like Scranton, Pennsylvania, and Wilkes-Barre. Coal miners lived up there, all working-class people.

These were small towns that had a variety house. So you'd do one show per day. You'd just have to hang in there and get through it. The theaters would have a four-piece band that couldn't play your music. And the pay was pitiful. By the time you bought your round-trip bus ticket, you would be lucky to go home with $20 or $25 apiece.

So we would do a few things like that, and some periodic television shows, although they also paid very low in the fifties; the top salary was about $150 for one show. To get a date at all, everybody had to go through in-house agents. If the job paid $60 and the agent took 10 percent of that, you had $54 left, which meant $27 for Honi and $27 for me. Twenty bucks could fill up a few grocery carts back then, but by the time you got some food in the house, bought a cold beer, and paid for carfare, you weren't much better off than you were before. Now, you were in real trouble if you had your own booking agent, because then you had to pay him as well as the in-house agent. After the gig, you'd look up and you wouldn't have no money at all!

Our television appearances in the States started while we were still with *Gentlemen*. Around 1950, Honi and I were in the first authorized color TV show in America. We were also the first black tap dancers to appear on the *Ford Hour*. The show had featured white dancers like Paul Draper and Fred Astaire, but it never had buck dancers, so we got permission from the producers of *Gentlemen Prefer Blondes* to perform our segment on television, which was a big to-do! We worked out a way to perform it without Anita Alvarez and all the columnists raved about how stunning it was.

Those little television gigs lasted off and on throughout the fifties. Producers never wanted more than three minutes, and Honi and I had so many little pieces of business . . . different songs that we could sing, different dance routines, and a lot of outfits. Consequently, we could do shows often, which was a big help when the rent was due. Every time things got lean, we knew we could probably get on the *Kate Smith Show*. She was pro–Coles and Atkins all the way. So was Morey Amsterdam. Gary Moore's show was another one that we could really count on periodically. I remember we did one of those with Harry Belafonte.

We also danced on the *Milton Berle Show* quite a bit. He used to introduce us by saying, "Here's one of the finest acts in the business, ladies and gentlemen, the Jewish Berry Brothers, Coles and Atkins." See, Honi knew a lot of Yiddish phrases and he used to talk that stuff with Milton. I think he started learning it when he was performing with Bert Howell. They did a lot of Jewish gags. Honi also hung out with some of the Jewish comics from time to time.

During this same period, we got a lot of theater dates. These shows were put on between movies. New York had little neighborhood circuits. On Tuesday night you'd be in the Bronx, Wednesday you would be in Jamaica, Thursday you would be down at Twenty-fourth Street. Friday and Saturday, you'd be down at the Fourteenth Street Academy of Music. We could always get that date because Honi knew the agent real well, who booked it. We got thirty-five dollars and he took 10 percent. We said, "What! Three dollars and fifty cents!" That was a serious cut back then. Sometimes we'd end up with a whole week's worth of work at the Academy, then the next week, here we come, the same two cats. We'd be Jenkins and Foster one time, and the next week, Mo and Joe; then Coles and Atkins or Atkins and Coles. Whatever!

We'd open with the finale, interchange our solo spots, ad-lib, change the music, you name it. On Fourteenth Street, the audience just didn't care. People came in the theater to get out of the cold or just have something to do. They'd say, "Oh, there's two more colored guys. They look something like them other two, but they got on different suits!" Those little jobs helped get us through some hard times.

Once Honi and I were working at a theater that featured *The Band Wagon*, a musical film starring Fred Astaire and Cyd Charisse. There was a lot of good dancing and it was all in color. After the movie, out comes this little three-piece band. The drummer couldn't half see the charts or keep the tempos, but we had to go on out there anyway. It was the first time people actually booed us. So we just kept dancing. About halfway through we danced on off and never came back.

Another small source of income during the fifties came from appearances in twenty-two-minute variety films, called two-reelers. There was a gentleman in New York by the name of Ben Frye, who was making these things for black theaters in the South. From a technical standpoint, they were really called short subjects.

Frye hired Leonard Reed to produce them in a studio down on Houston Street, and he also depended on him to select top artists like Ruth Brown, Dinah Washington, Sarah Vaughan, Joe Turner, and Bill Bailey. People who were real pros at performing and were available. Willie Bryant acted as the master of ceremonies in all of the clips. Since we were good friends with him and Leonard, Honi and I did about five. Ben Frye made a million of those things and gave the artists peanuts, no residuals, nothing. The pay was thirty to forty dollars per person for each one. Leonard didn't even get any royalties, and he wrote the scripts. All Frye did was put up the money. Those old films are still aired sometimes on cable TV, and every time I see one, it makes me mad all over again.

Between engagements scheduled for Coles and Atkins, I started dabbling in teaching. Honi and I were still friends with an attorney named Martin Leonard, who we'd met during *Gentlemen Prefer Blondes*. I'm not sure exactly what it was, but he had some kind of legal connection with the show. Back then we would go to dinner with him or just out for a drink. There was a little bar right beside the Ziegfeld where the cast usually hung out.

Sometime in '53, Martin had this brainstorm about my teaching a tap class at the Katherine Dunham School, on Forty-third Street, between Broadway and Eighth. He called me and asked if I'd be interested. I said, "Yeah, I wouldn't mind being a part of that school, but those kids are not into tap." He said, "Well, that could change, because there's a good possibility that it will be coming back to Broadway again. You want me to speak to Katherine?" So I told him to go ahead. Since he was her attorney, I figured he might be able to pull it off. She agreed with the idea and began canvassing the students, but the job didn't really materialize until the next year, 1954. I started out with about ten people, then a few dropped out because they couldn't afford the fee for her technique and tap, too.

Katherine Dunham was a very lovely person, exceptionally friendly. Sometimes she would get up in class and do a little time step. She could do just enough to say, "I can tap." But she respected what I was doing and promised to help me increase enrollment. Most of her classes were led by people from the company, but whenever she was giving a master class, I would be sitting right there, watching her teach. Believe me, it was quite an experience!

She was a marvelous instructor, very strict, and, boy, she kept track of every single student in the class and would actually point people out, "Are you with us? The arm motion is here, not here." She had no qualms about telling you that you were doing it wrong! You know, some teachers worry too much about hurting the students' feelings. But her main concern was that they got it right, because she was a perfectionist all the way.

The whole atmosphere of the school was strictly business. There was very little conversation about anything other than what the students were there for . . . the techniques and the problems they were having with them. She would give classes on the meanings of the dances and where they originated geographically. Watching those sessions was a real education for me.

One of the persons that I became real friendly with at the Dunham School was Karel Shook, who had danced with the Ballet Russe de Monte Carlo and the Dutch National Ballet. Karel later became a major figure at the Dance Theater of Harlem. Some of the students taking Dunham technique were studying ballet with him and they were having trouble paying for two courses, like my students, so his enrollments were down, too. After I'd been there for about three months, Katherine decided to dispense with the tap and ballet classes.

Since Karel had suspected that this would happen, he'd already started looking around for a spot close by that we could set up together. He ended up doing most of the legwork because little dates would come up for me and Honi, and I'd run in and out of town. We finally found a place on Eighth Avenue, close to the Dunham School. It was a second-story studio, about 30 feet by 30 feet, with ample space, and reasonable rent.

Karel was pulling students from the Broadway shows and some of the dance companies like Martha Graham's. He even had a few people from the International School of Dance at Carnegie Hall. Although his classes were great, they didn't cost as much as the name places. So he was able to get quite a few students, including some black dancers, like Mary Hinkson, from the Graham Company. Arthur Mitchell and Louis Johnson were there, too. I think that was the first time I met Louis and we wound up working together many years later on the production team for Aretha Franklin's concerts.

A lot of dancers used to hang out at our studio and visit with each other. We had a real mixture of ballet students, but the black kids really helped build my thing because they were the ones initially who wanted to take tap classes. The majority of the white ballet dancers were not into much tap. They liked to devote all of their time to the one technique, but when Karel taught the movements to his students, often the white kids would be off musically. They might be a little late or ahead, because they seemed to be thinking more about positions than really listening to what the music was saying. The thing is, they admired the feeling and musicality that some of the black dancers brought to their ballet movements. So Arthur and Louis explained to them that taking tap dance would make them more conscious of rhythm and they would be able to apply it to their ballet technique. Then, too, Karel would tell them, "Look, you need to take Cholly's class to work on your timing." Consequently, the white kids went out, bought little shoes, and pretty soon my enrollments went up.

The people that Karel and I rented from were Greek importers who had a big restaurant on the first floor. They eventually decided to use the studio for something else, so we received a notice asking us to be out by a certain date. We were just glad they didn't throw us out because we definitely couldn't contest the notice. They had taken care of that by refusing to give us a lease in the first place.

By that time it had become necessary for me to find my own space. We'd had a real nice partnership for about a year and a half, but I was starting to do a little vocal choreography and some of the groups needed to be scheduled around the same time Karel had ballet classes. Therefore, he looked for a place uptown and I wound up in the CBS Building at Fifty-third and Broadway, where Mary Goldfarb ran a studio and office rental operation.

A lot of vocal coaches, band agents, and arrangers rented little office spaces from her. Each room had a file cabinet, a desk, a couple of chairs—and your name on the door! When I got clients, I would pay for a studio. Otherwise, there was no overhead, except for the office rental. You could receive calls in your office or the switchboard operator would take messages for you. I paid about fifty dollars a month for the space, which was fine because my business wasn't big; I just needed a home base, a place to hang my hat.

If Honi and I had to go out of town, it wasn't like closing the thing up completely, so the Goldfarb Studios offered a much better option for me. And the other good thing was that Dotty could drop by and watch me work with the groups when she had time off from work. I kept that little office a long time and when Coles and Atkins had a lean period, I'd come right back to it. Occasionally I would need a studio for four or five days so I'd call in and Mary would lay it all out. She gave me a good deal on one particular room large enough to work with five guys, and that became my regular spot whenever I needed it.

I talked to some of the other teachers at Goldfarb and they had students interested in taking tap. Now here again I had a big decision to make, because Honi and I were still getting a few dates. I could handle the vocal choreography thing, but I wasn't anxious to get hooked up with parents who wanted to bring their children every Wednesday and Saturday. See, I didn't have any assistants. There was nobody to take over and you can't keep those kinds of classes going if you have to leave periodically for weeks at a time, so I decided to just stick with the vocal choreography at the Goldfarb Studios. But I still taught incidental tap classes at other locations.

One place was a dancing school in Jamaica, Queens, run by a former chorus line dancer, Bernice Johnson. When Dotty and I were dancing in Chicago back in the early forties, her husband, Budd Johnson, was there working with Earl Hines and we became good friends. Budd was just an outstanding saxophonist and arranger. He did fabulous arrangements for Earl's band. I figured he was the one who told her to contact me, which was good at the time. Although I didn't love to teach children's classes, I was glad to get the gig since Honi and I were going through another dry spell.

Bernice had a nice little neighborhood school with three studios and quite a few kids. They'd come running in with their little tap shoes on, ready to go. One of them was Michael Peters, the late choreographer who did Michael Jackson's early videos. He must have been around seven back then.

I also taught tap at the International School of Dance at Carnegie Hall, which was a pretty good place to work; real friendly. Agnes de Mille was on the ballet faculty. I used to run into her quite a bit. Sometimes dance education conventions were held there for movement teachers from all over the country. Joe Price, an acrobatics teacher at the Goldfarb Studios, got me involved in that. I think he had done some things with Cook and Brown and he also knew Honi real well because Joe's studio was where Coles practiced every day when he first came to New York.

At the conventions, all of the routines had to be notated for the students, but the idea of writing down steps was completely foreign to me and I felt that rhythm tap was way too complex to write down. So I was getting ready to turn the gig down, but this ballet teacher helped me out. She said, "The thing they want the most is style. You've got to simplify the taps because most people won't be able to interpret this." So I went along with the program and made the steps more elementary because, after all, it was very kind of her to do this. But I also didn't think you could get the feeling and style of it from the notation. It can be extremely difficult for many students to pick up the style when you're standing in the studio demonstrating!

Around that same time, I also got some assignments to choreograph numbers for the June Taylor Dancers, who were with the *Jackie Gleason Show*. The pay was real good, but I never received any recognition for my work. If June Taylor needed some new material to put on television, the producers would hire somebody to do it, then put her name in the credits. These jobs were always like a one-shot thing. I'd go in, choreograph and stage the dances, pick up my check, and leave. Then maybe four months later, she'd ask me to do another thing, you know. Par for the course. I guess I did the choreography for about three shows.

In the meantime, Honi had opened a tap studio with Pete Nugent. I think it was on Forty-ninth Street between Sixth and Seventh or somewhere in that vicinity. Their place became a little hangout for the buck dancers. All of them used to go up to that little third-floor studio and take their shoes. I didn't drop by too often, but I remember one time I was up there and Pete said, "Come on, man, let's dance around in front of the windows, so people walking up and down the street will think there's something happening up here."

Honi and Pete opened it on a shoestring, so they were struggling hard to keep the thing going; and a new dance studio is especially difficult, because you have to finance it for six months or a year until you get a steady flow of students. Also, in that particular area, it was real rough for them to get off the ground since there were so many schools. Henry LeTang had a studio down there. There was a slew of dancing schools that had been there for ages!

Their whole setup was a one-room thing, with a little office space blocked off in the corner. Although they didn't ask me, I really wanted to be a part of what they were trying to do at first, since a lot of studios were used for teaching several different techniques. I figured the vocal choreography could help generate revenue to maintain the place. But I never brought up the idea of joining them because the studio was also a hangout for tap dancers and I realized that I couldn't choreograph for vocal groups with all of them buck dancers standing around. Besides, it turned out that Pete and Honi wanted their business to be strictly tap.

In 1955, Honi and I went out to Las Vegas with Tony Martin for six weeks. A good friend of ours named Ty Sales knew Tony real well, so he hooked us up and it turned out that Tony was a real nice cat to work with. The pay was excellent and our run at the Flamingo was pretty good, except for one thing: Honi and I spent half our salary on costumes!

Tony had seen us in *Gentlemen Prefer Blondes*, and he wanted us to use those same white tails and top hats, but they were long gone. Those costumes belonged to the producers of the show. So we got ahold of the tailor in Philadelphia that we'd worked for in the forties, Lieberman, and he made the tails for us. Then we ordered the opera hats and white shoes from Capezio and figured we were all set.

When we got out there, we wore some sports outfits for the first show. Second show, we put on the tails and we didn't go over nearly as well with the audience. That happened for about three nights, then Tony came to us and said, "Fellows, let's dispense with the white tails thing. There's something about it." Well, we felt it, too. He said, "Try something like what you wore in the first show." Since we didn't have anything else sporty, we had to head downtown and buy black mohair suits, shirts, and ties. Man, that date cost us a boatload of money!

When we got back to New York, gigs were harder than ever to find, but we continued to rehearse. I was coaching vocal groups on the side and Honi went back to his studio, although tap was on its way down and he and Pete still weren't getting enough students. I remember saying to Honi one day, "If I don't catch you at home, I'll catch you up at the studio." He said, "Well, I don't know how much longer we're going to be there," without going into detail. It wasn't long after that—maybe a couple of months—that Pete and Honi closed their tap school.

What really saved me was the vocal choreography, because those jobs had been steadily increasing. The very first group I worked with was the Regals, from Cleveland, Ohio: Gerald "Jerry" Holeman, Tex Cornelius, Albert "Diz" Russell, Sonny Wright, and Billy "Junior" Adams. They were the Modern Sounds when they arrived in New York, but after seeing a Regals Shoe Store on 125th and Seventh Avenue, they changed the name.

These cats could sing! I got together with them through my buddy Leonard Reed, who had become the production manager at the Apollo. Leonard caught a performance of the Regals in Snookie's Lounge, at Forty-sixth and Broadway, and he was so impressed that he took them up to the Apollo and introduced the group to Bobby Schiffman, the owner's youngest son. After the Regals beat out Roy Hamilton at the Apollo's amateur night, Bobby and Leonard became their managers, and I was hired to tighten up their moves and stage etiquette. I remember Leonard and I wrote a song together for the Regals, "Oh, Oh, Oh, Oh, My Baby's Coming Home." I think the first record I choreographed for them was "Got the Water Boiling," with Ben Webster on tenor sax and Philly Joe Jones on drums.

This was the fall of '55 and right after that I started working with the Cadillacs. What happened was, I had a friend named Walter Thomas, who was a former saxophonist with Cab Calloway. When Cab's band broke up, Walter went to work for the Shaw Agency, which used to book a lot of acts, especially singing groups, during that period. He had seen the choreography that Honi and I were doing on vocals in our act, so he thought, "Hey, the way those cats move . . . if they could get a vocal group to do that kind of stuff, it would be fantastic." So he told Esther Navarro, the Cadillacs' manager, to look me up. She sent a copy of the product, I played it, scheduled a studio date with those guys, and the rest is history.

They became so sensational that they would go on stage and blow everybody away. All the record producers that had a group came looking for me and I knew how many records those companies were selling, so I was sitting right there in my little office, with my receipt book . . . waiting, "Well, that will cost you so-and-so-and-so." Working with the Cadillacs basically got me off the ground and opened doors at several agencies.

This was one of those special groups that could do everything well. I didn't have many groups as classy as those guys. They had what I call inborn sophistication. Earl "Speedo" Carroll was the lead singer, backed up by Bobby Phillips, LaVerne Drake, Buddy Brooks, and Earl Wade. The first day that I went into the studio with them, they were just tickled to death because they had seen Coles and Atkins many times.

All five of the Cadillacs grew up on the streets of Harlem and got to see a lot of acts at the Apollo Theater. Earl said he would sit up in the buzzard's nest and dream. That was the last balcony, where the spotlight was located. He would cut school, sneak in the basement of the theater, where the bands rehearsed, then slip on up to the balcony, and stay the whole day. Catch all the shows!

We hit it off real good. At first Speedo said, "Listen, Cholly, we ain't no professional dancers, man. Let's get that straight right now! I've got two left feet. Bobby's got two right legs . . ." I said, "Look, if you can count, you can dance." Sometimes we practiced six and seven hours a day. Those cats jumped directly on those moves, started doing them beautifully.

I found out later that Speedo had been putting on little shows all through his childhood. Each Saturday morning he would earn soda bottles by doing a little buck dance or the applejack and camel walk for the ladies in the beauty parlors. He also did a little hat-and-cane dance in school shows, and by the time he was a teenager, he had earned a reputation for his dancing throughout the neighborhood.

Right from the beginning, my ultimate goal with the Cadillacs was to change them into a standard act. At that time, a vocal group was only as good as its last record. If it didn't have a hot record, it wasn't worth too much to the promoters. I wanted to help them make the transformation from rock-and-roll singers into versatile performers, so they would have a wide range of venues available to them.

In addition to their hit records, we'd put standard tunes in the act. And during that process, if we found that somebody had a flair for comedy, we would add some visual and verbal things to highlight it. Then we'd use those talents for the hit songs, too. For example, instead of doing the tune "Speedo" in an ordinary way, I gave the lead singer a hat and a cane. Although he was singing a rock-and-roll song, I taught him how to twirl those props, which added to the group's appeal. And Earl could really cook on that stuff. Well, when you think about it, he had been watching it for a long time from up in the buzzard's nest!

During the first block of rehearsals, I wound up choreographing about four numbers. The Cadillacs were opening for Frank Sinatra at the Paramount Theater, in New York. Then I started doing everything they recorded and they became known all over for their choreography as well as their vocals.

They were sharp, too, one of the best-dressed vocal groups of the fifties. All of their outfits were made at F and F Clothes down in the Village. Esther Navarro saw to it that they had a rack full of uniforms when most groups just had one. I would watch them from the wings and they'd be smoking! When the show was over I'd say, "Okay. Let's go down in the basement." Those guys really took corrections well. I'd tell them something one time and the next time they hit the stage, it was perfect.

During the mid-fifties, I hooked up again with a good buddy from my army days, Rudy Traylor. He and I formed a partnership training and building acts, like the Dyerettes, a dancing group made up of five girls from Chicago. The group was really started by Sammy Dyer, who was a well-known producer of shows at the Regal and a lot of other clubs in Chi-town during the thirties and forties. But this turned

out to be a short-lived management thing because most of them started getting married, and one by one that group fell apart.

In February 1956, Frankie Lymon and the Teenagers were
booked at the Palladium in London. I think they might have been
one of the first rock-and-roll groups to sing there, so their manager
brought them to me well in advance, about four months. Around
that time Frankie began trying to do a little tap. He'd come to a studio where I was teaching a tap class and watch because he was real
eager to learn it.

I started him out, but Pete Nugent is the one who took over his lessons and taught him tap routines. And that's when Frankie really became a good rhythm tapper. Actually, he was already a good dancer,
but he just had to convert that into tap dance. He used to hang out
with Baby Laurence a lot, too, but I don't think Baby coached him. At
least I never heard that he did. Right up until the time he passed away,
he continued to study with Pete.

Fifty-six is also the year that Dotty started singing again. She took
a leave of absence from Gertz's to do a State Department tour in the
Middle East with Dizzy Gillespie's band. I think Quincy Jones went
on that tour. Dizzy put together a big band to do a goodwill tour of
several countries and selected Dotty as the female vocalist. After the
tour ended, things began to pick up. She went to Bermuda, Miami,
Montreal, and quite a few places near home. One was a small club
down in the Village, that used singers and did what they called "ups."
There was a series of singers presented each night. When it was your
turn to perform, the MC would come backstage, "You up!"

Some weekends Dotty worked at Peg Leg Bates's resort in the
Catskills. LeRoy Myers found a place up there in the fifties and tried
to get the Copasetics to buy it, but when that didn't work out, Peg,
who was in the Copasetics, decided that he'd take it. He really developed it and was successful for quite a while. Honi and I appeared
there, too. See, when Peg was trying to get started, a lot of the guys
would go up and help him out. Back then all the white resorts were
closed to our people, so on the weekends busloads of folks would show

up. Maggie said one time she went up with a group that had rented seventeen buses.

The vocal groups kept me pretty busy in '57. But what I wanted more than anything was to perform. Since the Tony Martin gig, nothing really big had happened out of town for Coles and Atkins. It's a good thing Leonard was looking out for us. He was still production manager at the Apollo and throughout the fifties he put us in a show every time he could swing it. Finally Mr. Schiffman got angry. "Mr. Reed, do you manage Coles and Atkins?" Leonard said, "No. Why?" He said, "I don't understand. Every show you put together, you've got them in here. You had them with Joe Louis, you had them with Count Basie, you had them with Lucky Millinder's New Year's Eve Show, and you've got them here now." Leonard said, "Well, they're the best I know!" There were many times when we needed a job badly, and he always came through.

Our luck took a turn in 1958, when we started a year-and-a-half tour with Pearl Bailey. She had her own revue with Louie Bellson's band; her brother Bill Bailey, who was a tap dancer; a six-voice choir; Coles and Atkins; and a chorus line of six girls: Anna Bailey, Martha Jordan, Mickey Adams, Blanche Shavers, Elsie Blow, and Joan Myers Brown, who eventually started Philadanco, a modern dance company based in Philly. We traveled throughout the country, playing mainly supper clubs and theaters.

I think in February we went to Blinstrub's in Boston. We left there in a blizzard, flew to Miami and did the Fontainebleau for a couple of weeks, then the Paradise Theater in Detroit, the Regal in Chicago, and on to the Chase Hotel in St. Louis. That was the first time any black star appeared in the Chase. We had to enter through the back door and nobody could live there. The whole cast stayed at a hotel in the black neighborhood.

Omaha, Nebraska, was our next stop, then on to Des Moines, Seattle, Portland, and Denver. We were flying from Denver to San Francisco and about to land when one of those little prop planes was taking off. Evidently he didn't see us, because our pilot shot straight up in the air.

Practically gave everybody a heart attack. Scared Pearl to death! She said, "My God, I didn't have time to pray!" When we got to San Francisco, Pearl turned in all her plane tickets and went to L.A. on the train.

Our gig in L.A. lasted for about a month, then we opened at the Flamingo in Las Vegas for a four-week engagement and ended up staying for three months. The owner kept picking up the options because the business was just tremendous. He had some cottages out in the back, so Pearl and Louis stayed there. By that time, they had been married for quite a while. The rest of us moved into a little motel right down from the Flamingo, which was totally unexpected, because when Honi and I went there in '55, blacks weren't allowed to stay anywhere on the Strip.

After Las Vegas, we went back to the Coconut Grove in L.A., before performing at the Lincoln Theater in the black neighborhood. A lot of times we'd play a theater in the downtown area and blacks wouldn't go because they had to sit up in the balcony and all that kind of crap. So, back in those days, to make the show more available to African Americans, we would generally play an extra week at theaters in black neighborhoods. That was by no means an economic decision, because we had good bookings. See, Pearl was very conscious of the problems encountered by blacks and she always wanted the revues to be accessible to her people.

While we were out on the road with Pearl, Dr. Hogan called to say that he had put Dotty in the hospital to rest. She was pregnant at the time and we were both real hopeful about being parents, because she had made it through four months. But I guess it just wasn't meant to be. The loss really took a toll on her. Right after she got out of the hospital, she went up to Utica to spend some time with her sister. Then she decided that she just didn't want to sing anymore.

Honi and I worked all the way back to New York with Pearl, then she ended the tour because she had been negotiating to do a television show. Between engagements, I'd come back in to work with different vocal groups. One time I did some choreography for Smokey Robinson and the Miracles. I'm sure it was in '59 because "Shop Around" was released that year and that was the first tune I choreographed for them. It was also the first time I saw Berry Gordy in New York, hanging around the Brill Building.

My buddy Walter Thomas set up the gig with the Miracles. He would try to convince all the groups handled by the Shaw Agency to hire me. And when the Miracles came to New York to work at a Brooklyn supper club, he had a long talk with them about the importance of getting someone to stage and choreograph their material because they had the potential to be a crossover act. This was early on, when there were five of them: Smokey Robinson, Pete Moore, Bobby Rogers, Claudette Rogers Robinson, who was married to Smokey, and Ronnie White.

Their only hit then was "Shop Around," but they wanted a big opening and some Broadway tunes to add to the act. I was working in conjunction with an arranger and vocal coach–pianist, and together we did some real nice things for them. I included show tunes like "Gee, It's Good to Be Here" with real high production stuff on the vocals, good choreography breakdown, and bluesy approaches, with a touch of Broadway.

We mentioned all the cities, like Chicago, Boston, New Orleans, even Kalamazoo; and Los Angeles, San Francisco. "But gee, it's good to be here!" The Miracles were primarily R & B people, so it was surprising that they adapted to those types of songs. Unfortunately, they never performed them. When they got back to Motown, their bookings were in places where the audience just wanted to hear records. The Miracles wound up giving all of that material to the Spinners, who did it successfully for quite a while.

Around this time, Dotty got a daytime job in a neighborhood Irish bar, where we all used to hang out. The owner's name was Walsh. We were in there one night and he asked me if I knew someone who would be interested in a job as a barmaid. Dotty said, "I'd like to try it." I said, "Well, what about mixing drinks? You haven't had experience doing that." But when we really thought about it, we realized that most of the people coming by the bar were mechanics from over at the airport. They ordered mostly straight shots and beer. So Dotty decided to try it out.

The show business jobs were getting so scarce that by 1960, Honi and I were thinking about breaking up our duo. The only really memorable thing we did that year was a summer replacement show with Andy Williams, who had seen us in Miami with Pearl's revue. After we finished our act, Andy came on and did the shim sham and a little challenge with us, which was a lot of fun. But that was the last variety television show that we appeared on. Then we basically went to pot, really. Nothing was happening.

We were a black *class act*, which in the tap world meant that you were well mannered, well groomed, your attire was excellent, and your material was extremely polished. We refused to play into any of the stereotypes, so a lot of the guys who controlled the swankiest spots thought of us as defiant. Back then many Americans were not ready to see two black men with an act as suave as ours. Another problem was the headliners. If they were singers or comics, they didn't like the fact that we were also doing those things as part of our act.

The promoters wanted us to come in, just dance, and leave out the rest. Typically they'd say, "You guys are good dancers, you don't need all that other garbage in your act." Honi would tell them, "This isn't garbage. We're getting laughs, the people seem to enjoy our singing and what we do is good, wholesome variety. You knew what we did when you hired us!" It was really quite a vicious circle. Still, Honi and I were determined to be accepted on our own terms, even though we were losing a lot of gigs because of what we stood for. Then there was always the concern, on the part of the club owners, that they might be bringing in some black male performers that would appeal to the white girls in the audience. That was one of the unspoken issues, even though everybody knew it existed.

Joe Glaser told us one time, "Look, once in a while a job will come along and you will be the only ones ready for it; the only ones they'll want to do it. Then they'll slap you down just like they let you up there. Because you're doing a white boys' act." And we would say, "Yeah, you're right." So, we came to the conclusion that no matter what we did, we were not going to get the kind of acceptance we wanted.

I went back in the studio and started coaching again. It seemed that the vocal groups were here to stay. Around the late fifties, I remember Leonard saying that he asked Mr. Schiffman when he was gonna bring back some bands and some chorus girls. Schiffman said, "Come here, I want to show you something. . . . It's raining, Jackie Wilson is in there with Brook Benton, and three or four other people. From that ticket booth all the way around 125th Street to Eighth Avenue, around the corner, almost up to the Braddock, people are standing in line in front of the *Amsterdam News*, trying to get into the theater. The day there's no more people behind this person right here at the ticket booth, then we'll make a change."

At the beginning of the sixties, the situation was the same. Harvey and the Moonglows hired me to put together an eight-minute medley of standard tunes, that they eventually passed on to the Spinners. I already knew Harvey Fuqua because I had worked with him in the fifties when I was coaching other groups of that era. There was a ton of doo-wop groups during that decade. First they had the bird groups, like the Orioles, then the cars came in. They were named after all kinds of things: musical terms, age groups, flowers, animals. I can remember working specifically with the Turbans, Solitaires, Five Satins, Cleftones, Five Keys, Harptones, Heartbeats, Ravens, Little Anthony and the Imperials, the Edsels, the Velvets, Shep and the Limelites, and Jerry Butler and the Impressions. There were a lot more that I can't even think of right now.

I usually choreographed a couple of tunes for most groups because there were just so many and like I told you before, I didn't have any assistants. The groups were just so hot and all the agencies were trying to grab them. Then they needed somebody to polish them up a little bit and put some kind of definition to their movement. So I got my contacts back together and went to work!

But not much was happening for Honi jobwise and to make matters worse, there were problems at his daughter's school. Dope dealers and hustlers were hanging around the grounds in the afternoon. He was going over there every day to pick up Isabelle. Honi was the type of person who would face problems head on, so he decided to approach one of the guys, "Hey, man, what are you cats hanging around here for? Why don't you leave these young kids alone?"

Three of the guys walked toward him. "Motherfucker, what's your problem?" Honi said, "Well, I've got a child in here and I'm worried about her." "Man, you just get your daughter the hell out of here, and don't be telling us how to run our lives." So Honi finally had to back down, but naturally he wasn't anxious to leave town on a gig after that; he wanted to stick around and keep an eye on the situation.

Then one night when Dotty, Maggie, Honi, and I were visiting Leonard and his wife, Barbara, Leonard told us that the two of them were moving out to California, which meant there was an opening for a production manager at the Apollo. So Maggie persuaded Honi to check into it since he was good friends with the Schiffmans. She said, "Look, I know you want to dance, but this job is connected with the theater, and I think if Mr. Schiffman realizes you want it, he'll give it to you."

Honi spent a lot of time golfing with Bobby, Jack, and their father, so one day he mentioned that he was interested in filling Leonard's position, and at first they didn't take him seriously, because they knew how much he loved performing. But soon after that he received a letter from Frank Schiffman offering him the job. I lived right around the corner, so he came by and we sat there in the living room for the longest time, discussing everything. As far as our act was concerned, we could see the writing on the wall, and I sure didn't want anything to happen to my goddaughter, Isabelle, so we decided to just throw in the towel. And if things didn't work out, we could always get back together, do three choruses or something and get a club date somewhere.

But it was a heartbreaking thing, because partners are like brothers. You share everything. That's the way we had grown up in the business. Honi used to say, "If you do Cholly wrong, you've done me wrong." I think our partnership was an exceptionally rich one because we were really able to collaborate on everything. He gave me what I needed and I gave him what he needed. See, Honi was a master at intricate tap steps. Everybody in our circle of artists recognized that he was a great technician and a great solo artist, but being black, the opportunities were just not there like they were for white dancers.

He helped me learn how to put a lot of complex taps into routines, but he was a very upright dancer. Now, most of my stuff had more of a jazz feeling. I was always more interested in how my body was moving, so I would eliminate a lot of taps in order to move well and he was influenced a great deal by my style. The combination of the two talents made a big difference. And we both recognized that. We knew that we added something to each other. That's one of the reasons we were able to stay together so long. And although our career as a team ended much too soon, I have the satisfaction of knowing that Coles and Atkins left a little sand on the beach. And one more thing, Honi and I always said that we'd never let the act interfere with our friendship—it never did.

7

RHYTHM TAP AND MORE

Aside from the Copasetics' shows and a few other appearances, the only performances that Honi and I did in the early sixties were with Billy Eckstine. Annually, since the late fifties, Eckstine's band had kicked off the new season at the Apollo Theater after its summer renovation. And each and every year, in spite of the fact that we hadn't worked for twelve months, Eckstine would insist that we be in the show with him. So we had to go to the woodshed and pull out an act. No matter what we said, the three of us always ended up on stage together. Finally, after doing that for about four years straight, Honi said, "Stiney, if you want some tap dancing on your show, *you* do it!"

But we were better off than a lot of rhythm tap dancers. At least we had jobs that could pay the bills. Most buck dancers and many of the musicians who had played with big bands were scuffling, from the mid-fifties right on through the sixties, trying to make ends meet. Most of them wound up getting day jobs or doing something like bartending.

I remember one time I ran into a very close friend of ours, Hilton Jefferson, down around Wall Street. Hilton had been a very wonderful saxophone player with Cab Calloway. When the band broke up, he was running messages for a bank. You'd see these things happening to dear friends all the time and it was so painful.

Some of the solo tap dancers were able to travel with the few big bands that were left. Baby Laurence went out a lot with Duke. And sometimes if Baby was busy, Bunny Briggs would go or Buster Brown. But basically that was a drop in the bucket as far as the guys were concerned.

The teams and the trios and duos are the ones that really suffered. One of the Three Rockets became a bank messenger, like Hilton. Then he finally left New York and went back to California. Binky Weaver became a super in an apartment house up in the Bronx. He was one of the Three Giants of Rhythm, that group Honi had danced with. The other guy in that trio, Dick Saunders, started doing an act with his wife up around the Boston area, and they bought a couple of buildings and turned them into rooming houses.

The guys were really spreading around because there wasn't that much work to do. Several of the buck dancers left the country. Ralph Brown went up to Canada. A lot stayed in Europe for a while, like Jimmy Slyde, who was in France. Some even got into teaching over there. So I guess you can't really say that tap stopped altogether, because there were some dancers who never took their shoes off.

A few, like John Bubbles, were on television periodically. Baby didn't do much television to my knowledge. Once in a while you might see Bunny Briggs or Bill Bailey on a show. I remember Arthur Duncan was on the *Lawrence Welk Show* every week, but television helped kill rhythm tap. See, it was very difficult for good tap to catch on televisionwise because it had more depth to it than TV could accommodate. Staging it was very expensive—a lot of money for rehearsals and adequate floors, so it just got eliminated.

Rhythm tap is not a simple art form. Most people just don't have a clue about how complex it really is. You have to develop complete control of muscles that you don't normally use in order to do your stuff in time, stay with the beat, and be creative enough to do the things that you think you want to do. And there aren't too many of us left to teach the real technique of tap dancing, all the ABCs. I strongly feel that the young tap dancers now need to include more shading, rather than pack in a million taps at ninety miles an hour. See, we based our rhythmic patterns on a melodic strain, to have something to say, create a change in syncopation. Mood changes. That's how you tell a story with your taps. Jimmy Slyde does that. And, of course, Chuck Green was one of the greatest storytellers ever. He could create poetry with his feet. Beautiful rhythms!

Back then almost all the dancers encouraged one another. You'd be fooling around and come up with a fantastic step. "Oh, man, that was a classic. That was a great step. Do it again." The cat would say, "Are you crazy?" We had more fun and I'm telling you, there was such a spirit of generosity. One of the many reasons why the dancers got along so well was that they were not really jealous of one another. At least that's the way it seemed to me. We'd show each other things, share ideas. Everybody could choreograph, but we didn't know the word. Had never heard of the word. I can't spell it now! You put your act together. That's what we called it.

One time Honi and I were performing and we both deleted four bars of choreography at the same time. Neither one of us could remember the steps, so we went back into rehearsal and created four more bars to insert in that spot. And we went along doing that for a week or so. Then we looked up one day and we were doing the first four bars again at exactly the same time. It was the strangest thing. We never could get over it. I guess that's what made Coles and Atkins. But we always created! The mind worked all the time. We never had to pay somebody for choreography. Although our act might have a spot where we improvised, most of our material was set when we went on stage.

Improvisation came into play more with the solo dancers. People like Baby Laurence and Bunny Briggs didn't do the same show every night. They'd do some of the same steps but put together a different way. You know how a jazz musician solos? Well, that's what they did, especially the bebop dancers. They were like drummers. Buster always says, "Tap dancing and drumming are twins. They just don't look alike."

Honi was a great improviser, but he didn't move into that bebop realm. Baby was the king of that style. Bebop was Bunny's thing, too. Walter Green was into bebop. Groundhog. Teddy Hale. Lon Chaney was a paddle-and-roller. There was another guy you didn't hear too much about, Albert Gibson. He was in the Chocolateers, a comedy act, but he could solo. I mean, he'd run all up the walls. I remember in California, around '36 or '37, we had jam sessions in the alley behind the hotel where everybody was staying and he'd do all those steps on concrete.

These were the type of dancers that influenced the musicians from a rhythmic standpoint. Now, that really happened, you know. Some musicians don't want to tell you about that, but they got a lot of their rhythms from tap dancers. What triggered the hoofers to move that way, God only knows. These things moved in cycles, based primarily on what John Bubbles had done earlier.

Bubbles influenced more dancers than anybody. He was the one who really started dropping the heels, doing a lot of different syncopations, prior to bebop. The dancers before Bubbles tapped up on the balls of their feet. We called them aerial dancers. They were another breed! That style had been passed down by Bill Robinson. But Bubbles lifted tap to another level by dropping his heels into cramp rolls and doing complex rhythm turns. Tap stayed like that for a while. Guys imitated him and learned.

Then came Honi Coles, who did the same type of things that Bubbles had done, but at a much faster tempo. When he came back to New York in 1932, as a soloist, all the guys were coming by the studio where he practiced to try to cut him, because he was introducing a new school. He was like Savion Glover is now. His dancing was just so complex and so technical, it was hard for the average person sitting in the audience to really understand what he was doing. He had nice rhythmic patterns, but they were so loaded with taps they'd all run together, instead of hard syncopated sounds. But it wasn't sloppy. Technically it was excellent. He'd stay on the highs and there wouldn't be any valleys, which affected the shading. The best way, I think, to blend your technique is with a variation of syncopations. The syncopation is lost when it's all technique. You have to alter the highs and the lows.

He'd be dropping heels and turning. When he did a spin, he never stopped making a lot of taps. Most of the guys, even Bubbles, would do a turn and there would be a spell in there with no sound. But with Honi, a turn would sound like, CHICKABOOBLUUYYAAAH. There were times when we would put little rhythm turns together and he would throw one of them things down. I said, "Man, you better get out of here." Because it was hard, you know. He couldn't break it down enough to show me where these sounds were coming from, what toe or what heel. I didn't even know what to *try* to do.

Between Honi and Baby Laurence, who was the next great trend-setter, there were a lot of guys who were fine dancers. There was a guy from Philly named Bo Jenkins, who did an excellent imitation of Bill Robinson. Bill Bailey had the carriage of Bill Robinson but did syncopated rhythms. Prince Spencer was a midwestern dancer who also did a lot of highly syncopated things. Freddie James was doing that style, too, with acrobatics added in.

There were many fine dancers during that era, but they did not take the art to another level and have things spring out from their contribution over a period of years, like you'd get with a Baby Laurence. When Baby came along, he was in a class by himself. He was very creative and very lyrical. I loved to see him dance with Ellington. His style fit beautifully with Duke's music, which could be abstract and have all kinds of innovative chord structures.

But truthfully, I enjoyed a whole lot of dancers. Pete Nugent was one of my favorites. I only saw Eddie Rector a couple of times. He was one of the few dancers that I saw at Shea's Buffalo when I first started dancing. Pete, Peaches, and Duke were classic dancers. Light. No real hoofin.' Precision was their thing. Bubba Gaines's group, the Three Dukes, was another good-looking, well-dressed trio. They did nice, novel things with ropes. The Condos Brothers were a white act that did fine dancing. They grew up in that same element as Honi, around the Pearl and Standard Theaters in Philadelphia, dancing on the street corners with black kids. Ralph Brown was somewhat in the Pete Nugent frame. He still had that old style, which was fantastic, beautiful dancing. He floated.

But, my all-time favorite dancer is Jimmy Slyde. If I could tap again and could choose one style, I'd want to dance like Jimmy. That type of dancing would make me happy because that's how my body likes to move. Slyde is an excellent proponent of *jazz* tap, any way you look at it, riding or walking! In my estimation, he's the best out there doing that particular style. There are a lot of guys going off of him, too, but this is what I'm talking about. The whole rhythm tap thing is like a tree.

You see, when it first comes up, a limb will go this way, another one will go that way, and the next one will go down, and then one will go up the center. This is what tap's development was really like. Everything was growing from what came before and everyone was searching for a fresher approach to whatever was happening.

But Baby Laurence, who came on the scene in the forties, was the last great innovator of that period from the twenties through the forties. He was the first bebop tap dancer. Believe me, nobody else was doing that kind of dance. When you watched him you could see in his combinations the basic techniques that everybody else came up with, but there was a way it was put together that made the difference; the language of it, the syncopation of it set well with the bebop music. And it was during that era with the change of music by people like Dizzy Gillespie and Charlie Parker—that's when Baby's dancing came to the surface.

In my estimation, there hasn't been anyone else until Savion. He has something fresh, something new, something added. Right now, it's exceptionally difficult for anybody—I don't care who the dancer is or how much knowledge they have—it's almost impossible for them to steal a step from Savion.

You might be able to pick something up during those little rest spots that he goes through. But when he's stretching out, all dancers can forget it as far as lifting a step is concerned. Because you have no idea where those taps are coming from. You never heard so many taps in your life. Not even from the innovators that came before him. And that's a gift! He's been taught well, but he's gone beyond that with his own ability.

He's taken what he's been taught and extended it three hundred fold. He's just taken it so much further. His sense of rhythm, his sense of timing, his ability to hear patterns that are interesting and not monotonous, with some sort of melody that flows underneath . . . he's just something to marvel at. I don't know any great dancers who have sat and watched him and didn't marvel at that young man!

He is definitely the greatest tap dancer, the greatest rhythm tap dancer in this world. And there will be a whole lot of people who won't give him that recognition—but that has nothing to do with it. Right now he's adding a huge limb to that old tree. And a lot of people will make contributions through their efforts to emulate his greatness. You establish something by trying to be a John Bubbles or Bill Robinson or Honi Coles or Baby Lawrence or Savion Glover. Some interesting styles will come out of efforts to achieve what these trend-setters have already laid out.

Not too many people talk about it, but there were some great black women tap dancers, too. Alice Whitman was as fine a tap dancer as anybody. She was better than a lot of the boys. In fact, she taught Pops, her son. All of the Whitmans could dance like crazy. They had a road show that traveled all over. In a lot of those road companies, the girls would get in the corner with the boys and learn all them steps and dance just like them. And then they'd get right back in the chorus. But they loved dancing and that's one of the ways they developed.

Pearl Bailey was one of the best black rhythm dancers that I ever saw. She was an excellent dancer before she started to sing. Frances Nealy was a good tap dancer. Jeni LeGon was excellent. She was influenced a great deal by Bill Robinson's style. Most of the girls in the Apollo line were wonderful. Marion Coles was a very fine tap dancer. Man, could she swing . . . still can! I always wanted Maggie to be my vocal choreography assistant, but since she and Honi were based in New York, we never could work it out.

I didn't see Louise Madison dance, but all my friends who saw her gave her a great bill of sale. Honi said she was excellent. As a matter of fact, he picked up some things from her. Like Louise Madison, many of those women dancers that ended up in the limelight were from Philadelphia. Remember, Dotty came out of that Philly bag. Ludie Jones was another Philadelphia girl who could really tap.

In Chicago there were the Rimmer Sisters. Also the Edwards Sisters. Their father had been a good tap dancer, and he passed his skills on to them. There was one very fine dancer out of Boston that Joe Louis was crazy about. She had a ballet background and was in the Eleanor Powell–Ann Miller bag, but she could do some nice little rhythm things, too. I know there were lots more; the names just elude me right now. But the guys dominated tap. There were many, many more male dancers.

There's been a lot of speculation around this issue and I don't really know all the answers, but I do know that there were some wonderful women dancers and they generally did not have as much access to performance and training venues as the guys. I'm going way back now, but what comes to mind is the difficulty Honi and I had trying to get Danny Miller to put Lois Bright in his act, the Miller Brothers. Believe me, it took a long time to make him see that Lois could be an asset to his team. Everybody who had worked in the group had been a male. Very, very few groups back then had a female buck dancer.

Honi and I knew that the kind of person Danny wanted to fill the spot couldn't be an apprentice but someone who was top-notch, and Lois definitely fit the bill. She was an excellent tap dancer and had wonderful projection. I knew exactly what she was capable of because out in California when we were choreographing for chorus lines together, I'd show her all of my pet steps and it didn't take me forever to teach them to her. She would work on them and say, "Have I got it?" "Yeah, baby, you *doing* it." And true taps. No jive taps. She'd make 'em all! Some things that I couldn't get the guys to do, she got right away. So I knew what a gem she would be in the Miller Brothers' act. In addition she had all of the basic training for doing the acrobatic stuff.

When we first proposed the idea to Danny, he said, "Hey, man, what are you talkin' about? Put a chick in here?" I said, "Yeah, man, she's better at this stuff than anybody you're gon' find. Give it a shot. Just take her into the studio and just work with her." Danny said, "I've seen her in the chorus line, man, and I know she wails, but I don't know if she can stand up to this stuff." I told him, "Man, give her a shot. I'm telling you, she can cook!"

Well, that debate went on for a long time, then finally one day he said, "Well, man, let's get together down at the Apollo in the rehearsal hall." And he showed her some things and she jumped right on them. Eventually Danny woke up to it. He said, "You cats were right. I'm very grateful to you, man." You see, the only reason he hesitated in the beginning was because she was a woman. Lois Bright was good looking and built and had the talent! She was just the wrong sex as far as he was concerned.

I guess another reason there were more men dancers had to do with the fact that tap requires tremendous devotion. It's laborious and you have to spend a great deal of time developing your technique. You just don't think it and do it. You have to really stretch out and practice it. Back then the common feeling was, "A woman's place is in the home." They couldn't devote their lives to tap as easily as the men. It's certainly not that women weren't willing to put the time in, but if they were married, for example, they were the ones expected to take care of everybody else's needs. And also they weren't allowed in places like the Hoofers Club—where tap experimentation was taking place and apprenticeships were being formed.

There were always some excellent women tap dancers who put everything else aside and worked at it real hard, but it appeared—to me—that most of them never had proper representation as far as agents were concerned. Most of the women represented themselves. They would go in little neighborhood clubs and audition for the jobs. In the better spots, the club owners were more interested in hiring male dancers, and even if a female was recommended for a job, it was hard to sell the idea. Sometimes when your gig was just about up at a club, the owner might say, "Who do you think I should get as a replacement?" You'd mention somebody like Juanita Pitts and try to convince him that this would be something new and fresh and different. The cat would say, "I want a man doing this thing." The agents pretty much felt that way, too. Those guys had absolutely no vision.

The same thing happened with the female comedians. You remember the song, "It's a Man's World?" That's how it was. And when you take into consideration the number of chorus lines throughout this country—millions of them—it says a lot that so few chorus line dancers became solo artists. You still have to wonder why. And that requires a lot more explanation than I can give.

I feel blessed to have come along when tap was at its peak. We practiced for days because it meant everything to us. I can't think of anything more satisfying. Nobody was standing over you with a whip—it was a love thing! We did it because we loved to dance and wanted to improve ourselves so that we could be as good as a Bubbles or a Bill Robinson.

But you see, all of this dance moves in a circle. The switch from choreographing rhythm tap to choreographing for vocal groups was a pretty smooth one for me. It was really a natural progression because of the way both are connected to black social dance, and really, all of it is jazz dance. One of the better groups that I worked with at the beginning of the sixties was the Vibrations, who did a lot of old tap steps, like over-the-top and trenches. They did *at* these things. They had concepts of them, but not a full understanding.

During the twenties and thirties, all big steps had names, like the cross-step, the front wing, trenches, over the top, the scratch wing, falling off the log. There were a million. I can't even think of half of them, but they were very popular steps and they all had affectionate names. But the Vibrations, a sixties vocal group, got pretty good at that stuff.

Their manager wanted to clean them up and teach them some theatrics. Also, they were running out of gas during their shows. About one third of the way through the act, they would use up all their energy. So it was about pacing. They brought me in to try to inject little things in between what they were doing, so they could catch their breath. This was a very different kind of assignment. I cleaned them up the best I could, and as usual, tried to meet the challenge.

This vocal choreography business was a real lucky thing for me because I could have easily been out there carrying messages back and forth, like Hilton. Instead, I was busier than ever at the Goldfarb Studios. You could come right up out of the subway, right into the building. And Honi was over at the Apollo handing out my business card every chance he got, because vocal groups were coming in there left and right. If a group looked like it needed help, he'd say, "Go down and see my partner, he'll straighten you out. He's done the Cadillacs and the Teenagers, the Solitaires, the Cleftones." He'd run 'em down. They'd say, "Oh, yeah, man! Them cats really step. Does he cost a lot of money?" "Well, he's pretty cool. Go and talk with him."

The average groups that came into the Apollo needed everything, because they were fresh off the street corner. They had to start learning all aspects of performance *after* they started performing. Many didn't know how to take a bow when they finished a song. Some would run off the stage, leave the other ones behind, or you might have five guys in the act and you'd hear two singing parts. Even though they had hit records, some didn't have sheet music, and they would come to the Apollo rehearsals without charts.

Honi inherited all of this. He said he used to hate Friday mornings because they'd have a rehearsal with the big band. Reuben Phillips was the house band leader at the time. Honi would call an act like the Dimensions, "Okay, Dimensions, let's get with Reuben now. You're doing three numbers. Your hit record you'll do last. Give Reuben your music." Those cats would say, "What music? You heard our record!" Reuben would just shake his head, because he was working with very talented jazz musicians, and time was important. He'd go across the street to the Record Shack, buy their music and play it for the musicians so they could hear where the drummers were coming in and the brass horns.

Some groups had no training whatsoever. Honi would tell them, "I want you to stay a little longer; I'm going to show you how to get on stage." The guys looked at Honi, "What's your record, man? You got a hit record?" The average choreographer would have charged them an arm and a leg for that information. So Honi just decided to leave them to the mercy of the second balcony.

Sometimes there would be three consecutive rock-and-roll acts on a bill, with three different musical setups. Honi would try to convince them to work it out so they wouldn't waste so much time between acts. "Look, why don't you use his drums? He's willing for you to use them." The drummer would say, "Yeah, man, but we have a *sound*. I got to play my own drums." Now you got another five-to-seven-minute break, and the audience is getting restless again.

One time he took a group downtown to see Count Basie. These particular guys sang and played instruments. They had microphones everywhere—on the drummer's foot pedal, you name it. Honi wanted the group's leader to see Basie's setup. That turkey got down there, looked over the thing, "Yeah, but he ain't got our sound." Honi said, "I gave up completely, then. I never said a word to another soul!"

Around that time, I was swamped with female groups. Girl groups had really caught on. We went through a transition period there, because all of the groups in the fifties, the Flamingos, Ravens, Orioles, Cleftones, they were all male groups. You had a few groups with maybe one female, like Ruby and the Romantics or Gladys Knight and the Pips. The Chantels first came on the scene in '57, I believe.

By the early sixties, the record companies were bringing most of the girl groups to me so they could be groomed for presentation. And because of my experiences with chorus lines, I knew a lot of the moves that I like to see girls do; moves that would make them look more feminine, and I could do them. I remember a few years later when I was working with the Supremes, Mary Wilson used to say, "Cholly, I don't understand how you can do that move better than *me* and I'm a girl. You've really got to stop. One of these days you're going to walk out, and that's all you'll be doing, those kinds of moves, and people are going to get the wrong idea about you!"

I said, "No way. That ain't never gonna happen, because when I leave you, I'm going directly to the Contours with their acrobatics and all that stuff. You just try to do it as well as *you* can do it, and make it more feminine than I make it!" Truthfully, during the early sixties, I had gotten a little concerned about how people were viewing me, because it was rumored that a lot of male choreographers were gay. I had to fight within myself to keep from letting that worry become an issue. So that's the reason I was thinking, "Hey, man, don't nobody get no ideas, because I'll bring you right down front!"

But, seriously, the biggest problem I had was getting the girls to change their approach because most of them wanted to dance like the guys. I said, "But you're not guys. You don't sound like guys. You don't look like guys. You're not supposed to be doing things the way you see the guys doing them." My work was cut out for me because some of them had been learning from the male groups and those cats didn't know diddly-squat about teaching females. They probably thought their approach was fine for everybody. It was all the same to them.

But I worked it out, softened them up; the Chantels, the Crystals, the Shirelles—any group I had a chance to work with. See, the girl groups had to be more concerned with what I call physical drama. Instead of trying to move like the guys, I wanted them to use the kind of body language that was associated with women—using your eyes, hands on the hips, and so forth, but not in a macho way. They had to really think about this feminine approach and keep that uppermost in their minds. And naturally, they were doing a lot of love tunes. If I demonstrated a feminine move that they thought was basically an affectation, they called it camping, which was the street term used at that time. When I was growing up, my mother and aunts used to call it putting on airs or being proper.

Now, the girls would do a little fall-off with a step and a slide up; they would slide up soft, drag the leg, push the pelvis forward, and drop the hand over like a girl would do. When the guys did that move, they'd *chug* into it forcefully. But the basic step was primarily the same. Only, the mental approach to it would change.

The other thing I gave a lot of consideration to was the places that the artists were going to be working; their engagements, the type of venues they were going into. And my whole thing was to have a happy marriage between the talent and the type of material they were doing. There was no sense in taking a group that was doing a lot of funky steps and try to give them a whole lot of sophisticated moves. Mentally, you have to be prepared for that. And a lot of the young girls weren't ready.

The Crystals were a pretty nice little group, but their material was really bubble-gum stuff; little teenybop stuff. You could give them nice little moves that were typical of what the kids were doing, but with a sophisticated attitude. Since they had a very strange management that didn't want to spend any money, all their material sounded pretty much the same. Consequently, they could take the choreography from the things I taught them and put it on the next release themselves. But that led to another problem. Then all the songs sounded the same and looked the same.

The first girl group I worked with was the Shirelles, and I coached them on a consistent basis because I had a certain kind of rapport with Scepter Records. The record company also managed the group. That's when I first worked with Dionne Warwick, Chuck Jackson, and Tommy Hunt, a former member of the Flamingos. All three were on Scepter, so I had a pretty steady account with that company.

When tap hit rock bottom, my vocal choreography thing was pretty lucrative. But I still felt that the sixties was the beginning of a very negative period for me. I'd had such a happy life up until then. Lucky enough not to have to go out of the country during the war or be shipped over while they were shooting and all of that crap. Finding a place in show business during the service thing! Then getting married to Dotty. We had created so many wonderful memories together. Man, my life was just going so smoothly, when all this sadness started to creep in. I guess it had really started with the breakup of Coles and Atkins.

Then on April 5 of 1962, Dotty passed away. It just about destroyed me. Everything fell apart in my life. She was still employed at that little Irish bar when she died. I had stopped by there that day to pick her up and the guy said she had left early. I went on home and she was in bed with a headache, so I said, "Why don't we take a little walk and get some fresh air? Maybe you'll feel better." There was a church about two blocks away called St. Gabriel's. When we got there, I told her, "Let's say a little prayer, Sugar, that you'll feel better, then we'll walk by the diner to get something to eat." But she was feeling real weak and wanted to get home.

So we went back to the house. I gave her some aspirin and encouraged her to just rest while I went over to the restaurant to get some Chinese food. Then, I came back and asked her if she wanted me to fix her a plate, and she said, "No, just let me sleep." I went on and had a little bite to eat because I wasn't too worried. Dotty had suffered with bad headaches before.

When she got up to go to the bathroom, though, she was stumbling and said she felt faint. So I helped her back to bed and sat there and talked to her for a while, but she was sort of dozing off. Then I was getting real worried, because that seemed kind of strange. She said, "I feel like I'm drifting off; I feel like I'm falling." I said, "Well, I'm going to sit you up and try to put some clothes on you because I want to get you to the hospital." She could barely sit up at all.

Finally, I had raised her up to put her coat on, and I had to hold her because she was fainting, like. Then all of a sudden, she just looked down at me, and she just dropped her head. I got the coat on her and laid her across the bed and called a cab. The cab station was about two blocks from us, so within minutes, the guy came by, blew the horn and I took her downstairs.

I had her in my arms the whole time we were driving there and I was trying to wake her up. When we got to the hospital, the driver went in and they sent an orderly out with a stretcher and he wheeled her inside. I paid the cab driver, went in, and when the orderly came out of the room where he'd taken her, I said, "How's she doing?" He said, "Mister, she was dead when you brought her in here"—and walked away from me. For a second, I didn't know where the hell I was. I must have stood there for ten minutes. Just the way he said that to me. Is life that cheap, you know?

So the woman behind the desk asked me if I wanted some water. Then she said, "Just sit down here for a while." She needed information on Dotty and asked me what she had eaten. After a little while, the doctor came out, "Well, we'd like to do an autopsy on her, try to find out what happened." I got on the phone and called Maggie and Honi. He said, "Get a cab and come on over here. Don't go back to the house now; come straight here." So I went over, and I sat there and tried to explain what had happened. Honi said, "You stay here with Maggie and I'll check everything out for you. I'll handle it."

We had a friend on the staff at the hospital, a guy we played golf with all the time, and he looked out for everybody's family. So Honi got ahold of him. From then on, Honi and Maggie took care of everything. She went over and packed all of Dotty's clothes and got those things out of there. I don't know who she gave them to. She put out all the lights and told my landlord, who lived underneath us. So, he let the neighbors know. Peg lived across the street and he came by Honi's. All of our friends started dropping by. The whole thing was such a shock to everybody because she was just thirty-nine.

Finally, Dotty's doctor told me she had a tumor on the brain and the pain became so severe that it just stopped her heart. That's when she collapsed in my arms; that's when it happened. She had slipped on the ice and hit her head against the bottom step one time, so the doctor thought that could have started the problem or maybe it began later when she was in Turkey with Dizzy. During that tour she hit her head again when she tripped and fell off of a bandstand. I remember after that, she started suffering from headaches periodically, so our family doctor ran some tests. But he wasn't the greatest doctor in the world, and they didn't have all the technology that's available now.

Well, 1962 was a real rough period. I stayed over at Honi's and Maggie's for a while after the funeral and didn't go anywhere, except back home to feed our little kitten, Princess. I'd go in there and she was so lonesome; there all the time by herself. So Maggie went over and got her. Honi and Maggie tried their best to get me going again because I was making I. W. Harper rich.

One day Maggie stood me up, looked me in the eye. "You got to pick up your life. Dotty would not want this. You got to get off of this sofa and get yourself back together!" Finally, I moved home. For the longest time, I was laying up at that little house getting drunk and some days I wouldn't even go in to work. I'd fix myself a bowl of soup, drink a couple of beers, and go back to bed.

8

IN WALKED MAYE

By the summer of '62, I was still coaching groups in the CBS Building, but I had given up my office and moved upstairs to Queen Artists. Dinah Washington ran an agency on the tenth floor that managed singers and since I was working with a few of her artists and taking care of her personal stage direction, she invited me to share some space up there.

I was coaching the Dells and five or six singles—grooming them, teaching stage etiquette, the whole shot. But I wasn't doing my best work. I was still struggling with the loss of Dotty, drinking real heavy and sitting around feeling sorry for myself. Honi and all my close friends were trying to help, but what the hell, they couldn't do nothin' much. I was my own worst enemy. The thing that really saved me was finding Maye.

We were introduced through Ruthie Bowen, who was very close to her and also a dear friend of mine. When Honi and I went on the road with the Ink Spots back in the forties, her husband, Billy Bowen, was in the group and she traveled with us everywhere. Ruthie was the president of Queen Artists, so she saw, first hand, what was happening to me, and like my other friends, she was trying everything to get me back on track.

Boy, she would chew me out, "You're just hanging around the house, not taking care of your work. You need to get on with your life." One of her plans was to set me up with a date. So she told Maye, "I have someone I'd like for you to meet. He's such a nice guy and I just think . . . well, his wife just died."

Maye said, "Stop right there. I don't want nobody crying on my shoulder. Forget it, Ruthie. You know I don't like blind dates anyway." "But he's so nice. His name is Cholly Atkins." Maye said her mouth flew open and there was a silence from here to the coast! She had been watching me perform at the Apollo, and basically Maye had eyes for me. But she was just coming out of a long relationship with a guy and needed another one like a hole in the head. Still, Ruthie was determined to get us together. One day at work she said, "Cholly, you have to get out of that house. My club is giving a dance and Billy is still on the road, so I'd like for you to go as my escort."

The night of the dance, when Ruthie stopped by for me, she mentioned very casually that we had to pick up her friend on Riverside Drive and asked if I'd mind running in to get her. When that door opened, she was stunned. I was knocked out, too, because she was looking fabulous in a pink strapless dress with black Spanish lace. We ended up dancing together the whole evening!

After that, we dated sporadically and played telephone games for a while. She would call and I'd tell her I'd been on the golf course all day and was too tired to come into the city, which was true most of the time, or I would call her and she'd say that she was planning to go out. Sometimes I'd make a date with her, not show up, then make all kinds of phony excuses. We went on like that for most of the summer. But I'll admit, I was the main one messing up. It was just so hard for me to shake that depression.

Eventually, we began spending more and more time together. She'd get off from work at Macy's and come by the studio. Then we would go to dinner and a show or maybe stop by Showman's. A lot of the time when we were out late and I didn't feel like getting a cab to Queens, I'd stay at her apartment. Well, one thing led to another. Finally, I gave up my place and moved on in with her. But, I have all the admiration in the world for Maye because she understood what I was going through and stayed with it anyway.

Around that time, my friend Walter Thomas talked me into working for an agency in Philadelphia, which meant some steady money, since my clients had fallen off in New York. The change was good because I'd gotten tired of teaching and I was still very confused about my future. Right up until the end of '62, I hadn't been doing the caliber of work that I was known for in the industry—and I realized it. I'd make appointments and not show up. A lot of the time I had hangovers. So during the early part of '63, I decided the best thing was to get away from choreographing and do something else for a minute.

The agency in Philly handled Curtis Mayfield and the Impressions, Gene Chandler, Jerry Butler, and a few other artists, and I was hired to check the shows, improve the lineups, and straighten out their moves. A couple of times I traveled to Washington or Baltimore with the groups. But commuting every day to Philadelphia was a lot of wear and tear on the body. It meant I had to get up real early, take a subway into Penn Station, and get in the office by 9:30. At 5:00 I'd head for the train and get back home around 8:00.

After six months of that grind, the guy I was temporarily replacing came back, which was a good thing because running down to Philly was getting to be a real drag. Luckily, I had gotten myself pretty much together by then. I started acting right again with my clients and things began to pick up in New York.

Maye and I had grown closer and closer, so we decided to just go on and seal the thing up. Now, remember I was going through a real transitional phase there when I met her, moving from tap to vocal choreography, and I had a lot of decisions to make. But she would encourage me to do things that I wouldn't have done ordinarily. Maye understood me and always knew what was right for my career. We became not only husband and wife but best friends.

She was forty-five and I was fifty, and both of us had been married twice. Her mother told her, "Each time you got married, you ran off somewhere to do it, and stayed with the guy two minutes. You're going to have a real wedding this time." Maye said, "Well, one thing for sure, Lilly, I'm not coming down no church aisle." So we decided to get married in her mother's living room and ask Ruthie to be the matron of honor.

My mother came down from Buffalo and my cousin Snook was the minister. Remember, he was my best friend when I was growing up. The place was all decorated with flowers, there was a caterer, three-tiered cake; a real beautiful affair. One of Maye's close friends, Martha Lewis, caught the bouquet.

Our wedding was like a big reunion; all of our friends came and most of them loved to party. Strayhorn was wonderful. He brought us a big basket of different whiskeys and wines as a wedding gift. Maye had decided to serve French 75 (a combination of champagne and brandy), mixed with strawberries. And it tasted so good, you know. Everybody's head was just torn up. Al Hibbler sang "Trees." He got up there: "I think that I shall never see . . ." and folks started crying. I said, "This ain't no wake!" Oh, we carried on!

My mother ended up spending two weeks with us. During that period, I was scheduled to perform at the Newport Jazz Festival, so Maye and I took her out to stay at Maggie's while we went up to Rhode Island. Marshall Stearns had invited me to go along with Honi, Baby Laurence, Chuck Green, Pete Nugent, Cookie Cook, and his partner, Ernest Brown.

Both Honi and I were very close to Marshall and his wife, Jean. In fact, we stayed with them as much as they stayed with each other! Marshall must have interviewed us about a thousand times for their book *Jazz Dance*. They were always coming wherever we were, or we'd go wherever they were. Sometimes Maye and Maggie would go with us down to their apartment in the Village. We were knocked out by the volume of material they had in there on jazz—all kinds of books, pictures, and just records from floor to ceiling. See, Jean loved jazz as much as Marshall did; she had been listening to it for most of her life when they met. I think they got together through Duke Ellington.

The '63 performance at Newport was our second time at the festival because we'd danced up there the summer before, right after I met Maye. I remember her friend Martha drove up with us. Although I had been interviewed by Marshall a couple of times, I don't think I knew him well prior to that trip. He contacted Honi about the festival, and then Honi brought me the news. We were real excited because it was fresh, it sounded interesting, and it was an opportunity to be included in some sort of historical documentation on tap.

A lot of people have taken credit for the resurgence of rhythm tap, but Marshall Stearns was really the one who generated respect for it as an art form and created a situation where serious music critics could see it in the right context. Marshall was trying to preserve tap, to show the connection between real jazz music and tap dancing from an artistic standpoint. Because, by the early sixties, even the music critics did not really associate the two. In New York, the Copasetics were still getting together and having annual shows with great jazz musicians, but for the most part, the general public thought of jazz strictly as listening music.

That first Newport summer, in '62, I went with four other guys: Honi, Pete, Baby Laurence, and Bunny Briggs. Marshall set up an afternoon program on the outdoor concert stage and called it "A History of the Tap Dance and Its Relationship to Jazz." The program was presented very informally, as if we were all sitting in someone's living room. Jo Jones and Roy Eldridge accompanied us, and they were cooking, as usual. John Neves was on bass. I can't recall who was on piano. We opened with the shim sham shimmy, then during the first half we covered the fundamentals of tap and its main innovators before John Bubbles. At different points, Marshall would tell anecdotes about dancers, like Uncle Bo, and we'd demonstrate their style. After intermission, we went right on through the evolution of tap right up to bebop and finished the show with everybody on stage improvising. That night Baby and Bunny had their own jam session, backed up by Duke's band!

The audience at Newport was wonderful and we got rave reviews from a lot of the jazz critics, including Whitney Balliett and Stanley Dance. One of the reasons we were so well received was because of the way Marshall tied it all in. He talked about the music, about who we traveled with. He associated tap with Basie, Duke, Erskine Hawkins,

Lucky Millinder—most of the well-known bands who carried shows at that time were from the East. People loved it. That's why he decided to go back in '63, when we presented "An Afternoon at the Hoofers Club," with Clark Terry and Howard McGhee on trumpet, Sam Woodyard on drums, Gildo Mahones on piano, and Wendell Marshall on bass.

We had a ball imitating those Hoofers Club characters, like Mushmouth, Shim Sham Blue, Motorboat, and Piano. Some of the guys showed how to steal a step. Then we demonstrated the different tap vocabulary used at the club and wrapped up the first half with the b.s. chorus, which includes the time step, cross step, front wing, over the top, and the trenches. In the second part, we started off with the Coles stroll, then went into "Famous Dancers and Their Steps," and a demonstration of tap styles, like eccentric, comedy, and class acts. That's when Honi and I did our soft-shoe, "Taking a Chance on Love." The finale was a killer, a "battle of rhythms" between the tappers and Sam.

In addition to his programs at Newport, Marshall conducted seminars on tap in different parts of the country. Honi and I did a lot of those. Once we went to the United Nations with him; Jo Jones was our drummer. Another time we appeared at the Arts Club of Chicago. But we had the most fun up in Cooperstown at the New York State Historical Society, where Marshall occasionally gave seminars on American culture. In '64, Maggie, Honi, Maye, Strayhorn, and I drove up from New York. Ernie Smith came up that year, too, and brought films from his jazz dance archives.

That trip was when Honi and I both left our dancing shoes at home. Maye and I were in our hotel room with the window up, and I saw Honi and Maggie walking down the street. So I yelled down to see where they were going. Maggie laughed and said he'd just discovered that he left his dancing shoes. And the only thing he'd brought was a pair of green sneakers. I said, "His *dancing* shoes? How could he leave his dancing shoes? The turkey knew he was coming up here to dance." She said, "Well, he accused me of not packing them for him. So we were thinking about going shopping."

When I went to finish unpacking my things, my shoes were missing, too, so we ran down to catch up with them, but by the time we got to the city all the stores had closed. We wound up demonstrating in little rubber soles, and the next day we had to go out and buy some shoes. They didn't have taps on them, but Strayhorn was the only one accompanying us, so we could still be heard over the piano. Stray was sick at the time and slept on a little cot in Honi and Maggie's room. He loved both of them dearly. As a matter of fact, Stray always referred to Honi as his father. When they showed him a single room up at Cooperstown, he walked in there for a minute, then he said, "Oh no, this won't work. I'm going in the room with my father and mother."

The people up in Cooperstown gave a lot of parties. All rich people. We were the peasants! But they were so hospitable; did everything to make us real comfortable. So did Marshall and Jean. She was especially kind to Maye and Maggie. We would go to the city during the daytime and just walk around or visit the museum to see the baseball exhibitions. At night we'd all eat together, then do the session; sit and talk, answer questions, and demonstrate steps that Marshall was telling the audience about. Strayhorn would tell what it was like working with Duke and having Bunny Briggs and Baby Laurence travel with the band. Ernie showed films of jazz dancers. It was really a heartwarming experience, and a helluva learning opportunity not just for the Cooperstown folk, but for us, too. Tap was a classic American form, man! And it was out!

Our sessions were always very relaxed. Marshall and Jean fostered that kind of atmosphere. I can't begin to tell you how fantastic they were to work with, and as people. We appreciated them so much because there were never any off-the-wall questions, like, "How did you start doing this?" No stock questions. Very fresh, interesting sessions; no tightness. They were that way with everybody. You can tell from their book.

My last trip to Cooperstown was '66. I was already at Motown then and Maye and I drove over from Detroit. I was so sorry Maggie and Honi couldn't make it that time, because Marshall died the following

December. He had just taken *Jazz Dance* to the publisher in September and was real excited about finally getting it all together, but he passed before the book was even ready to come out. Jean had to do all of the proofreading and take it through the final steps, which took about two years.

If it hadn't been for Marshall and Jean, half of our dance history would have gone straight down the drain. They worked like crazy, traveling throughout the country doing interviews to gather that material. He would ask the questions and she would write everything down, by hand. It was amazing just to watch them operate together. I still talk to her by phone from time to time. When I look back over the years, my association with Marshall and Jean is one of the things that gives me a real warm feeling inside.

During the early sixties, I choreographed for Norma Miller and Her Jazzmen. Norma originally had a company of male and female dancers. Then in 1963, she trimmed it down to four guys: Chazz Young, who was Frankie Manning's son; Billy Ricker; Raymond Scott; and Billy Dotson. That was a fine group of male dancers who could perform just about any style . . . jazz, tap, Afro. They did specialty numbers and whenever they would be working someplace, the buck dancers would go and check them out because they were just an excellent act, by anybody's standards.

Norma was quite a performer, herself, and very articulate. She could do the introductions and set up all of the specialty spots in her show. And, man, was she a taskmaster! She wanted perfection in every sense. That's the way she was groomed in the business. Early in her career she was a chorus line dancer with Leonard Reed and you definitely had to be on your toes with him. He was that type of choreographer and producer. Same thing with Bill Robinson. And later with the Lindy Hoppers, because they were trained, you know. Everything was in unison. They had uniforms and were highly organized.

As I said before, my friendship with Norma went back to the thirties when she danced with the Lindy Hoppers in the *Hot Mikado*, and even before that out in California. Norma was also good friends with Honi and Maggie, and she just adored Pete Nugent. So whenever she needed a dance for her guys, one of us would get a call. Pete not only did choreography, he performed as a single in her shows and was even the company's manager at one point. Nobody was better than Pete at military-type staccato dancing, so he taught the guys something in that vein. One thing I did was a tap routine off of "Cute," for Chazz, and Honi put together a slow tap piece for two of the guys to the number called "Shiny Stockings."

I remember one year they did some of those dances in the Co-pasetics' annual show. Norma was very supportive of our fraternity and always at the shows, as either a spectator or a performer. She lives out here in Vegas right now and we're still good friends. Every time I see her she says, "I want Chazz to bring back 'Cute' and show 'em how it's really supposed to be done!"

Around the same time I was working with Norma's group, I began coaching Gladys Knight and the Pips. The Pips included Gladys's brother, Merald "Bubba" Knight, and their two cousins, William Guest and Edward Patten. We rehearsed morning, noon, and night. I worked them to death! Bubba is always kidding me about the time I came down the aisle at the Apollo and started giving corrections during the show. I had put so many hours into those cats, and I was obsessed with perfection. I didn't want to see even a finger out of place. This was back in my drinking days! So watch out!

Now, you have to picture the theater. This is a full house. I ran from the back of the Apollo to the side of the stage yelling, "Didn't I tell you to hit the angle?" People were looking, "Who's that crazy man down there?" Bubba said it was the most embarrassing moment of his life! But they took it in stride, and all of them started working ten times harder on their homework. They didn't want any more public lessons from the teacher.

Gladys and the guys began preparing in the early part of their career for the better spots. They didn't fare too well on those marathon shows at the arenas and coliseums, where there were forty acts in the show. Their mental approach was very different from most of the other groups who just went on stage and did two or three hot songs. Gladys Knight and the Pips were not about that.

I'd take them through some real rough choruses because I never really had enough time to stretch out and choreograph at a leisurely pace; there was always some deadline we had to meet. But they learned fast, they were real studious. They would go home at night, practice, and have everything down perfect. The next day they couldn't wait to show me the moves. I'd say, "Well, yeah, that's all right, but we could work on it a little more." That was to keep them on their toes. I was never one for a whole lot of stroking and complimenting. I wanted them to go way beyond what they ever dreamed they could do, because I knew they were prime class material.

At first, Gladys didn't want to talk on stage. She'd say, "Cholly, I just want to sing, please don't make me talk to the audience." I said, "Look, you have to build a relationship with the people you're singing to. You have to make each one feel you're communicating with them directly." "Well, what do I say to them?" I said, "Ask them how they're doing!" Through the years, we worked on that thing so much that eventually she was writing her own spiels. Now you can't shut her up!

A lot of the people in R & B didn't know much about theater etiquette, deportment, how to take bows, what to do if you made mistakes on stage. In other words, they knew how to sing but not how to perform. I had to do a great deal of work in that department. Then, too, you had to be kind of a father figure. If somebody was having problems, you'd say, "What's the matter with you? Come on, you can talk to me." I always wanted them to feel that I was someone they could confide in. As my relationship developed with Gladys and the guys, they began calling me "Pop" and later on the other groups picked up on that. Some of them changed "Pop" to "Pops" and a few of the girls called me "Popsie."

Then there was that other thing that had to do with the group's backstage needs. Naturally, being close to real theater, I learned a lot about lighting, sound, and working with a technical crew when I was dancing; these were aspects of performing that Gladys Knight and the Pips didn't know much about. Before they could afford their own technical crew, somebody had to be there to get the cue sheets made up and dictate to the head house people, the spotlight people, and so on.

See, if Louis Armstrong had a date to play a certain theater, he could show up an hour or so before curtain time because the band would be in place, the lights and sound checks would be taken care of, and everything else. He didn't have to do nothin' but put his horn under his arm and go. Which is a great asset for the star of anything, because you don't have those little incidental things to worry about. I say incidental, but they're as important to your act sometimes as your act is.

Groups that can afford it have one person for each of those functions. So when Gladys and the guys had an engagement, I'd go in a day ahead of time and do those little extra things, and I became their production manager as well as their choreographer. I had no problems with that because I loved working with them. They had the ability to showcase the very best that I had to offer. And from my point of view, when they stepped out on that stage they were representing Cholly Atkins.

I was working with them in Bermuda when Harvey Fuqua first tried to contact me about joining Motown Records. The Moonglows had broken up and Harvey was in Detroit producing records for Berry Gordy by this time. When he first got the job, he started planting the seed about setting up classes to groom their singers. They were mostly concentrating on getting the record business really going right, so he kept digging at them and digging at them. I would see him when he'd come to New York, and he'd tell me what his idea was. He said, "If I get it to go through, man, I sure want you to come out and work with me on it." I said, "Yeah, well, you keep working on it." At the time I thought it was like lip service.

Anyway, I had promised Harvey that I'd call him when Gladys Knight and the Pips finished up in Bermuda. And I had the damnedest time getting home. I came back on the British airline into a blizzard. We flew around New York for hours. The pilot said, "Well, we're going to go to Boston. Everything between here and there is closed." The next minute, "Well, Boston is closing up, so we're turning around and going to Philadelphia." Then, "Philadelphia is crowded. We might have to go to Pittsburgh."

"No, we're not going to Pittsburgh; we can land in Washington." It was still snowing in D.C. The whole East Coast was a blizzard! I was a nervous wreck with all that flying and circling, and panicking. Worrying that those guys were going to run out of fuel up there and we'd wind up in somebody's backyard! But the flight attendants were real nice—they gave everybody plenty of liquor and food to try to keep them calm.

We finally got down and were told they'd put everybody up in a hotel and they could reach their destinations the next morning or we could get a train out that night, so I took the train and slept all the way in. We got to New York about three or four o'clock in the morning. You talking about *tired*! I must have slept for two whole days.

Then I called Harvey in Detroit and he said he had finally gotten permission from Berry Gordy to open up a new department at the company called Artist Development. By this time, Motown was the fourth-largest record company in the country and black folks were real proud of that fact. And no other company had developed a department to groom the singers. No company was even thinking that way, so Motown was on the cutting edge in the music industry. At the time I was very conscious of the black movement, and to be a part of something destined to become a first and contribute to the future of black artists was a wonderful opportunity.

So, we made arrangements for me to go out and get together with the powers at Motown and discuss the possibility of my becoming part of the operation. He lined me up fine in a great hotel. They had a bar set up in there. It was like a suite hotel. Harvey would come and get me, show me around the place—the studios and all. He just ran the whole thing down to me. They were in the process of getting the Marvelettes together to go down to Bermuda to sing at the same place Gladys and the Pips had just left. And I mean they had torn it up down there. So I saw the Marvelettes and told Harvey, "Look, man, they're nowhere near ready!"

There was a quality control meeting scheduled around the time I was visiting and he took me to that—I sat next to Harvey and his wife, Gwen, who was Berry Gordy's sister. So at those meetings they would play all of their new products and everyone would make comments. Gordy was sitting up there near the operators, playing this stuff. He says, "Well, it sounds like there's too much bass or the background is too heavy over the lead singers." Different people were commenting, but I didn't say a word. Then he asked me how I liked one thing. I glanced over at Harvey, and he was looking all nervous like, "Please don't blow this thing!" It reminded me of the time Honi was trying to get me in Cab's revue. I told Gordy that I didn't particularly like the vocal background, and he said, "Yeah, that's what's wrong with the record for me, too. We can go back in, work that background up more, and give them a little bit more to do in there." So I made it past that test!

Next I had a personal meeting with Gordy, his attorney, and Harvey. Berry Gordy talked about his artists and what he wanted to happen for them. He didn't want them to just be rock-and-roll singers. So rather than just drop them when they didn't have a hot record, he wanted to take the ones that had the ability, turn them into good performers, and put them in classy places.

` He was familiar with that type of show business because he used to vacation in Idlewild, Michigan, during the summer. A black guy owned a place up there that featured a revue with a black vaudeville format. I remember Ziggy Johnson produced the shows from time to time. That's where Gordy first saw some choreography I did for the Moonglows and he asked Harvey who had done it. That was in the fifties.

Around the time I went up to Detroit, Motown's music was becoming real popular. All the little young college kids were listening to the Supremes' tunes and Stevie Wonder's tunes. By this time the white kids were hooked on Motown's music. See, back in the day, the company wasn't even putting the pictures of the groups on the outside of the album covers. This was so they would cross over. A lot of the kids buying the records didn't necessarily know whether the artists were black or white—they had never seen them. But they loved the music. At least that's what they told me at Motown. When I visited, that picture policy had changed.

Nineteen sixty-five was just the right time for an artist development department to really thrive, so the deal sounded pretty good. I told

Gordy I would have to talk it over with my wife and get back to him, because he wanted me to move to Detroit. This was a real touchy thing. A lot had to be thrashed out since Maye was ten years away from retiring with a really decent pension. But she and I decided that I would go ahead and accept the position in Detroit, and that she would stay in New York for a few months to see how it worked out and just visit once a month. The whole thing took about six months. I left in March of '65, then she gave up her job at Macy's to join me the following fall. Although I was pleased with the way I was accepted in Detroit, I felt bad about Maye having to give up her job and all.

So I've always regretted the deal that I made with Motown. There should have been a stipulation in the contract for her. She was more than qualified to work in the finance department or to do anything in the management division. But what the hell did I know about talking to executives at a big corporation? At the time I was just happy to get a job that was going to pay me every week and give me a chance to pull myself together.

I figured I had a new wife and a new life to start in Detroit. And I was still suffering through that negative period because leaving New York was real difficult—moving away from Honi, Maggie, the Copasetics; leaving a neighborhood that I really liked and a city with so much theater. Of course, all of Maye's friends were in New York, too, and the move was even harder for her because she was accustomed to working. She had been in the banking department at Macy's for many years and the benefits were just fantastic; the employees had profit-sharing and all that kind of stuff.

But the one thing that I was really pleased about was a stipulation in my contract that allowed me to keep Gladys Knight and the Pips as personal clients even though I would be an employee of Motown Records. To tell the truth, Gordy wasn't too happy about it at first, but this was definitely something that I would not compromise under any circumstances. By that time, Gladys and the guys were like my own children!

So that was the initial transition from New York. It happened in the latter part of September '65. Mary Wilson had a home that was a duplex. She lived on one side and her tenants were vacating the other, so she offered the apartment to us. It was real nice. We moved in right away and stayed for ten years.

Sometimes Maye and I would sit up until daylight listening to albums of Basie and Duke and Dinah. We'd get into it, and the time would just go by; we'd look up and the sun would be coming out. Really, really nice. We both liked the same kind of music. We never sat and listened to rock and roll, because that was work, you see. Jazz was something else; jazz was full of memories.

9

HITSVILLE, U.S.A.

M otown was jumping in 1965. It ran like a twenty-four-hour-a-day factory and everybody was trying to get in on the action because hits were bouncing off the production line. During my first week there Harvey organized the personnel for our department. As I said before, Artist Development was his brainchild and that was the first time any record company had created a component designed to prepare artists for personal appearances by hiring specialists in choreography, vocals, and theatrical etiquette.

Maurice King was one of the mainstays of the department. He was a superb vocal coach and arranger with a rich history in black music. Maurice had traveled all over the world as musical conductor for the International Sweethearts of Rhythm. And he was the first black musical conductor at the Fox Theater, a major house in Detroit. Along with vocal arrangements, he was in charge of all the musicians that worked with the artists, like the rhythm sections, and also the musical conductors for each set of artists.

Maurice worked very closely with Johnny Allen, who was the main rehearsal pianist. Now, Johnny had that rich background in music, too. He had played with Lucky Millinder and a lot of other great jazz musicians during the thirties and forties and his whole thing was to try and get the kids at Motown to match the excellence in performance that he had witnessed back when he was playing in clubs all around the country. In addition, he really knew what I was trying to achieve dancewise because he'd seen me perform with Dotty and with Honi. Johnny understood the relationship between the music and the dance. He was familiar with the chorus line thing and had played in shows with people like Baby Laurence and Buck and Bubbles, as well as singers like Billie Holiday. So having him around was a tremendous asset. I think he had been associated with Motown since '62 or '63.

Maxine Powell was hired to groom the artists. She gave a lot of helpful tips to the guys, but she worked more closely with the girls—how to walk, how to talk, how to dress. She had been the owner of a local charm school, the Maxine Powell Finishing and Modeling School, where Gordy's sisters had studied modeling. I remember she was always giving the kids little pep talks and telling them they had to get ready for places like Buckingham Palace.

My title at Motown was "Choreographer-Director." Anything that had to do with choreography, stage presentation, and musical coordination with production came under that heading. The other thing that I was in charge of was all scheduling—vocal rehearsals, choreography sessions, and all meetings with the artists on their new material. We reported directly to Harvey, but there was very little dictation from him. We knew what we had to do as far as the operation was concerned and we took care of it.

Leonard Reed was hired around the same time I was. Harvey told him, "Look, Leonard, we're going to bring you in to work with Marvin Gaye." See, Marvin was a balladeer. Harvey said he wanted to be like Frank Sinatra. So, Leonard came from California and pulled out all these songs; I mean he was ready to go. But Marvin stayed on the road singing his hits so much that after a couple of months, Leonard decided to go on back home. While he was there, though, he was kicking everybody's butt on the golf course, because a lot of the upper brass played and Leonard was just top-notch. He'd take 'em out there on the course and wear 'em out.

Although Motown had a budget for Artist Development, we couldn't bring in outside consultants. So there ended up being just one vocal coach/arranger and one choreographer. The rehearsal pianists were also part of the arranging staff. Since there was a shortage of musical conductors, all of us occasionally made suggestions to Maurice.

About three times a week we had production meetings of all heads inside the department. But it could be more often depending on the availability of the singers, their new product, and their priority. There were twenty-seven major artists and the most popular ones were se-lected for the Motown Revues—eight to ten who had a hot product out at the time. There was not much point in putting some group on the revue if their song wasn't getting any airplay. Then you also had the cost of transporting and maintaining the tours, so there was no way to take everybody on the roster. A lot of acts eventually grew up and were eligible to be considered for the tours, but basically you aligned your show according to popularity.

The first priority was to stage and choreograph the tunes and to put special endings and introductions on the new records. At that time sin-gles were top priority. Later, when albums became more important, the training was more extensive. Especially when you had three or four things that you wanted to do on one album. Groups like the Supremes, Temptations, Smokey Robinson and the Miracles, and Martha and the Vandellas were scheduled more often because they had top priority. About a year and a half after I'd been there, Gladys Knight and the Pips came on board and they eventually fell in that category.

Once the most popular groups would go out on engagements, then the studio was available for the lesser lights. Scheduling all of this was extremely difficult and I lost a lot of sleep during those days trying to get the job done. But I gave it my best shot and I'd say the whole thing ran pretty smoothly.

As a rule, all of us had to do much more than what was listed in our job descriptions. Counseling the kids was a big part of it because we had to cope with attitudes and families and issues at home. See, you've got to take into consideration that you're dealing with a lot of personalities, all different. Groups of three, groups of four, groups of five. Getting through to them was my first priority. I had to establish something where I gained their respect and could keep their attention and make them interested in absorbing what I was trying to teach.

But this process was not new to me because I had gone through all of that with groups before going to Detroit. The Motown singers were accustomed to doing whatever they saw some other act do or just putting things together themselves. The choreography wasn't professional and most of the time what they were singing about had nothing to do with the way they were moving. Also, some of them were a little inhibited, so you had to build their confidence. I'd say, "Look, you walk, you play ball, you do social dancing. You can get this. We just have to break it down some."

So we'd go through those changes because it was very difficult to choreograph and stage down to the weaker link in the chain. You had to try to strengthen that person so that you could get the best out of the group from a visual standpoint. This generated another problem because those that were able to get the step right away would snicker at the slower ones, and you had to bring them down front too, you know.

There were all sorts of little tricks I'd learned for handling situations like that. I'd just call those people up and give them some steps they couldn't do and let the others laugh at them and that took care of the problem. You were never just a choreographer and a director— you were a psychiatrist, a diplomat, and the whole thing.

There's more to being a choreographer, in my estimation, than just teaching dance steps. You have to understand the people you're teaching, and you have to either possess or acquire the ability to teach. You have to try to learn the personalities that you're working with and not show partiality, not discourage the ones who are slower picking up the material. You spend more time with them, but not too much, because that could be a thorn in their sides and I was trying to build their confidence. "But, man," one guy used to say, "you have to work harder with me than the other people."

So you pick somebody in the group that they are close to and you put them on the case. "Hey, man, get with Joe on that last step and see that he gets it before we move on." And you go off and take a little break or something. Or you go over and work with somebody who catches on fast. You don't really need to work with them, but you can tell if they're not quite sure of something, so you work with them to make the person who is more inhibited feel, "Well, he ain't so smart either." Then they can start concentrating on learning the moves!

I think if you're going to do the job right, you have to become that involved. That's been the foundation of my success with most of my clients. I usually have a real closeness with each one. Naturally there's got to be one or two here and there that might not think I'm okay. Maybe I've made the steps too hard for them. . . . Then there're some people who are just born complainers and some people who criticize everybody else. If I have a problem, my philosophy is the first person to look at is yourself, and you find out generally whatever's happening is your fault!

If I saw some of the guys doing things that were detrimental to them, I'd pull them aside . . . just the same as a good teacher, "You stay after school. I want to talk to you." You pick the right time and you don't do it in front of the others. I'd say, "Listen, you got to stop using the cologne and start using some soap! When you come in here, you're sweating and the guys don't want to say nothin' to you, but you're smelling up the place." You talk to them like a father would, so automatically they start thinking about you as a father. "Okay, Pop, I get the picture."

Most of the kids were real excited about having someone around to teach them some new steps. I think the first group I worked with at Motown was the Marvelettes: Gladys Horton, Wanda Rogers, Katherine Anderson, and Georgeanna Tillman. Remember they were getting ready for that engagement in Bermuda. I choreographed "Don't Mess with Bill" and a couple of other major tunes, but I didn't have much time, just a few days. Later I did a lot of work with them.

So they were first. There was another little female group called the Velvelettes that had something big coming up. Mudcat Grant, the Boston Red Sox pitcher, was also a singer; he was in show business then and needed some background voices, so Motown booked the Velvelettes as an opening act with Mudcat, then they'd come back and sing with him on some of his tunes. That gave them priority for a hot minute because Berry Gordy was very sports-minded, and he was friendly with Mudcat, so I assume it was more or less a favor to him.

For the first six months the Supremes and the Temptations had a pretty tight rehearsal schedule. Now, the Temps I already knew. Back in '64 I met them at the Howard Theater in Washington, D.C., while I was there on another assignment. They had been on a bill with the Cadillacs, and they got blown away. So when they met me, Otis said, "Man, we been trying to run into you; we sure would like for you to do some stuff for us." So he asked me if I could help them between shows on their new song called "The Way You Do the Things You Do."

At the time, Paul Williams was in the group along with David Ruffin, Melvin Franklin, Eddie Kendricks, and Otis Williams. Paul had been doing the choreography. So it became a very touchy situation, because he had done so many wonderful things for the guys. He gave them the "Temptations' walk," but that didn't stop them from wanting to do some moves like the Cadillacs or the Pips. Well, I think I handled it correctly. I tried to keep a good feeling between Paul and myself. But I could understand his feelings about me. After all, I was infringing on his territory. Even so, I never really had any major problems with him. He and David and Eddie have all passed, and there have been a lot of changes in the group's membership, but the guys still come to me when they get a new song.

Whenever the Temps got last-minute bookings and had to leave, the Spinners would come into Artist Development and ask if they could use those rehearsal slots. They were managed by Harvey and naturally he'd say, "Yeah, let's take the Spinners and spend two or three hours with them." So they were stopping shows even when they didn't have a hit record, because we worked out a lot of good production things. At that time, the group consisted of Bobbie Smith, Billy Henderson, Henry Fambrough, Pervis Jackson, and Edgar Edwards.

Martha and the Vandellas had some little moves on "Dancin' in the Streets" when I first got there, but the visual part didn't have anything to do with the tune. We made a little production out of it because the record was already out and it was a hit. That group really took directions well. Betty Kelly and Rosalind Ashford were doing backup then, and of course Martha Reeves was lead singer. Their style was very appealing to white student groups, so they had a lot of pop dates before the Supremes.

Anyway, by dressing up "Dancin' in the Streets" a little bit, the choreography became more meaningful. And this was real good for the girls because they had a lot of repeat engagements, and since the choreography was spruced up, the tune had a fresh look to the audiences the second time around.

I did that with a lot of the acts. Like "Mickey's Monkey" with the Miracles. They already had some choreography on that, too, because the guy that wrote it, Mickey Stevenson, gave them some movement ideas. We cleaned that up, dressed it up, and made it look a heck of a lot better from a choreographic standpoint. One of the Miracles' pieces that really stands out in my mind is "Going to a Go-Go." We did it with tambourines and I had those guys throwing them up and catching them behind their backs—a real crowd pleaser.

We also put together some real nice production numbers to "Wives and Lovers" and "Days of Wine and Roses." That's when the Miracles had a table upstage and they'd dance from the mike back to the table, get a sip of wine, head back to the mikes—all in rhythm with the music.

I was giving those guys some great moves until that whole thing came up with Berry and we had to trim them down. He said he wanted the Miracles to cut out all of their choreography, just stand there and sway, because nobody was paying attention to Smokey. I mean those guys were *cooking* in the back! And everybody was watching them. They were singing like crazy, too; beautiful, great harmony. I remember they used to come over to my basement and work with me on their own. I had a little studio in the duplex that I rented from Mary Wilson.

The company obviously wanted Smokey to be the focal point. He was Berry's friend and also vice president. That helped. Berry called me over to his office and explained this to me. Now Pete and Ron and Bobby had been working their butts off so I figured I'd try to humor him. I said, "Mr. Gordy, have you ever looked at those guys just standing there doing nothing? One is short and skinny, the other is big and tall, and the third is standing up there pigeon-toed. You better let these guys do some moves!"

He said, "Well, okay, but just don't get too clever with it. Just give them something simple." I said, "What is your reason for doing this?" He said, "Well, I'm selling Smokey Robinson. He's my main product in this group." Then he said, "So you take care of it, and that's not a request, that's an order." I said, "Yes, sir," and left. But we continued to do our thing in a modified way. I cut out a little because we did not want to seem that we were not in compliance with the powers, but it did cause a bit of friction there. All of that was happening around the same time they were preparing Diana for her emergence as a solo artist. Later, when Smokey left the group, we got Bill Griffin and kept on stepping.

Now Marvin Gaye was a multitalented cat. He played the drums, piano, and was a good dancer. Although he did a lot of movements, they were all pretty much sensual moves. But he was more than able to get down. See, Marvin was an excellent athlete. He played good baseball, football, and golf. But his music didn't have all that jumping around. Still, he danced much more than a lot of R & B single artists like Sam Cooke or Otis Redding. The kids at Motown loved the way he moved.

I did teach him some little soft-shoe things and a hat-and-cane dance to "I'm Biding My Time." During that period Harvey Fuqua was his road manager and Harvey would do the soft-shoe with him because he learned it at the same time. So Marvin really enjoyed it when he was dancing with Harvey. But it was choreographed for him to do by himself in supper clubs and nightclubs. He didn't do it on those concert tours. We worked a lot together. I set all of his lights, aligned the repertoire, the whole shot.

Marvin was very studious, and he learned fast, but he was also moody. He would be having a ball with something today, and tomorrow he'd say, "I'm not doing the dance tonight." And it would have nothing to do with the choreography; it would just be something laying on his mind and he just wasn't into his show at all that night. "Oh, I'm not going to do the piano thing; I'm not going to play the drums tonight." For no reason.

We had all of this stuff in his nightclub act but you never knew what to expect. We would be in the smartest supper club in the city and around midnight, when his second show was over, he would leave there and go, as we say, across the tracks, over to some smoky joint that stayed open all night. Marvin would throw his cuff links and hankerchief and junk into the audience. He loved doing that, but he never tried it in supper clubs, just those little joints. He'd get in those places and sing and carry on until daylight.

Then he would come to the hotel and wake us up, "Come on, let's go to the golf course." We would have been asleep for maybe six hours at the most. But socially Marvin was a very likeable person, so we'd get up and go to the golf course and play eighteen holes. Then he'd come back and sack out until time for his first show!

He loved golf. Although he was a beginner, he noticed right away if you were a better player, so we'd tell him, "I'll give you a stroke a hole." Marvin would say, "No, man, don't give me nothin.'" He would play even-up with the boys. The guys told him, "Okay, man, if that's the way you want it, you can give me the money now. Just hand me the bet." So we'd take the money, then buy the lunch, drinks or whatever. He said that made him play better.

Another single that had high priority was Stevie Wonder. Man, I had a whole lot of laughs with Stevie. I used to call him Singer Boy. Stevie was a rare specimen. When you're working with him, it's hard to believe that he can't see, because his whole approach is just like a person that has eyesight. You can say, "Stevie, your right hand should go up, and when it's halfway there, turn your thumb around so that your palm is facing front." And he would do it exactly like you said it, just from hearing it.

He was around fifteen when we started to work on a tap routine and he had about sixteen bars down. Generally he picked up the right sound. Once in a while he would hear the heel when he was supposed to hear the toe, but he would get the sound, so I'd tell him, "You got it!" We never did finish that routine. They sent him out on tour so much, there was no chance to do it. But the time we spent working on tap was a lot of fun. Just shows what you can do if you make up your mind.

When I was coaching the girls who sang in back of him, he'd want to get into some of their little moves, like on the exits, and I would just take his foot in the rhythm of the thing and just BOOM, "turn it, step over here, step on your right foot, bring your left foot behind your right foot, don't step on it, just touch it and bring it back out and step on it." Then I'd say, "Now we're gonna do it within the rhythmic pattern." He'd get right on in there and do it. Perfect, too. As far as the movement was concerned, it was no big deal for him.

Stevie was tricky, too. If I came into a party, somebody would say to him, "Cholly Atkins just came in," and he'd ask, "What's he got on?" "He's wearing a blue shirt with a multicolored tie; it's got green in it, orange in it, and blue." So he'd remember that. When I'd get to him, "Hey, Singer Boy, what's happening?" "Hey, man, you sharp as you want to be. I love that tie you got on with all them pretty colors in it, the blue, the orange, green." I'd look at that cat, "Man, come on. You know you can see."

He'd say things like, "Hey, man. See that chick over there in the green dress? She's really stacked, ain't she?" Now see, somebody had told him that. He'd know just where she was sitting and the whole shot. God knows, if he could see, Singer Boy might be too much for this world!

One group I never did get through to was the Four Tops. Those cats would see me coming and run the other way. They were wonderful singers, but all they wanted to do was that little side-to-side bend. The other kids called it the "windshield wiper." But the Tops were from an older generation and I guess they figured they already had their identity when they came to Motown. Still we had a very special relationship, because Honi and I had been on bills with them at the Apollo and I helped get them ready for their first appearance on the *Ed Sullivan Show*. The Pips got a whole lot of extra sessions in Artist Development because every time the Tops cut rehearsal, I'd call up Gladys and the guys right away, "Come on over. The Tops didn't show. You got their time." In five minutes flat they were hustling through the door, grinning for days.

While the Four Tops were ducking choreography sessions, the Contours were dying to get in there. They were great big guys, tall, and 260,

275 pounds. Really nice guys. They looked like truck drivers and they did all of that heavy acrobatics-type stuff. They would leave the stage hot in those revues. But the company was concentrating on acts that they thought could cross over and they were satisfied with what the Contours were choreographing for themselves. I was always sorry I didn't get a chance to really work with them on a regular basis.

As the artists began to grow, they were booked in fancier and fancier places. So rather than some little sideman like many vocal groups used, they needed conductors with extensive musical knowledge. We did production numbers on show tunes and standard tunes that had nothing to do with their recordings, so that they would be classified as entertainers rather than just singers of songs.

Now remember, one of the main reasons Motown created the department was to prepare the artists for venues other than where R & B singers normally appeared. We were trying to target places like the Copacabana in New York City and theaters-in-the-round. Actually, Motown artists were the first to really get into the theater-in-the-round circuit. One was located in Westbury, Long Island. Then up around Boston there were a couple. Several were located up and down the West Coast. And there was Mill Run in Chicago, Pine Knob in Detroit, one in Pittsburgh, one in Baltimore, one outside of Washington.

I think the Supremes went first and the Temptations were their opening act. This became a boomerang thing because the next year the Temptations were going around headlining, and the Spinners were riding their coattails. We had to really work on those artists who were being carried along, so that they would be attractive enough to the promoters and operators to return as headliners. That was all planned and that's how we worked our way into appearing at the Copacabana on a regular basis.

We groomed the Supremes for four months to get them ready. Even though their product was very hot at the time, they had to be given the proper material for that particular venue. We taught them show tunes, including songs from *West Side Story* and old nostalgic things like "Rock-a-Bye, My Baby." They did a tap routine with hats and canes to that tune. Then we did another taplike routine to "Girl from Ipanema" with some bossa nova steps. We added that kind of material to give the audience a well-rounded show.

Diana Ross was given most of the leads because it was the opinion of the executive producers and the people in quality control that she had the voice that would sell records. So we were told that she was to lead the production numbers, too, although that wasn't always our cup of tea. We thought that Mary Wilson and Florence Ballard were just as talented. Even though they had very different styles, we felt strongly that some of the development should have gone to them. But that was not the view of the company administrators, and we had to adhere to their wishes.

Whenever Maurice and I expressed what we had in mind, they would come back and say, "Well, we think you ought to approach it this way." Bear in mind now, there were no children in our department. We were all experienced, intelligent guys who could see where the company was coming from, and regardless of how diplomatic they were in explaining it, we could all see that in a minute it was gonna be Diana Ross and the Supremes.

On my recommendation, Gil Askey had been hired as the Supremes' music director because Maurice King was overloaded with responsibilities in Artist Development. Gil, Johnny Allen, and I rehearsed them to death! When we got to New York right before the opening, we held rehearsals in the Plaza, where most of the Motown crew was staying. Every bit of that coaching paid off because they were a definite smash. They hardly played any more R & B shows after the Copa.

The *New York Times* ran a review saying, "Berry Gordy had choreographed the girls beautifully, and it was sensational choreography." I read that thing and I couldn't get over it. *Berry Gordy?* So, he made a big speech, "I know you guys do a lot of work that other people are going to get credit for, but I'm not going to forget it." After the opening he gave all of us a $500 bonus, which at that time was pretty good money. But that kind of thing was par for the course. He had told the artists many times to say, when they were interviewed, "We do our own choreography."

After the Supremes, we had to get right into preparing the Temptations. What I did with the Temps was try to polish them up. We started doing some production things on "Old Man River," and we did a medley of all rain tunes, like "Singing in the Rain" and "Raindrops Falling on My Head." We did it with umbrellas. They used them like canes, almost like a tap dance. I choreographed tricks with the umbrellas—twirling them around their necks and tapping them on the floor. I mean they were clean, too—decked out in British homburg hats!

Standard tunes were injected into their rock-and-roll show. And all their big tunes, like "My Girl" and "Papa Was a Rolling Stone," we really tightened up and made more precise and a little more sophisticated choreographically. But later the Temps changed their image and went into the psychedelic bag. Then all the material they had built up for supper club appearances was taken out. Unfortunately, back then the psychedelic stuff couldn't take them into smart supper clubs because the people didn't know what the hell they were singing about.

After getting the Temps ready for the Copa, we worked on the Miracles, then Marvin Gaye was next, then Martha and the Vandellas . . . Gladys Knight and the Pips. But all of the acts, with the exception of Gladys and the Pips, had to be groomed in every respect. Remember I had worked with them for two years before I even moved to Detroit. As I told you before, Gordy allowed me to work with them on the side. That was part of my original deal.

Generally, the groups had a major entourage when they opened somewhere like the Copa. I usually went for opening night and maybe a couple of nights after that. Then I'd go back to Detroit and work with somebody else. If there were any problems, I would fly back in for a day or so. But members of our staff always accompanied them, which generated some problems at first because prior to our department, the personal managers of each group went on the tours.

Their department was called ITMI, International Talent Management, Inc. With the formation of Artist Development, Gordy decided that we should travel with the groups since we were, in a sense, the technicians. As a result, the managers felt that their wings had been clipped. But some of them ended up going along when they were willing to take the expenses out of their commissions.

In addition to places like the Copa, smart supper clubs started opening their doors to R & B acts. The Supremes were definitely the front-runners and they laid the groundwork in places like Detroit's Rooster Tail. Then across into Canada—Windsor—where there was a real nice supper club that featured stars like Lena Horne, Tony Bennett, and top comics.

Once television appearances were a part of the picture, there was additional staging and choreographing to be scheduled. And we had to stay on top of all of that. All of the Motown groups had to be taught how to handle an interview or what to have an opinion on and what not to have an opinion on. Maxine got them ready for those talk shows. She taught them how to sit and how to talk, and what to talk about. Because when you go on a lot of talk shows, they try to put you on the spot and ask you all about the private lives of the president and other company VIPs.

Now, many of these singers were young kids, so they had to be schooled. But Maxine tightened them up and it was wonderful, because when our artists appeared on TV they wouldn't go, "Well, uh, you see . . . uh. . . ." They were on the ball. And every time somebody would use the wrong grammar, she nipped it right in the bud. Nobody was talking about, "I seen . . ." because Ms. Powell wouldn't stand for it!

The Motown organization was riding high in those days. Any time their artists appeared on a bill with other vocal groups, they made it very rough for everybody because of Artist Development. Those training sessions made the Motown artists unique: they had everything available to them that was necessary for progress. And it really paid off, and everybody in the recording industry had to sit up and take notice because those groups were smoking! They sounded good, they looked good, their talk was good, and their movement was precise. But the other record labels didn't know the formula. Consequently, we were the only company that had this type of thing going. And it was completely out of the question for us to work for anybody else. Motown wouldn't stand for that.

After I'd been in Detroit for a couple of years, Harvey Fuqua left. During the time it happened, I was in New York. Maye's mother was very ill. That's when she passed away . . . in '67. So I was called and told that Harvey was out, and Ralph Seltzer, who was in charge of personnel, said to me, "How would you feel about the job?" I said, "Well, Ralph, Harvey was the guy who brought me to Motown, so I really wouldn't feel right about taking it." He said, "I just had to ask you about it in case Gordy hasn't made up his mind about a replacement. I just wanted to personally find out how you felt about it."

I told him I was real sorry to lose Harvey, and with my mother-in-law dying and all, I was at a low point. Then I asked him what happened and he didn't want to explain it. He said, "Cholly, you'll have to ask Berry Gordy about that." Obviously something happened, because Harvey was one of the major producers. But see, he and Berry Gordy's sister were separated and I guess problems came out of that because, hey, that was *family*. As far as I could see, Harvey was running things the way he always had. I couldn't see that he was doing anything differently.

The next thing I heard, Gordy was bringing in Lon Fontaine. There was nothing I could do about that except quit, but I decided not to. I didn't expect him to last too long, anyway. So with death in the family and the transition at Motown, I figured I'd just stay there until I got my head clear because the whole record industry knew who had choreographed all of those acts for Motown, although the company had tried to arrange for everybody else to take the credit.

That change in Artist Development was the beginning of another real difficult period for me. In '68 I became very ill and it sent Maye through a lot of changes. That's the year my mother died from lung cancer. I had gone to Buffalo during my Motown vacation because my brother, Spencer, called and told me that Mama was coming out of the hospital and she didn't have too much time left. The cancer had spread so much that the doctors couldn't really help her any more. I was fortunate to be able to spend a few days with her prior to her death. When she passed, I was right across the hall, a few feet away.

Both of us were real devoted to Mama, and never really knowing our biological father, the loss of my mother was extra hard. She always stuck by me and my brother and it was just difficult to imagine a time when she wouldn't be there for us. My brother and I drank so much whiskey in back of her death, I didn't know what I was doing half the time. And I already had a long-term drinking problem. It had become a daily thing for me.

Shortly after the funeral, Spencer and his wife, Evie, left me alone while they went out to take care of some business and while they were gone, I packed up all my clothes, went to the airport, and flew back to Detroit without saying a word to anybody. At the time I was in the process of preparing for the Temps' and Supremes' "TCB" concert on television. I left all those papers right on the table. I don't even know how I got home. I was stoned. I just woke up the next morning in my bed. No memory of the plane trip at all.

My whole family was in a panic. Evie said she walked in the house and she had this eerie feeling. Then they realized that I was gone, but my papers were still there. She and Spencer were running around, calling everybody, trying to figure out if something terrible had happened to me. They phoned all over Detroit . . . every place they even thought somebody knew me. Then someone came over to check the house and they called Maye, who was in New York.

Not too long after she got back, Maye had to put me in the hospital because I woke up one day and my whole body was out of control, shaking and jerking, so she ran across the street and got some whiskey to calm me down. Then she checked me into this little place that was a rehabilitation center and it wasn't doing no good at all. I was hallucinating and the whole shot. On my birthday Maye came to bring me a cake and I wasn't doing any better. That's the night I imagined Honi had come to visit me. He said, "Man, what is wrong with you? You going out of the world backwards. You better straighten up, man, and fly right." Then he said, "I don't want to come back and see you in this condition. I'm leaving now. You get yourself together and get out of here!"

And as he started to leave, I jumped out of the bed and ran to the front door like I was following him, "Don't leave me, Honi. Don't go." Then I opened the door and ran out. This place was located near a lot of torn-down buildings and I was running across the field calling Honi. The attendants from the center found me in somebody's backyard in my pajamas. They called Maye and told her to come get me because it was obvious that I needed more extensive medical treatment.

So she got ahold of my boss and his assistant, Junius Griffin, who was so good to me. He left his office, picked up Maye, then came over and picked me up. He got in touch with the doctor that took care of most of the Motown people, Donovan Givens, and took me to his office. So Dr. Givens examined me and put me in the hospital right away. I was in such bad shape the nurses had to strap me down in bed, because I'd be walking around hallucinating. I'd stand at a blank wall, and think I was standing in front of a window, "See, that truck over there. . . ." Maye would say, "All right, come on, baby, you got to get back in bed."

Every time something like that happened, she'd go to the front nurse and in a few minutes the doctor was there. He kept on working on me and each day I would get a little better. I remember around that time the World Series was coming up. Two of the Pips, Bubba and Baby Brother, went by the house and got the little television from Maye so I could watch the games. I had improved just that much.

The company was so supportive. I had the finest hospital and the finest care. They told Maye, "Anything you need, you just call us and let us know. If you don't have a way to get to the hospital, we'll send a car for you." Motown paid all the medical bills and my salary never stopped. Mr. and Mrs. Gordy, Berry's parents, came by to visit. She thought a lot of Maye. I really appreciated the fact that there was no big broadcast about my condition, no gossiping. Of course, some people knew because at times I became so desperate, I would knock on the neighbors' doors at six in the morning asking for whiskey. I'm not sure how much the groups knew about the extent of my drinking because it didn't really affect the quality of my work and I was never drunk in front of them.

I came out of the hospital in twelve days. All that hallucinating was over. After the first week, Maye took me to the doctor and he said, "Now, let me tell you, I can do one of two things, Charles. I can send you a case of I. W. Harper and kiss your butt good-bye or I can give you a list of things that you're gonna have to do if you want to live because if you have another one of these things that's going to be the end of your life. So you have to make up your mind. What do you want to do? You want me to send you the case of whiskey?"

I said, "Oh, no-o-o. I want to live. You just told me what I gotta do to live and that's what I'm gonna do." He said, "Now, you probably will need some help. It's pretty rough going cold turkey." I said, "You just gave me all the help I need." He said, "Well, you been doing this drinking for thirty years. And what you've done is injure the nerve in your brain that controls your equilibrium. Now, it's not irreparable, but if you continue to drink, it's going to happen this way again." So I told him, I said, "I don't need no help at all, man."

I went back to see him a week later and he was really pleased with my progress and the way I was handling it. He asked me whether I felt the urge for a drink. I said, "Nope, not a bit. I don't feel any kind of need at all." I guess the following week I went back to work. Now, we're into the latter part of October. So we're working on the annual Christmas show at the Fox Theater in Detroit. It took place around the end of December.

At that time, I hadn't touched anything and on the thirty-first they were busting out the champagne and "Happy New Year!" and all that stuff. Finally Gil Askey said, "Aw, c'mon, man, take a glass. It won't hurt you. Just one." The guys said, "Hey, man, a little taste of champagne on New Year's Eve. If you ain't got one in your hand, you ain't with us." And sure enough, I took that one, and before I knew it, I was having another one; and it was cold and icy, and now I got to drive and the whole shot. So, I was very lucky. I got in that car and I drove home and the minute I walked through that door, Maye could see I was tanked.

Right away she started fussing. We had guests there . . . relatives. I said, "Well, you know, it's New Year's Eve and I had a couple of glasses

The Regals in rehearsal with Cholly Atkins (1955); *seated:* Leonard Reed *(left)* and Bobby Schiffman *(right)* make plans for the group   CHOLLY ATKINS COLLECTION

The Cadillacs (1950s); *from left:* Jimmy Bailey, Early Wade, Charles Brooks, Earl "Speedo" Carroll, Bobby Phillips, Rudy Bailey (chauffeur), Jesse Powell (band leader)   COURTESY OF CHARLES STEWART, PHOTOGRAPHER

Scenes from the Apollo Theater (1959); *center picture:* Coles and Atkins swing to the sounds of Louie Bellson's band in the Pearl Bailey Revue   CHOLLY ATKINS COLLECTION

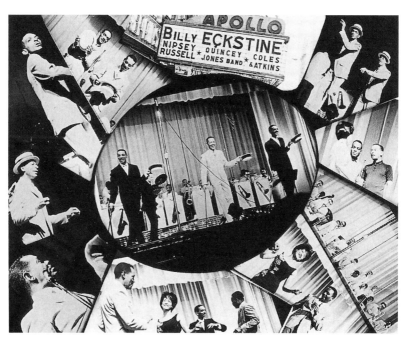

Scenes from the Apollo Theater (1950s); *center picture, from left:* Cholly Atkins, Billy Eckstine, Honi Coles   CHOLLY ATKINS COLLECTION

State Theater, Hartford, Connecticut (1945); *seated*: Buck Washington; *standing, from left*: Bill Bailey, Louis Armstrong, Buck Bubbles

Newport Jazz Festival
(1962); *from left*:
John Neves, Jo Jones,
Baby Laurence,
Pete Nugent, Honi Coles,
Cholly Atkins,
Bunny Briggs

Newport Jazz Festival (1962); *from left:* Duke Ellington, Bunny Briggs, Baby Laurence

Lecture-demonstration with Marshall Stearns, Cooperstown, New York (1966); *back row, from left:* Jean Stearns, Maye Atkinson, unidentified participants, Marshall Stearns; *front row, from left:* Cholly Atkins and Ernie Smith

Cholly Atkins coaches teenager Aretha Franklin, then a new artist at Columbia Records (c. 1960)   COURTESY OF THE FRANK DRIGGS COLLECTION

Cholly Atkins meets with members of the Marvelettes, Monitors, and single artist, Jimmy Ruffin, in Motown's Artist Development division (c. 1966); *seated, far left:* Cholly Atkins; *female artists, front to back:* Wanda Rogers, Gladys Horton, Sandra Fagin, Katherine Anderson; male artists, *front to back:* Richard Street, Jimmy Ruffin, Maurice Fagin, Warren Harris   Courtesy of the Motown Archives

Gladys Knight and the Pips perform in Detroit (1966); *from left:* William Guest, Edward Patten, Merald "Bubba" Knight, Gladys Knight

Courtesy of the Michael Ochs Archives

Temptations (1966);
clockwise from front:
Eddie Kendricks,
Paul Williams,
Melvin Franklin,
Otis Williams,
David Griffin

Supremes and Temptations, TCB television special (1968); *front row, from left:*
Mary Wilson, Diana Ross, Cindy Birdsong; *back row, from left:* Eddie Kendricks, Otis
Williams, Paul Williams, Melvin Franklin, Dennis Edwards

Cholly Atkins in rehearsal with the O'Jays (1970s); *from left:* Sammy Strain, Cholly Atkins, Walter Williams, Eddie Levert   CHOLLY ATKINS COLLECTION

Cholly Atkins coaches Tavares in Bermuda (1974); *from left:* Terry Tavares, Arthur Tavares, Cholly Atkins, Feliciano Tavares, Ralph Tavares, Antone Tavares
COURTESY OF RALPH TAVARES

Tony Award–winning choreographers of *Black and Blue* (1989); *standing:* Cholly Atkins and Frankie Manning; *seated, from left:* Fayard Nicholas and Henry LeTang

Cholly Atkins's "Memories of You" in the Broadway hit, *Black and Blue* (1989); *from left:* Bernard Manners, Dianne Walker, Kevin Ramsey

Jimmy Slyde, National Tap Dance Day Extravaganza, New York City (1992)
Courtesy of Karen Zebulon, photographer

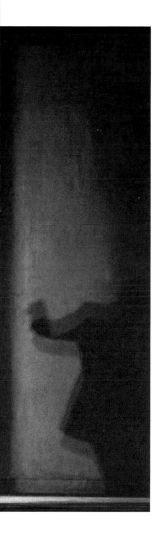

On stage at Swing 46, New York City (2000); *from left:*
Savion Glover and Buster Brown

Cholly Atkins teaches a vocal choreography class in the School of American Dance, Oklahoma City University, where he received the Living Treasure in American Dance Award (1999)   COURTESY OF JO ROWAN AND JOHN BEDFORD

Cholly and his wife, Maye (1998)

of champagne." Maye stared at me, "You know what the doctor told you. You know what I went through. You're not even thinking about me." I said, "Oh, that's where it's at?" See, that liquor made me so contrary, it just changed my whole personality. Maye had to put up with so much foolishness and verbal abuse, but she stuck by me all the way. Even when I was making her life miserable.

Well, that episode woke me up. For about three or four days after the party I was getting that urge. And just like the doctor told me, "When you take one, it's going to call for another and the desire will just keep increasing." I felt like I wanted a drink and I had to bite my lip and just forget about it. And, I'm telling, you, after that *no-o-body* could get me to take a drink, I don't care how close they were.

Gil and I were like brothers. And I could understand where he was coming from. I looked healthy to him and he really thought I could handle it, but Gil knew I had a problem, because he'd told me many times before, "Hey, man, you got to lighten up on that slush; it's taking charge of you." I'd say, "Aw, man, shut up. You drink as much as I do."

But being close friends, I knew what he was saying because I'd start slurring my words and all that. See, you reach a point where you don't want to stop drinking until you're out and that's the point I was reaching. If you don't go completely out, you start doing things out of your head like leaving Evie's. I could have gone on out of here and joined Mama . . . I was just lucky.

But that was the end of my drinking. And Dr. Givens couldn't get over it. He'd introduce me to all his doctor friends at the medical complex, "Remember that patient I was telling you about that had the drinking problem? This is the guy. He's the one that teaches all those great Motown acts." They said, "Oh, yeah, we admire you, man. You got a lot of strength." Well, all that was very encouraging, too. I said, "Looks like I got another reputation I got to uphold! Here I go again, picking up these reputations."

10

BACK TO FREELANCING

We had a lot of success with Artist Development until the groups started to feel their prosperity. In other words, after three or four years, most of the acts became complacent because they were making more money, had more fame, and everything was a big party. We'd schedule the different artists and they wouldn't show up, so the personnel department started asking why certain tunes weren't choreographed. Then they would get on the artists about it.

Finally, Berry sent individual notices to everybody informing them that the company had decided to stop providing those services and if they felt they wanted grooming in the future, they would have to pay for it. Well, all the artists were upset about it, but his decision was final. So that's the way it was set up in '70, and by the end of '71 most of the lesser artists just stopped going to Artist Development altogether because Motown started to concentrate solely on the ones that were making it. The Jackson Five had come into the picture. I never worked directly with them, but they used to stand in the wings during performances, and at Motown they would sit on the stairs and watch me rehearse the other groups. Marlon had such a photographic memory he could duplicate the moves almost immediately. The Temps came to me and said, "You've given them all our routines!"

At that time, the company was going through a transition from Detroit to California, and they were branching out, doing bigger projects like motion picture production and television production. They were putting together a lot of those specials with the Temps and the Supremes. Then there was one on the Four Tops . . . Marvin Gaye. All of those things were new for R & B artists, and it was more convenient for Motown to operate out of California because that was where most of the producing was done.

They shut down a lot of the Detroit operation, not all though. That was a gradual thing. Finally they dispensed with the Artist Development Department, which meant the end of my job. Most of the big acts like Gladys Knight and the Pips kept me, the Temptations kept me, the Supremes, Martha and the Vandellas, the Spinners, the Miracles. Eventually, they were the major clients I handled. The company had sent them all letters advising them to continue working with me because I had been the backbone of their personal appearances.

At one point I was offered a job as an assistant to Suzanne de Passe, who came on board initially as Gordy's creative assistant and later as advisor to the Jackson Five. She was beginning to move up in the ranks and Berry was giving her more and more authority. But it sounded like a flunky job to me and that wasn't good for my ego either. At the time I didn't feel like taking a job under someone whose expertise I had no respect for, which shows you how wrong I was. It seemed to me, Suzanne didn't know a lot about the business then. And truthfully some of the things she was suggesting when she came through Detroit were for the birds, and everybody was laughing at her ideas. But obviously, she grew into it, because she's had a great deal of success since then.

Still, I certainly didn't feel like I needed the change in role because I could make as much money as I was getting at Motown, and more, by freelancing, especially since I had many of their top artists. Besides, a lot of the Motown people that left Detroit for California ended up in a bind. They sold their homes and everything, and soon after they got out there, they were fired. So then there was this exodus back to Michigan.

But despite all these ups and downs, it was a great experience working for Motown. I appreciated the opportunity to be a part of an all-black operation until it was basically infiltrated by people involved in the takeover process. Every day you'd look up and you'd see three or four new white people around. There was a lot of controversy as to what was really happening with the company around this time, but I will not get into that because actually all the information I have on it would be classified as rumors. And I'm not one to pass on rumors, you know. Only the facts.

I brought all of this up since one of the main reasons I wanted to go work at Motown was because it was basically an all-black company that had made terrific strides and become the fourth-largest record company in this country. When they eventually moved to California, it seemed like half the personnel was white. To see it change over like that and not be completely controlled by blacks was very disturbing to me.

After Artist Development shut down, I stayed in Detroit and went to work for another record company but continued coaching my old acts on the side. Brian and Eddie Holland, who were great writers at Motown, started their own business and hired a number of the people who were cut loose by Motown. They had two labels, Invictus, which was distributed by Capitol Records, and a smaller label called Hot Wax, distributed by Buddah Records out of New York. There were good artists on both labels. Freda Payne was one of them. There was a trio of girls called the Honey Cone on the Hot Wax label. They had several groups, including Chairmen of the Board, Hundred Proof, Eighth Day, and they had the Jones Girls, who later became backup singers for Diana Ross.

I ran Artist Development at Invictus like the one at Motown, only I didn't have as efficient a staff. Holland and Holland were great record producers and writers, but their business ability left something to be desired. They put their company in the hands of people who were really not in their corner. Also, a lot of the people in key positions had no knowledge of the industry. For example, the head of the legal department had a background in criminal law, which had nothing to do with corporate law. They didn't know enough about things like running copyrights, and as a result there were a lot of lawsuits.

When I left, the company was having serious financial problems. See, when you have major record companies helping you, like Capitol, you bring them a certain number of new tunes and you get advances on these, then you work on some more. The company got in so deep with advances that they couldn't deliver on time, so finally Capitol dispensed with the association. Invictus just went under.

Still, I enjoyed working there. It was a nice little company and I loved the guys. But the contacts that I had with most of my personal clients, like the Temptations, and Gladys Knight and the Pips, I continued even when I was at Invictus because I still had that studio in my basement at home. Those clients and the ones in other places kept me busy. I got the Love Committee out of Philadelphia, and First Choice, which was a fine act. I choreographed all of their new tunes. I had a group called New York City. Their backup band eventually became big recording artists—Chic, on Atlantic Records.

I was also working with Aretha Franklin periodically. Actually we started when I was still living in New York. She was about seventeen and I had to get her ready to appear on the *Ed Sullivan Show*. We didn't do much dancing, mainly stage movement, mike technique, and so forth. When I moved to Detroit, Aretha used to bring her background singers down to my basement studio to work. She would hire these singers right out of the choir at her father's church. We'd get down there, work out all the moves, and get everything right on the money.

I'm still in contact with her. In Aretha's book, she calls me her favorite teacher, but really I feel honored to have played a part in her career because she is one of the greatest artists of our time, by anybody's standards. We rarely work together these days, but I love her dearly.

In '72 I was still freelancing. I took Maye to San Juan, Puerto Rico, where I was working with the Supremes. This was a new trio—Mary Wilson, Jean Terrell, and Lynda Lawrence. I thought that was really the most talented set of Supremes. Everybody had leads in the show. It wasn't like Diana Ross and the Supremes. Lynda was an excellent singer, and Jean and Mary, of course. With that version of the Supremes, Mary finally had a chance to branch out. The trio played top-drawer clubs. Their movement was sophisticated, too, no teeny-bop stuff.

In 1973, the O'Jays came into the fold. While I was doing a lot of work with Gladys Knight and the Pips, the Temptations, First Choice, and New York City, Ruthie Bowen contacted me about putting together a tour for Queen Artists. She was sending out a show with Millie Jackson and several trios, called "Steamrollers' Revue." The O'Jays were the headliners. All through the seventies, they were one of the number one R & B groups. They started to become real popular when they got with a company called Philadelphia International and began doing message songs, like "Love Train" and "For the Love of Money."

The "Steamrollers' Revue" was my first time working directly with the Jays. I was dictating to everybody in the package—the Chi-lites, Detroit Emeralds, the Moments—telling them what to do and cleaning up their theatrical etiquette. Instead of using Millie Jackson as just a spot in the show, I noticed her flair for comedy and I made the whole presentation her thing. She'd play with the audience, "Now, all the guys in this show . . . these are my men, so, girls, don't start getting ideas. I might let you fool around with a few of them, but see that little curly-haired one on the end? Don't mess with him, honey, because he's all mine!" It was a real production thing; very successful.

During the tour, the Detroit Emeralds caught the eye of the O'Jays' managers, Barbara Kennedy and Edward Windsor Wright. I had done some moonlighting with the Emeralds back in '72, so they were really looking good in the revue. Barbara and Edward asked me if I would meet with the Jays and talk to them about developing their act. At that time the group consisted of Eddie Levert, Walter Williams, and William Powell, all from Canton, Ohio. Eddie and Walt had strong roots in gospel music.

When we got together, I spoke to them about the direction they should take. I said, "It won't be easy. You got to understand that this is backbreaking work. But you have the potential to be the biggest act in the business!" And they went for it! So after I returned to Detroit I continued to correspond with their management. This was a pretty busy time for me. I was doing a lot of local coaching and some choreography for the new young singers along with my regular clients. So I was making enough money to pay the rent and put some food in the house. And Maye was working at the hospital, too. Finally, Barbara and Edward hired me to work with the O'Jays on a regular basis.

The first date I was on with them was a concert in Houston. And boy, those Jays were cookin', I'm telling you. Gladys and the Pips had just done a date with them in Omaha, Nebraska, and the Jays kicked their behind. Bubba said, "God! What happened with these guys!?" When they got down to Houston, Gladys's manager went to the promoter and insisted that they be on early in the show. It was in a ballpark and there were acts for days. They didn't want no part of being down in the heat of the thing. They wanted to do their spot and get out of there.

And they definitely didn't want the Jays laying up on top of them. None of the other acts were doing any Cholly Atkins stuff, so the Jays were really the only ones they worried about. Well, the Pips ended up third and the Jays were about eighth. Gladys and the guys were standing in the wings watching them and those cats were turning it out. People were saying, "They're outstepping the Pips, man!" It was real good publicity for the group because everybody was running their mouths about how the Jays were cooking. I think that might have been the spring of '74, because that same year I'm sure I did a thing with them on *Soul Train*.

We also did "Ship Ahoy" at the Greek Theater in '74. Now, that was one of our biggest productions. The Jays' managers called me in Detroit and said they wanted to do something sensational at the Greek because it was their first time appearing there. At that time headlining at the Greek Theater was very prestigious.

Management had a pretty good budget, so they were going to try to make this a big showcase for the guys. Well, I was going out of my mind with this thing, thinking and thinking and thinking. I told Maye when I was on my way to the airport, "Baby, I don't know what I'm going to do out here. My mind is just cluttered up with so many different things, and basically nothing." She said, "Charles, I know by the time you get off that plane, you'll know exactly what you want to do. Just don't worry about it. Just relax and let it come to you."

And that's what happened in flight from Detroit to L.A. I just laid back and I visualized. . . . I thought about this tune. I had a little tape recorder with headphones and I was listening to "Ship Ahoy" over and over. Then I realized what I wanted to do, and how I would have to do it—all of that just came to mind. I knew a lot of time had to be spent on the treatment, so we wouldn't end up doing the conventional thing.

So I'm thinking, "If you don't do your overture first, people are going to say that's out of order. Do you want to gamble on that? Yes, I want to gamble on it because it'll work. They've got to accept it." See, you've always got to be certain that the overture is fantastic. You've got a big orchestra. You've got six fiddles, two cellos, two oboes, two French horns; you've got all of those things to work with and Dennis's arranging ability.

Dennis Williams was the musical director. I laid it all out for him. Dennis said, "Man, you must be crazy; all of this stuff you're talking about!" I said, "No, I'm not, man." He just gave me this look, you know. Then he said, "These people won't go for this!" I said, "Yes, they will. They'll buy it, man. It's got to be a good five minutes. And if the cats ain't ready, you've got to mark a spot in there where you go back for a repeat." He said, "Aw, man!"

Now, the Jays never liked to rehearse before twelve noon and they finished up at six. So at night Dennis and I would be doing the creating. We had a suite in the Continental Hyatt House. Dennis was on one side and I was on the other and there was a living room in between. So we would stay up half the night working on that thing. We'd go through each and every possible song. He'd say, "Now, what do you think about this one?" I'd say, "No, that tune don't mean nothin.' Let's don't even try to get that in the medley." All of these production things were based on their tunes.

Then in the daytime during the rehearsals, when we would take breaks, I'd have the other technical people come over, and I'd talk to them about ideas for other numbers. For example, on "Wildflower" I wanted six of those rotating slide machines mounted in the ceiling downstage. We had interchanging slides of beautiful young black models projected onto miniature screens upstage. And behind the screens, on a scrim, we had color slides of vegetation—wildflowers. The slides of the models changed all during the course of the song. It was very striking and one of our most successful numbers.

Those are the kinds of things I'd be discussing, and "Ship Ahoy" turned out great. It put those cats on the map. At the Greek, we had an act in front of us, then an intermission. We brought down a fire curtain so that we could have smoke on the stage when the curtain opened and the outline of the ship. The orchestra was split, it was on dollies. So you could see the ship and all of the smoke. . . . It started with the sound—the creaking of the ship and the waves and everything.

There were four dancers who were slaves on the ship, but it looked like a whole bunch of them because it was backlit. I worked all that out with the lighting people. When they moved to the front, the image became bigger and when they moved back it would be smaller. Then all of a sudden you saw these heads coming up out of the smoke. One over here. One over there. And the audience didn't know what the hell was happening. And the timing was perfect. They'd wiggle their way around and you would see one head, then it would go back down . . . now the Jays are escaping from this slave ship! And finally, they all wound up right up front, in back of the mike stand.

It was sensational, and the audience just went wild when they went into the song. The Jays did this whole tune in tattered clothes. When the song ended, we had the sound of bullwhips—WHAP, WHAP, WHAP! Then the searchlights came on and they started running, and the smoke came back up. They were running away, you see. Finally the whole ship disappeared; the backdrop faded out completely. And the timing of the smoke was just right. There was a standing ovation.

Now we go into the overture. The split band moves together, the regular lighting starts coming in, and Dennis is into his overture. That lasts five minutes while the Jays are changing into their uniforms. You hear all this great music, then BOOM, the lights are up, and here come them same three cats out there in white tuxedos, and popping like crazy, "Put Your Hands Together" . . . Hey, man, shoot! This is production. This ain't no jive stuff like they've been lookin' at.

But that's the point I'm really trying to make. Sometimes you have to gamble and move away from the conventional if it proves a point and you feel that you can make the people accept it. All the groups, especially the Temps, were saying, "Why don't you do something like that for us?" I said, "Because your record company won't pay for it." At that time Motown was hiring all these big-name choreographers. They had this guy who was the first black choreographer on the NBC roster. I knew him very well, because I had done some things with him when I was at Motown, and I dug him.

The Temptations were in rehearsal at that time and when they came to the Greek and saw that show, they fired that cat. They sent Cornelius Grant, their musical conductor, up to the hotel to see if I could finish the thing up because they were opening somewhere for Bill Cosby. This guy had put together some sort of medley that ran for eighteen minutes and the Temps weren't too happy with him right from the start, but the record company was dictating. Motown became so name-conscious when they moved out to California; they were "progressive," "moving on," "a higher plane," all that kind of crap.

Anyway, Cornelius asked me about taking over and I said, "No, man, I ain't got time. I'm going to relax when I get through with this here." The Temps were worried because Cosby had told them, "Now, you guys got to be hot up here. You can't be screwing around because you'll be wanting me to bring you back." Well, they bombed with that and they hurried up and got back with me! It was amazing. I remind them of it sometimes. They say, "Aw, man, don't come up here with that old stuff again." Boy, I just crack up, "You guys don't be telling me about your mistakes."

After the Greek, I worked with a group called Tavares. I was preparing them for the Princess Hotel in Bermuda. I remember that date because Duke Ellington's band and a number of jazz artists were playing at a convention there. Duke had just died. Working with Tavares was one of the most delightful periods of my career. They were great guys, all brothers: Ralph, Arthur, Terry, Feliciano, and Antone. I also really liked their manager, their record company, and the whole shot. Actually I coached them off and on for four or five years.

When I finished with Tavares in Bermuda, I came back to do some directing for Gladys Knight. She was opening for Goldie Hawn at the Las Vegas Hilton, and Maurice King was conducting Gladys's band. Since the show had to be short, I chopped the numbers up, changed the eight-bar introduction to a two-bar introduction. It was like a *Reader's Digest* version of her regular show, but it looked like a whole complete presentation. Goldie was changing her show every night to get out from under the hammer, because our show was tight and there was no fat. Nothing but lean. You know what I mean? It was punchin' and kickin' and the cats were sharp and Gladys had on beautiful gowns.

That's the show that Barron Hilton saw. He said, "I'll tell you what I want to do with Gladys and the Pips. I'd like to bring them in here next time as a headliner, but I'm going to book them first in the Waldorf in New York and see how that works out." And it was a smash! She had all them gospel people from up in Harlem; everybody coming in there. The Waldorf looked like the Savoy! Business was great and the response was just terrific.

I left there and went to Miami with New York City. Took Maye down there with me for the weekend. Now, that was a real good group. One of the guys from the Cadillacs ended up in that group. It was a quartet—all males. Good singers; good dancers, too. And they responded to dictation beautifully. They did a lot of little production things. One of the guys used to dress up like a girl on stage—just a wig and a blouse, he'd keep his pants on. Man, that cat did some real comical stuff.

During 1975 they were my main clients, along with the O'Jays, Temps, and Gladys Knight and the Pips. I also did some things for the Miracles and for First Choice. Then it was back to Gladys and the Pips. In March I worked with a former member of the Delfonics, a singer named Major Harris. I put his show up, produced it, put in background singers, choreographed their moves, and selected tunes for his repertoire. I gave him all production numbers and a medley of tunes from the Delfonics. Finished up with him in May; then in June, Gladys and the guys started working on their NBC summer replacement show.

Their manager was real friendly with the agent that NBC hired to find potential artists for the series and he decided to suggest Gladys since she had been such a hit at the Waldorf and the Hilton. I was completely in charge of production for Gladys Knight and the Pips, so I'd make all the production meetings, review what they were being asked to do, make corrections, then get with them to explain the procedures.

The producers and writers might have something in the script that was corny, completely out of character, or derogatory from a racial standpoint, "Yah-suh, how you do, suh?" You know, one of those kinds of things. I'd say, "No, he won't say it. Maybe you'll be successful if you try it with a British accent." They had a lot of skits for them to do and some of them were okay. It was just the wording and the intonations that they would come up with. There were no black writers on the scene.

But this summer show was a real strange piece of business for me. NBC had a choreographer named Tony Charmoli, who was well known in the TV business, and he was in the process of becoming a television director. This show was his first directing opportunity, but he wanted to watch his back and hang on to what he already had, so I was brought in as assistant choreographer. That was the credit that they gave me, even though I was doing all the choreography and staging.

I didn't expect that because I knew Tony. We had met in New York long before this show, and we basically had a friendly relationship. As the director, he was supposed to be directing me. That was the procedure. He would call sessions just for the two of us to talk. He said, "Look, man, it's not like I'm trying to take advantage of your position, because I want to work with you as much as possible. See, I'm trying to make another step up, and I don't want to lose what I've got." Then he said, "It has nothing to do with your color or anything." Well, that's always the story, so I let that roll off my back like water off a duck. But I knew he wasn't going to let his needs be secondary to mine.

Gladys and the Pips were real upset about it, but the only thing they could have said was, "We won't do the show." And I definitely didn't want them to do that since this was the break of their career, so we had to go along with the program. And really, the people in that business didn't have a whole lot of respect for R & B artists.

Now, when Sammy Davis came in as a guest, he raised hell about it. Bob Henry told him, "Hey, man, you've got to go way upstairs to peep this thing and get to those people." Sammy said, "I can get to them. Get them on the phone. I want to talk to them!" So they went through the whole rigmarole. They were apologetic and all that. Sammy said, "This man has worked all these years with this group to make them what they are and he ought to be getting credit for it." They agreed with him, but they wouldn't change.

Sammy Davis was big, but he wasn't as big as NBC, especially at that time, in 1975! We had just gotten through the civil rights period. But we were still in the back of the bus. The only difference was that we had a door that we could go in and out of, and our own conductor! But the show provided a real boost for the group. It ran for four weeks and I was able to double my fees afterward, even though I didn't get the proper credit. But that's politics. Nothing much had changed since the June Taylor days.

In the fall, I decided to do an act for a group called Creative Source, from California, three girls and two guys. Then I got another new account—a family act—the Sylvers. They were on Capitol Records. I did their first two or three hit records. Then they hired this white manager who wanted them to have a TV choreographer. When he shifted them over, their popularity started to wane. Bill Cosby gave them hell. He said, "I don't know why in the world you ever left the man who made you successful."

Near the end of '75, I went back to Detroit and helped Maye with the packing. We had decided to move to Las Vegas and she had already found a house out there. Maye was fifty-eight and I was sixty-three, so we wanted to live some place that would be good for retirement . . . good for senior people . . . in a house that was ours. The other thing was to get away from that cold weather . . . shoveling snow, trying to move around. Then trying to get in and out of there all the time was a drag with the blizzards and all. The year before we left Detroit, the Temps moved to L.A. and most of the other major Motown artists had left.

Maye really wanted to move to L.A., because she had friends there. But I didn't want no part of that scene, not only because of the earthquake thing, but Los Angeles was an import town. They had the greatest musical directors right there, but they would go all the way to Paris and get some little jive apprentice director, named Jacques DuBois or something, and give him a whole lot of money . . . it was an import town!

At that time Vegas was very inexpensive. The housing was good, no state income taxes, and it was a show business center. I figured I was forty-five minutes from L.A. So I could jump on the plane at 6:30 in the morning, have a session, get home in time for dinner, and still be considered an import. But Maye was miserable at first because she didn't know a soul here and maintaining a house was no picnic either. We were apartment dwellers, so handling repairs and all was a major problem. But in the long run, we agree that this was the best move for us.

After we settled in, I got busy again with the Jays. Around '76, William Powell was replaced by Sammy Strain. Sammy had been with Little Anthony and the Imperials for twelve years. He was an excellent addition to the O'Jays: a seasoned performer and a wonderful singer and dancer. Over the years, I've had so much fun with those guys. I remember one time I was doing something real hard and I looked up and all those cats had disappeared. They went down the hall to another room. So I walked in there, "Hey, man, I'm out here demonstrating like hell and you guys . . ." They said, "Man, you expect us to do that crap? You out of your cotton-pickin' mind." I said, "Okay, I'll give it to the Pips or I'll give it to the Temps. That's okay. Come on, do this." Then I did something stupid, you know, very elementary. Eddie looked at the other two, "Now he's becoming a comedian!"

I said, "Well, I didn't think Walt was going to be able to get it, so let's try this." Walt said, "Come on with it, man. I'll show you. If you can do it, I can do it." So if Walt jumped in there and got it, then them other two guys started scuffling. Oh, it would be so funny. But the psychology of getting these things to happen is something else. I feel real good that I can get across to them, regardless of how it's done.

We have our differences about a lot of things. But I say, "Hey, I work for you guys. If this is the way you want to do it, it's perfectly all right with me. I don't suggest that you do that, but don't tell anybody that I did that part." "It's that bad, huh, Pops?" "No, it's not really that bad, but it just has no relationship to what you've been doing." They say, "Oh, okay, man, let's do it your way." And that will be the end of it.

But basically, Eddie is very creative, and he wants to have something to say about what the O'Jays are going to do, which I admire. Sometimes he'll suggest things and I tell him, "Yeah, that sounds great. Let's try it." And generally if I do that, it works. But if he comes up with something off-the-wall, it's my job to tell him, "That shit you're talking about is for the birds, man. But if you want to jump out of the window, I'll be the first one to give you a push." Now, when it bombs, he's not like some people who will say, "Well, man, it's working for me; I like it. Let's keep it in." He never does that, but I know exactly where he's coming from. He wants to exercise his creativity.

The one thing I don't want to do is stagnate their creativity. One of the most important things in this business is to teach them to take care of themselves whether I'm there or not. For instance, if they get a new record and they need some choreography quick, I want them to be able to put some things together, even if they have to steal from steps they already know. That way they don't have to learn all new steps, just new placements.

And the Jays have learned this well. Walt doesn't particularly like to do that. He'll say, "Well, we won't fool with that till we get with the old man. He'll take care of that." But Sam and Ed will work on different little things. And they're qualified. The same was true with the Pips, especially Bubba. There always will be one or two in a group.

Now the Jays are highly competitive when it comes to their vocals and the choreography. Which is healthy, because that takes a lot of the pressure off of me. If a group wants to do the material so well that they compete with each other, you're in good shape, because they'll be more attentive and get help when they need it. If one of the Jays has a hangup, he'll bring it to the surface right away.

Walter will say, "What am I doing wrong?" I tell him, "Well, you came in here this morning. That was your first mistake. I think you need to go back to bed and sleep about thirty-two hours, then get up and maybe you can learn this step! I said *maybe*!" He says, "Come on, man; I know what I'm doing wrong, man." And he gets mad with himself and winds up doing it perfect. But that's the kind of attitude they all have about it. They're three distinctly different types of personalities, but each one is a perfectionist and all of them are very profound guys.

And it shows, boy. When they hit that stage, I'll tell you, they're cooking because they come out of every rehearsal period with 65 percent perfect, and that's all you're probably going to get from anybody in a rehearsal hall. The other 35 percent you have to get from performing it with an audience and repeating it over and over. The most important thing is to try and make sure that when you're going over and over the same choreography, you're not allowing them to go over bad concepts of certain moves. You let them run through the songs several times just for the sake of continuity; then you go back and pick the choreography apart.

But if you continue to let them do bad things, the mistakes become embedded, and then you have to spend another whole session to break those habits. That makes the sessions lengthier because bad habits are very difficult to erase once they get them in their muscle memory. And in many cases, they'll tell you, "Well, man, I've been doing that for three days! Why didn't you say something?"

Now, basically, Sammy has more of a dancer's look. I mean, like a student of dance, and I primarily depend on him to be a yardstick for the whole group, a standard bearer. But sometimes he will drift off into what is more comfortable for him. But I don't have any problem getting him back, because he realizes what he's doing. I always remind my clients to approach the choreography with an open mind so that they get a chance to understand exactly what it is that they're trying to learn.

I say, "Don't do it like it's just another step, because each one of these steps has its own character, and you have to bring it to life. I'll give it to you, but you have to make these moves *live*. None of them will come to the surface unless you bring them to the surface. You have to treat all of the steps like individuals, and don't play any of them cheap, or it's going to be obvious."

In addition to the Jays, I continued to work with the Miracles, Spinners, and all my other regular clients, like the Temps and the Pips, right on through the seventies. My schedule was pretty tight. I was bouncing from one thing to the other, crisscrossing the country . . . in and out of the country. For an old man, that was quite hectic. I was hardly ever home. But in this business, you have to make hay while the sun shines, because you never know when it's going to be all over.

I worked with Graham Central Station for a while in '78, went to the Greek Theater again with the Jays, then brought my buns on home and started negotiations on a show called *Red, Hot and Foxy*, with Redd Foxx. We'd been friends for years. Honi and I were on a lot of shows with him in the late forties and early fifties. We appeared together with Count Basie's band and Billy Eckstine's. I'd been one of Redd's fans for a long time, even back in the days when he and Slappy White had a team.

Red, Hot and Foxy was my first major directing job on the Strip in Vegas, although I'd staged and directed Gladys Knight's shows. Norma Miller was working for Redd around that time, so she suggested that he hire me to do the show. Norma gave him my number, he called, and that started the ball rolling. We took about a month to organize it and get the technicians. Bob Bailey, who used to sing with Basie, was my stage manager.

I did all the directing and staging, no choreography. Beverly White was the choreographer; we had a line of girls and Gerald Wilson's band. This was a big revue with lots of stars—Della Reese, the Nicholas Brothers, the comedian Johnny Dark. There were also a couple of magicians, Goldfinger and Dove. The show ran about three weeks and business was real good; then they changed entertainment directors at the Silver Bird and the new guy got in a hassle with Redd. He started calling him "boy" and all that kind of stuff, so Redd canceled the show. We tried to get it in another place, but it just didn't pan out. I finished out that year working with Gene Chandler, the Jays, the Pips. Then I was home for Christmas, which was great. I always liked being home on the holidays.

Right on into the eighties I was in and out of production meetings with Gladys Knight and the Pips. That's when I was still doing road dates with them. In addition to staging and choreographing, I was still in charge of production. They were back to using in-house technicians then, so rather than hiring individual specialists, it was cheaper to take me along to deal with the sound, lights, and production people. I had to check on-stage monitors, mikes, props, and special curtains.

I supervised all of that. See, the in-house technicians don't get lackadaisical if they see you. So you walk in, you go by the lighting booth, "Hey, how's everybody tonight?" Then you go backstage and you talk to the stage crew. They know you're there, so they'll stay pretty much on the ball. Because if they mess up, they know they're going to hear from you and they don't like bad reports going to the entertainment department. It's all a psychological thing, so the idea is to just let them see you.

I did that kind of thing at Motown, too. I even went to the TV shows and explained what we would like to have. Bob Farrell, who was with the *Ed Sullivan Show*, used to say he was glad when he saw me around because I'd have some kind of fresh idea for presenting the talent. Generally, I would go in about a day or so ahead of the artists. But you had to have the right type of personality to talk with those people.

You'd rub them down, "I know you'll be exercising your own creativity here, but I just want you to know what we'd like and, of course, I welcome your input." And, hey, they would cooperate, "Is that all right?" I'd say, "Yeah, that's fine, but if you could bring it in a split second earlier. . . . Okay, you got it." So it's all about diplomacy. You don't go in there acting like you're God. Because those people can mess your show up.

For a while, I did a lot of that for the Temps, too. Then if I happened to be out on tour with Gladys when a date came up, the Temps wouldn't have anybody who understood all that backstage stuff, so they eventually got their own individual technicians. Which was great because there was less pressure on me. I was jockeying from one hotel to another, and the wear and tear on the body was something else. In December of '79 when I was on one of those dates with the Pips, I had to be rushed to the emergency room. The doctor said I wasn't getting enough potassium in my system to counteract my high-blood-pressure medicine.

When I got home on Christmas Day, I still wasn't feeling well and at that time I hadn't stopped smoking. But my doctor couldn't figure out what was wrong. To make a long story short, Maye sent me to her doctor, and he detected a spot on my left lung. I said, "Well, I've got a job with a group in Freeport and when I come back . . ." He said, "You're not going to Freeport. If you spend a month down there, there's no telling how big this thing will be when you come back. You're going right in the hospital."

After a lot of testing the doctors determined that I had cancer. They took the top right lobe off and I didn't have to take no chemotherapy or nothing. I had to stop smoking. But that had really stopped when I first went in there, because my godson, Jimmy Peyton, came over and stole my cigarettes to make me stop. I was up and out after about three weeks. The doctor said, "Well, you can go out to the golf course. Don't play but eighteen!"

I had smoked for fifty years. So '80 was a very lucky year. And I was just so grateful to Maye, because I probably would have gone on back to that first doctor and said, "Hey, man, what the hell is happening here, baby?" He'd say, "Aw, there ain't nothing wrong with you." And I'd be six feet under right now.

THE WAY I DO THE THINGS I DO

People often ask me how I get the groups to look so different, even though they're all doing my style. Now, that takes me back to one of my mottoes: Let the Punishment Fit the Crime. In other words, you go primarily with the talent that you have to work with. Certain groups get more intricate steps than others. The choreography that I give them depends on what they are able to absorb and execute well.

Also, the material that they're noted for, the songs they're noted for, the producers, the writers—they are not the same. What those producers put in the musical tracks is a factor. They all say different little things. Now, I could give a new group the same moves that I give the O'Jays, but they would not necessarily look good doing those moves and the choreography would probably look different altogether because the Jays are just so on top of it.

With this kind of choreography there's always a thin line between getting the singers to do what I show them and getting them to still express their individuality on stage. See, I don't want the choreography to be performed exactly like I teach it, although I am working for precision. I want you to inject yourself. I want you to get involved in it and do it your way. Don't change it, but *give* it something that belongs to you. It's just like me giving you a Cadillac. You're going to get your driver's license, you're going to have to drive it, put some gas in it and maintain it. I don't care how fine an automobile it is. Those things you're going to have to do! Otherwise, it's just going to be something that sits in your front yard.

What I really mean is, you have to create your own personal style in this business. Like the song says, "It ain't what you do, it's the way that you do it." Even though you're part of a collective, you've got to make sure that you're contributing something to the group that only you can give. That's the bottom line, because if something unforeseen happens—if the group disintegrates—you're in a position to get into another one or form your own. So you can't allow yourself to become complacent even if the group is very popular, and you definitely don't want the others to feel that they are carrying you and you're just along for the ride.

When I start putting the choreography together for a song, I make an effort to get a lyric sheet so that I know what they're singing about. So the physical drama is given a lot of consideration. For instance, "Keep On Lovin' Me, Baby" is a funky, bluesy, R & B–type thing, very earthy. When you read the lyrics and listen to the music, your movement has to correspond with those things. And you start formatting different types of moves in your mind for that particular subject matter.

Then you go to the main source, which is the musical track, and you extract the rhythmic patterns, and make sure your movements correspond with them. Not all of them, but what we call in the music game "the hooks," the little syncopations down in the musical tracks that will psychologically stick out in the minds of the listeners—little rhythms like RE-BOP-ADU BE-AH, DAH-DE-DU-BAH-BAH. You try to put a funky move to that rhythmic pattern.

This is the thing that distinguishes the type of choreography that I do from the vocal dancing that you usually see. I make a major study of all of this, and I spend a lot of time before I get with the artists. And being a tap dancer has made it very easy for me to adhere to rhythmic patterns. It seems to me that tap dancing set up a lot of yardsticks for musicians, particularly drummers and horn players, and arrangers. When they get stuck for rhythmic patterns, they can watch dancers like Honi Coles or Baby Laurence, or Bunny Briggs—any good tap dancer who has a good sense of composition and is not just making noise.

Somebody who understands that tap can be lyrical and melodic, as well as noisy.

But I'm not thinking about tap when I hear the rhythmic patterns in the music. It's just automatic. I've been educated to always be aware of rhythmical complexity. Now, the vocal melodic lines—the general pattern of the songs themselves—are somewhat repetitious. In other words, the melody of each verse is the same, the melody of each channel is the same, and generally the rhythmic patterns are the same in those. So once you get one verse choreographed, one channel choreographed, you see what the pattern is throughout the song.

In many cases, the arranger will inject an instrumental section, which runs anywhere from four bars to sixteen bars. If there is an eight-bar instrumental and the singers are doing something real energetic, they'll only do that for four bars. The last four bars before they have to come back in to sing are not as energetic. Generally the instrumental is either a keyboard, like an organ or synthesizer, or it's a saxophone. Saxophones are very popular now for instrumentals. So that gives you another rhythmic pattern that you have to be concerned about.

But usually, when you set the choreography on the first verse, you do a channel and you're going to do another verse after that. You revert to the choreography that you did on the first verse. That's why it's very important that you make your choreography strong enough to be worthy of repeating, rather than just an ordinary piece of work.

When I'm working with the groups I break everything down beat for beat and I teach them to listen to the musical track, which will cue them as to what the rhythmic pattern is. That's a major part of the process. So when I'm doing the step, I sing the rhythmic pattern, then I make them sing it. I say, "What is the music saying right here? BUH-PAH-DEEDO-PEE-PAK, DE-DU-BOP, BUH-DO-BOOP. Now you move to those things." "Yeah, Pop, we got it." Since they are singers and they sing like that, it's just a matter of showing them that they have to learn those patterns that they're going to move to.

I make sure they spend an adequate amount of time listening to the instrumental music and not themselves when they first get the product. They're so busy listening to their own voices and tearing them down, saying, "I could have done this better," and so on, they don't even hear what the background music is. When they don't do their homework, the choreography gets real difficult for them. And it's a little hard to get some people who are approaching sixty to do homework. When they get through rehearsing, some of them don't want to hear it again until the next day when they come back into rehearsal, but the ones who actually study the musical tracks are going to shine. And it's better to shine than to reflect—in any walk of life!

Now, the other thing you need to understand is that the audience can feel those rhythmic patterns. It's like when you see African dances, you can't hear the rhythmic patterns of the feet like you can with tap, but you feel that rhythm . . . you feel the contrast between what the body is doing and what the drum is saying, and you see the consistency of staying on the beat in spite of the contrast in rhythms. Which is very mathematical when you really break it down. You're listening to one rhythmic pattern, and you're working against that.

The same thing is present in my work. The audience doesn't realize half the time what's actually happening with vocal choreography. The vocal part is on one melodic line. It's a whole different melody. And the body is moving to the musical background track. In other words, while your body is moving to one rhythm, your voice is moving in another rhythmic direction. The melodic line will be altogether different from what the background is doing and it becomes exceptionally difficult for a lot of individuals to do that—sing one rhythmic pattern and move to another.

It's all about different syncopations. In the track you have descriptive rhythmic patterns. You might sing, "I love you," and the band will go *de doodly boo bop*, "This is the night," *bang de doo doo*, "I love you," *de doodly doo wop* . . . those little nonsensical things you move to. They could be played by the rhythm section . . . the horn section, but you move to those things, which means your body is moving in a different tempo from your vocal line or what you're singing. Oh, man, it's like BLUH-BLA-BLUH-BLUH-LUH-DUH. To register both is not the simplest thing in the world. But it is the Cholly Atkins style. When

I came on the scene, nobody else was choreographing moves to the *doodly doo wop*. They'd just stay in the pocket—choreograph to the tempo of the vocal line.

You have to devise systems to get artists to sing one rhythm and move to another because immediately they say, even when they're excellent singers, "Hey, man, I can't move this way and my voice is going in another direction." I tell them, "Yes you can. Let's learn them separately, and then we'll do them together. So forget about the singing for a minute. Just learn the step. Let that become automatic. Think about what you're hearing in the track . . . move with that. After we learn the moves and smooth them out, we'll just do a vocal rehearsal. Then we'll put the two together." This is very time-consuming, but it's worth it. And all my life I've tried to do my work in such a way that it will not only stand out, but stand the test of time.

That's why I spend a lot of time with orientation. Mary used to get on my case at Motown, "Come on, Cholly, please. Just show me the step. I'll get it. We spend two days picking the foot up and two days putting it back down!" I said, "Look, Mary Wilson, you're not the only one in this group. They're two other people that make up the Supremes. You understand? So if you have a problem dealing with the orientation, leave the room. I'll call you when we finish." She said, "In other words you're telling me to put the zipper on the lip." "Yes, please. If you've got a problem, keep it to yourself." But you know, that's Mary, and I love her to death. But she don't want to know about what makes up the thing or how you should approach it. "Just do it and let me try to learn it!"

With the single artists I had other problems, like mike technique. If they held a mike in one hand, they didn't know what to do with the other hand. They didn't have no pockets to put it in or nothing; you're out there in this sleek evening gown—"So what the hell do I do with this *hand*?" It became a question of how to demonstrate different moves that would add to the presentation. You put both hands together, and then you would move the other hand out. Then you interchange the mike again.

And you'd take the lyric of the tune and try to teach them that there are certain things in that lyric that you can describe with that other hand. For instance, if you say, "In the *dis*-tance." There's something about moving that hand out, up and above, away from the body, that demonstrates movement. That helps to sell what you're singing about.

So you take that lyric and you work with them on the physical drama. And it's not done on everything. You don't want to be literal. You might say, "Come close to me," just pull your shoulders up and snuggle, like. You don't stay in it, but you just imply it, then you immediately come out of it because the next lyric might say something else, so you don't want to be hung up in this other thing.

In many cases it's not the simplest concept to get across because it becomes too technical for some artists. They say, "Hey, man, this is too deep. It gives me a headache. I have to think too much and I'm trying to think about how I'm going to sell this song!" I say, "This is a part of your selling the song." "Yeah, man, but my mind isn't ready for that right now." But see, you can't stop there. You have to continue to tell them about this and when they go to see a Lena Horne or a Joe Williams they say, "That's the stuff Cholly was telling me about; I've got to get with that stuff."

There is a difference and they recognize it. Then here they come, "Hey, let's get back on that physical drama stuff you were talking about. I think maybe I can get with it." They don't tell you what changed their mind. But you're going from experience, so you know what brought them around. They begin to realize it's all a part of taking charge on stage.

I told Tavares, "I'm going to teach you guys a lesson on how to handle an audience. I mean, you're not up there like tin soldiers. When they're 2,500 people sitting out there who have paid X amount of dollars to come and see you, you are in command. They're not in command and you must take charge up there!" "I don't understand what you mean, man." "Well, it's the same thing that happens at the down-home Sunday morning church service. The preacher is in command and the lead singer is something like a preacher. It's as simple as that. The people in the audience have come here to see you and hear what you have to say. When the lead singer says something about, 'Baby, let me make love to you,' and somebody jumps up and screams, 'Hallelujah!' is what she's saying." So you are in charge. But by all means, don't take advantage of that.

I have to warn some of the groups about the use of profanity on stage. Sometimes they figure they have the audience in the palm of their hand and they can say what they want, but I tell them, "That's just the time some producer will be sitting in the audience — somebody who wants to book you in a hotel or supper club, and that's all they'll remember. The people in those places don't want to hear that kind of language. So don't be telling me about some other artist who is vulgar on stage, because they have a certain crowd that follows them and they are in the minority. Redd Foxx was just as funny doing a clean show, like *Sanford and Son*, as he was doing filth every night. And Cosby never had to resort to that. He'll have you cracking up with just simple things that happen in your everyday life. It's best to keep your act as clean as possible; then it can travel."

Another real important aspect of vocal choreography is creating places for the singers to catch their breath. For instance, if they're singing an up-tempo tune, it's important to have rest spots. In those places the movement can't be as energetic. Since I'm a dancer, I have to keep reminding myself that these are singers and I want to make sure that the movement in those rest spots is still exciting, but elementary enough for them to breathe.

Now, that breathing time has to be done carefully to keep the level of choreography pretty much up to standard, so there are not too many hills and valleys — from a visual standpoint. And that's not simple. But it can happen within, say, two or three bars of music. So if you take them out of the mike area, when they're not singing, to do a very energetic step, then you do a clever thing, not as energetic, though, getting back into the mike area. During that brief space of time they get a chance to catch their breath.

I think the continuation of movement is what initially attracted the different groups to my choreography. And all of that has to do with the ability to study the music and get the singers in and out of each segment. When I started doing this back in the fifties, I knew I had two and a half or three beats to get them out there and do something fantastic and rush them back in to sing DOO-WAH; then back up again and do something else, rather than just stand there and wait for DOO-WAH again. The movements were a pure jazz thing, set into the frame of the rhythmic pattern.

I wouldn't try to tell the story in dance or describe the words. The lead singer would do that stuff: "The moon over the earth," then "the horse ran this way." But most of the groups were doing that at first. They'd point to the floor and say, "Down to the river," then point up, "up to the sky." They were doing literal interpretations of the words. When I incorporated interesting background movement with the rhythmic patterns, it was a happy marriage, nothing obvious, no clichés.

So, this is not as easy as we make it look. We like to give the appearance that these things just come naturally, which God knows that they don't! In the early days with the Cadillacs and the Pips, and more recently with the O'Jays, I set a piece completely in about four days. But take a group like the Temptations, I would need a week because of the number of people in the group. You're dealing with two more people, and they have different personalities, different attention spans.

I used to do a great deal of the choreography before I got with the group. But I have learned over the years that as soon as I make up my mind about which rhythmic patterns I want to catch choreographically, I don't have to completely work the steps out ahead of time. I can do it right on the spot with the guys. And if what I create is too difficult for them, I can create something else that's pretty much going to say the same thing movementwise, but simpler.

So that's not a problem for me anymore and it hasn't been for the last fifteen to twenty years. Sometimes I have trouble deciding which move I want to do. I used to make the mistake of choreographing to the lowest talent in the group, but I didn't stay with that too long because I wasn't satisfied with what I did. So I went the other way. I choreographed to the top talent and spent a little more time with the ones that were slower at picking it up.

In dealing with vocal groups, I've found the most important thing is to relax them and build up their confidence at the same time. See, my main clients tend to use me as a yardstick. They say, "Well, you're a dancer, man. You can do it like that; we'll never do it like you." I say, "Yes, you can. All you've got to do is understand it." So I pull it apart section by section. The next thing you know, "Hey, yeah, man, I look as good as you doing it!" Immediately, they begin to work better.

Another problem that we have during rehearsal periods is the interference of management. They set up gigs that really rub the group the wrong way, and they give them a long spiel about how important it is for them to make these last-minute commitments. Not only does it upset the group as far as their learning new material is concerned, it just messes with their emotions. That's management.

Then the record company gets in the picture by insisting on promotional appearances, which means if you are rehearsing from 12:00 to 6:00, and they want to do one at 2:30 on the other side of town, your time gets chopped up. They tell you it will take an hour, but they don't mention that it takes an hour to get there and an hour to get back. It's six o'clock before you know it, and these guys have families and evening commitments. So you look up and most of the day is blown. But the record companies are primarily in the driver's seat and their schedules take precedence over rehearsals.

Most of my contributions to the various acts that I've worked with have been in the jazz and tap vein. Remember, before I learned to tap, I had a good authentic jazz background. What I mean by "authentic jazz" is what they basically now call street dancing—things that black neighborhoods came up with. We've been doing those moves for a thousand years!

Tap dancers basically use portions of authentic jazz dance so they'll look good as well as sound good. I'm talking about dances like the Suzie-Q, Charleston, and black bottom; things that created excitement as soon as we came up with them. Now, right away there were adaptations of these dances and they were claimed by other people and presented in places where we weren't permitted to go. But we all know where they came from.

A lot of the moves that the young kids are doing now are very familiar. They have a different beat and all that, but you look closely and you see steps there from African traditional dances. They just have another little twist added. The kids are doing all kinds of moves, shaking and coming up and down, hopping and skipping, and hands flying. You see all those things.

In some of the pictures that I've seen of dances during slavery time, you see the same kinds of moves. You see the arm movements and the legs kicking, the strut. You know, moves typical of *us*! And when you analyze it further and see these *National Geographic* films of the dances of Africa and the Caribbean islands, you can see the roots of these dances that became popular, like the Charleston, truckin', and the twist. If you're a student of the dance you can look and see where them steps came from! The basic movement is there, but I guess you have to really know dance to look that deep into it. But it is all recognizable. You can look at it and see it come right on up.

I just saw a real old clip of a little boy dancing on a platform, and the dances that he was doing are the same kinds of things that Michael Jackson is doing now. Take the moonwalk for example. Michael probably had never seen it before, but Johnny Hudgins and Bill Bailey had been doing it forever. It was Bill's stage exit sixty years ago! All of a sudden, it's Michael Jackson's moonwalk. Every bit of that break dance that you've seen the guys doing on the sidewalk, spinning on their heads and all that—done a thousand years ago! Every single step of it. But that's neither here nor there. It's brand new to these generations. Brand new to them, ancient to me.

But the connection is there—those rhythms. You can go all the way back to primarily just drumbeats. And the dances were just as interesting when you didn't have saxophones, and trumpets and trombones. All of that was just more whipped cream on the Jell-O. That rhythm from those drums was the foundation, the basic beats; and the inspiration, in many cases, because when they would increase their volume, it would inspire the dancers to do more energetic things.

When I used to watch classes at the Dunham School on Fortythird Street, I'd sit there and I'd look at that stuff, and it would fascinate me. Then years later I'd look up and see a thing like *Soul Train*, and there were the same moves. I said, "We will be us. I don't care what the beat is, we're going to dance to the music."

And when you really start to think about it, a lot of this modern jazz dance came from us, the foundation of it. When I started to be exposed more to different techniques of various teachers, I could see the relationship of authentic jazz to most of the things that modern jazz choreographers were doing. I could see the origin of all of these things not only from the islands and Africa, but also the Far East. There are only so many positions you can put the body in. And at some given time in doing a dance, you're going to hit on a movement that can be found in other techniques, like Balinese, or something, feet and toes sticking out. You know what I mean?

Now all of this to me was part of knowing what I was doing. I never had a formal lesson in my life. I never took a class, but I always exposed myself to various dance techniques, just through observation. That's pretty much the way I've always learned. It wasn't a chore. It came from a genuine desire to find out what dance contributions had been made and by whom. And I'm still in the process of doing that. Even after all these years I'm still constantly looking at different things produced by different people.

I recently watched an award-winning thing on Bob Fosse, who I respect a great deal. And I could find things in Bob's work that I saw in acts during the thirties. There were millions of little nightclubs throughout the country in almost every neighborhood, and they all had little chorus lines with four to eight dancers. The numbers were choreographed by people who later became popular as producers and choreographers simply because they were given the opportunity to exercise their creativity.

And when you look at the work by well-known choreographers like Peter Gennaro and Jerome Robbins you see a lot of the moves that were done by those nightclub dancers back in the thirties and forties, and all the way back to the twenties, in shows like *Shuffle Along*. And most of those black dancers learned on the street, in nightclubs and ballrooms, and at parties; wherever people were getting together socially to have a good time. Generally speaking, they didn't go to technique classes. Of course, a few dancers attended dancing schools when they were growing up, like the Mary Bruce School in Chicago, that I mentioned before, but most parents didn't have enough money to send their kids to those kinds of places. Maggie said when she was growing up in Harlem, she'd see the little girls with their dancing bags walking to class and she wanted to go, too, but her mother just didn't have the money to send her.

Years ago, you could sit up and look at all of the chorus lines, all of the dance steps that they were doing. Eventually somebody would come along and lift one of those combinations out and make a dance out of it, like the Suzie-Q or the boogie-woogie. I think that's how truckin' came about. Now, truckin' could have originally been a step that some choreographer or producer saw a kid doing on the street. Maybe it didn't even have a name at first. On the other hand, some dancer in the chorus could have made it up. Most of the time we couldn't trace exactly where these authentic jazz steps and dances originated. It's clear that they evolved as part of black dance styles. But all we really knew was that they were here!

Take the Charleston, for example. We think it came up from South Carolina with its name intact and was introduced in a Broadway show, *Runnin' Wild*. That's what I was always told. But see, this thing is real complex because of all the interweaving and overlapping that happened. There was so much cross-fertilization from one venue to another—from the street, to the theater, to the dance hall, to the nightclub.

But getting back to what I was saying, chorus girls have been doing those moves for decades; the moonwalk, all of that stuff—done all over the country in chorus lines. All of those little dances came right out of authentic jazz dance and were choreographed for the stage. And like I said before, this kind of dance is partly the foundation of what we call modern jazz dance, which came mainly from a mixture of authentic jazz and ballet, and then you came up with different techniques like the Jack Cole technique and the Bob Fosse technique. Everybody had a concept of how they wanted to combine things. I can also see an influence on modern dance. Even in the work of somebody like Martha Graham. I recognize some of those moves in her dances, except that she gave them a different treatment.

When I put my choreography together for the vocal groups, I was mixing authentic jazz with whatever the street moves were at the time plus different little things from the other techniques that I had observed. The group members might be doing a street thing with the upper body and a cakewalk with the lower body, keeping the legs in front and going to the ball of the foot. But the physical attitude up top was like a now thing, which is basically a different rhythmic pattern. So you're mixing two variations of black dance and it looks like a new creation. But you're not really conscious of it until you break the movement down and realize what you've done.

Sometimes I use takeoffs on the boogie and setups for the boogie, backing up and coming forward. But your sense of direction is very important here because you have to hit the 45-degree angles rather than lateral, north, south, east, and west—the boxy-type things. You use your angles so that the body opens up to different sections of the audience. The change of direction automatically makes the body dance! You don't have to think about it. And it's all guided by the position of the foot. Where you turn your foot is where the body will follow when you finally arrive at the spot that you want to go to.

When I point those things out to students at the dance festivals, it simplifies their understanding of vocal choreography technique. In many cases, choreographers either don't take the time to do this or they are not knowledgeable enough to know how they're getting to where they're going themselves. Because a lot of choreographers find it difficult to break things down and keep them in context. They can get up and do the hell out of the moves, but when they start teaching what they've done, it's another story. They lose something when they tear the rhythmic pattern apart. That's why some of your greatest dancers cannot be good choreographers or teachers because it's about transmitting what your knowledge is to the people you're working with.

I wish the young artists out there now had more mentors to fine-tune them for the business, but so much has changed in terms of presentation and all the rest. The type of music that's out there now makes it easy to do dance movements and sing because vocal quality is for the birds! I mean, nobody is listening to singing quality, so it doesn't really matter whether you have a lot of breath or not. The tunes the older groups sang were more melodic, and you had to sustain notes, you had the passing tones. This is generally true except for groups like New Edition or Boyz II Men, who are primarily youthful copies of the Temptations. The Temps are their idols. But they do very little choreography. They need help in that area, but they haven't gotten around to realizing it yet.

Most of these groups hit a plateau and they just stay there unless they get help. And with that help you can develop longevity. Back in the fifties most of the groups were happy to just be making a record. First you come on, you're a bunch of singers off the corner, singing under the stairways, out under the streetlights. There was no finesse, no sense of continuity as far as show business was concerned. Those who lasted got help. They didn't do it by themselves. And they learned how to make it without necessarily having hit records. That's why I was at Motown—that's what the company president wanted.

12

BLACK AND BLUE

In the early eighties, 1983 to be exact, I hooked up with Motown again for the documentary celebration of their twenty-fifth anniversary. We had the show in L.A., where it was taped, then edited for video and later aired on television. It was designed to be a two-hour documentary that would recognize many of the people who helped make the company a success. They laid out a nice little piece of business for me with Smokey Robinson. I sat in the audience while Smokey set the thing up on stage, then he said, "There's Cholly Atkins right down there. Come on up here, Cholly." And I went up on stage and we got to talking about how we had worked together and what it was like coaching the different acts. I teased him about his dancing. Told him how grateful I was that he was the *lead* singer! Then he asked me something about who I thought was top-drawer today, and I said, "The two groups that we're about to introduce now. Individually they're exceptionally powerful, and collectively they're super-powerful. So let's say hello to the Temptations and Four Tops!" It was that kind of thing.

I really enjoyed doing it, but they cut all of that out during the editing. So, actually I didn't appear in the documentary at all. I don't believe I was even mentioned, but I was paid. They apologized. Called me four hours before the show was aired to let me know. I'll never forget that day . . . I had a feeling about it when the phone rang. I told Maye, "I guess they cut me out of the show." She said, "Oh, Charles, no. No!" And sure enough that was the message. It was a heartbreaker. We just sat there on the couch for a while and held hands.

And what was so painful about it was that they aired people like Adam Ant, who didn't even have a record on the Motown label. But that's corporations for you. What can you do? There's just no room for fair-mindedness in those big companies because the people putting those types of things together don't care what's left on the cutting-room floor. Suzanne de Passe, the executive director, was very sorry about it. She kept saying that she hoped I wouldn't hate her for it. But, see, things like that have happened a lot, but I don't hate anybody because I pray on that. I pray to God every night that I won't have that kind of feeling in my heart.

One of the highlights of the eighties was the Olympic Arts Festival when I got a tap award with Honi. This was a huge affair, the cultural component of the 1984 Summer Olympic Games. They had a slew of performances. There were companies from eighty-seven different countries. Bella Lewitzky directed the festival and she insisted that American tap be included so that future audiences would know about the roots of dance in this country.

I was coming into L.A. from Reno at the time. Honi didn't know anything about it. They were trying to surprise him, so they hid me in my room just in case he was wandering around the hotel. Then LeRoy Myers took me out to lunch. When they were sure Honi had left the hotel, I snuck back in. That night when he was on stage talking to Brock Peters about *Camera Three*, a TV show we did with Marshall Stearns in the sixties, I walked on. "No, man, you're not telling the guy right. See, you don't even remember how it happened." Honi said, "Aw, you turkey. Who brought you down here, man?"

We talked a little about *Camera Three*, and Brock was saying that they had one segment from it, which was our soft-shoe. Then Honi says, "It went something like this. Cholly let's go." And we danced on off the stage just as the film started. Brock and his wife, Didi, did a wonderful job of putting that tap component together and they also wrote a real informative piece on the history of American tap dance for the program booklet. It was based mainly on Marshall and Jean's book.

But that was a very nice thing down there at the Olympics. A real nice reunion. Each night they honored one of the "Tap Olympians." July 30 was Coles and Atkins, the thirty-first was Peg Leg Bates, the Four Step Brothers were August 1, John Bubbles was August 2, and the Nicholas Brothers were August 3. Honi and I were in real good company! I hung out with the Copasetics. All of those guys were there and a whole lot of other tap people: Skip Cunningham, Leonard Reed, Leon Collins, Frances Nealy, Jonelle Allen.

Jonelle had been my little student back in the fifties. When she was seven, I choreographed a piece for her with Sammy Davis when he had a spot on the *Walter Winchell Show*. Sammy wanted to do a Bill Robinson thing with a little black boy, in suits and derby hats like Uncle Bo wore. Since he was in the Broadway show *Mr. Wonderful* and very busy, he said, "Cholly, you find a little boy, teach him the routine, then I'll come in and learn it for the show."

So I was searching around, and I couldn't find a little boy. I went to Sammy and I said, "Look, man, I've checked all around and I can't find no little boy who can do this thing with you. But I've got an idea. I've got a cute little girl I'm working with now who can *dance*, man. I can dress her up as a boy, and put her hair up, and when you finish she could take off her derby and let her hair fall down. You'll have an element of surprise there." He said, "Great idea! Go to work on it. Call me when you've got the routine all set and I'll come up and learn it."

Which I did. We only needed about a chorus-and-a-half—the stock Bill Robinson steps—like the things the Copasetics did. It took me about a day to teach it to Jonelle, because she was quick. So Sammy came over one afternoon and nailed it down. Then they did the show and it was sensational.

That was right before Honi and I went on tour with Pearl Bailey. I remember it was around the same time I worked with Gregory and Maurice Hines. Their mother, Alma Hines, brought the two boys to my studio and asked me to choreograph their first professional act. See, their father, Chink, knew about Coles and Atkins and I guess he wanted a similar kind of thing for his sons. It took me about six months to get them ready to tour.

After the '84 Olympic Arts Festival, I worked with a group that I know you've never heard of—Process and the Doo Rags! Rick James was producing them and he wanted them to have the old Temptations look. So I worked with the guys in Buffalo for about three weeks. That was an excellent group, good talent, but something happened with their management and I never heard from them again. Also, in '84 I started working with the Manhattans: Gerald Alston, Winfred "Blue" Lovett, Kenny Kelly, and Sonny Bivins. Even though they were already very successful as singers, they wanted to move the group to a higher level. So I was hired as their first choreographer. We spent some great sessions together and they definitely took care of business. When we finished up, it was back to Gladys and the Pips. I always sound like I'm repeating myself! Either the Temps or the Pips or the Jays . . . were there no other people?

I don't think I ever told you about that movie I did in '87, called *Tapeheads*. The way I got this gig was through Don Cornelius, from *Soul Train*, because he was one of the guest artists in the film. The story was about a couple of young white guys who wanted to become video producers. I think they called themselves the Video Aces. They were fans of two sixties rhythm-and-blues singers, played by Junior Walker and Sam Moore of Sam and Dave. When the Video Aces hit it big, they decided to sponsor these guys and make them big stars.

That's where I fit in. See, my job was to do the choreography for Junior and Sam and a group of girls who were their backup singers. Junior I knew very well. I had met Sam and Dave years before when I staged a show for Aretha Franklin, but I hadn't spent much time with them. Between dates with my regular clients, they'd have me come down to L.A. Unfortunately *Tapeheads* never hit the movie theaters; there was some kind of problem with distribution. But it eventually came out in video.

Right after that I wanted to stick close to home because Maye had just gone through a hip operation. So it was a good thing when I got a directing job with Robert Guillaume because we were able to start rehearsals in Vegas, then move to L.A., where Robert lived. He was putting together a new show to take on a concert tour. I had worked with him once before when he and Gladys did a duet on his show, *Benson*.

This directing assignment was really a fun project. We had a wonderful setup and great communication. Tex Richardson was the musical director; he was a pianist, vocal coach, singer—great talent. Tex happened to be working in Vegas, so in the beginning he'd come up to my house with Robert to format the show and select the material.

We had backup singers, two of the Jones Girls, a singer from Atlanta, and Robert's son. There were a lot of little specialty production numbers where they had to do lines with Robert, and on days when he was busy, Tex would work with the singers on vocals in the morning and I'd work with them on choreography in the afternoon. When he had them, I took the tapes and worked on choreography, and when I had them, he worked on musical arrangements. We had it all laid out.

Robert had a little estate-like, with tennis courts, a big Olympic swimming pool—a lovely house. There was a huge living room with a grand piano. That's where he worked with Tex on his vocal thing and I would be working with the backup group in the guest house. I did a little choreography for him; not too much because of the type of material and his sound and everything, but he was dying to get in on the dancing. I had a lot of fun with that cat.

He'd say, "Hey, man, when you gonna work with me? You're not spending time on my choreography." I told him, "You're not in this part." "Aw, man, why can't I do something in there?" I said, "It won't look right. Now, you gonna let me do this, man, or do you want to get somebody from NBC to do it?" "No, you got it! Call me if you need me." I told him, "I need you to take us out to lunch!" He said, "See! See! You need me!"

This wasn't a jazz show, but a variety show. We did top-forty tunes and situation things. I went crazy in this one. I did an old thing that Nat Cole used to sing called "Calypso Blues," in conjunction with "Sitting on the Dock of the Bay." The background singers were dressed in colorful things, little straw hats. I designed the costumes, too. Spent hours on this piece. As the lights faded out on the background singers doing "Sitting on the Dock of the Bay," Robert made his entrance.

Then there was silence . . . the lights continued to fade out. Next you heard a conga, BUP-A-DUP, real soft, then it got louder, and over on this side of the stage, in the distance, you could see this guy walking with a white shirt on and rolled up black trousers, and his shirt open, you know. This whole "Calypso Blues" was done with just one conga; no other musical accompaniment. It went, "Sitting by the river, me heart's a pierced so sad. Don't got the money to take me back to Trin-i-dad. Whoo-whoo, I should feel so sad." Boy, it was a great number!

And the ending was so surprising; caught the audience complete-ly off guard, because they were in such a mood. But I knew it would create that feeling. We let the music die out and Robert's walking in the distance, and there are no lights, just this spotlight that followed him and faded. And the last thing you heard was BAP-A-DIP, BOP-BOO. . . . And for, say, five seconds there was nothing, there was per-fect silence, and then it dawned on the audience that that's where he had taken them. Then they started to applaud, and they applauded, and applauded. Then the house lights came up, so everybody started standing and applauding.

That was the type of thing we were doing. But the tour didn't pan out too well because he had the wrong people booking it. We were playing stadiums and coliseums. It was ridiculous. We should have been playing Philadelphia's Shubert Theater or the Pantages in Los Angeles, the Fisher in Detroit, and the Palace in Cleveland. These are all legitimate houses. The type of people who were familiar with Robert Guillaume wouldn't be going to the stadiums. The whole thing was out of whack. But, like I said, it was a whole lot of fun.

Big opportunities to direct like that have been some of the highlights of my career. And I'm very proud of them. Robert's show and *Red, Hot and Foxy*, I'm especially proud of. I liked what I did. Although I've di-rected shows for the Temps, the Pips, and the Jays, that's another kind of directing. It's not as extensive, but it's still very fulfilling.

I also liked what I did with solo artists like Shirley Jones. There were backup singers like we had in the Robert Guillaume project and we did short vocal skits. I remember one scene with just a guitar player. Shirley talked a little in the beginning, while he was put into position in the blackout. The musician sat on a stool beside her, but we were using what you call a block spotlight, a square, and it was just on the fret of his guitar.

Shirley had told me, "Cholly, these people won't sit still for this." I said, "Girl, the people *will* sit still for it, and you're gonna make them listen to every word and just love it." And that's what happened. But when you gamble like that and it works, you have a real sense of satisfaction and a feeling that your abilities are being appreciated.

Now, with *Black and Blue* in '89, I had a lot of success, but I wasn't necessarily going for the nonconventional thing, I was really trying like crazy to satisfy the producers' visions. In the beginning I wasn't even inclined to take the job because of the time element thing. I was very busy with my vocal choreography clients and I had to protect that because it was my livelihood. I figured *Black and Blue* might not open and if it did, who knew what the critics were going to say? Also, 1988 was the first time I had put tap shoes on my feet since 1965, so when I really thought about it, I said to myself: "'65 to '88! Naw, man, no way in the world I can get involved in no major tap thing. For a Broadway show? You crazy?"

The first time I met with the producers was early March '88, and I wouldn't make any commitments. I remember the date because around that period I started wearing hearing aids, on the advice of my wife. Ol' Sarge was always on my case, "You can't hear! You don't know what's happening! Go get some hearing aids." See, Maye has always been a "take charge" person, which has been a good thing for me in a lot of ways. When we got married, we were too old for that "sweetie pie" stuff, so I started calling her "Sarge," after my first sergeant in the army.

I happened to be working with Mike Mailloux when the *Black and Blue* discussions started. He was putting together an act in Vegas and I was staging a tap thing for him to a Count Basie version of "Cute." Mike said, "Pops, you ought to go ahead on and do this. You don't realize what your ability is. The way you put all that stuff together for the O'Jays and Temps, you could do this. You're doing tap for me." I said, "Yeah, man, but that's different. I mean, I do eight bars, then I sit down, then three bars—that's a different thing."

And Sarge was on my case every day, "Daddy, stop straddling the fence. You can do this. All you have to—" I said, "Well, that ain't it. I'm not in any shape." She said, "Well, get in shape! You've got time. I know you can do it. It'll be great." I told her that they were expecting this to be as great as Coles and Atkins. Sarge said, "Well, not necessarily. But anything you do is going to be in that category." Oh, she was pushing me like mad!

Now, Honi and Dianne Walker were the real instigators behind this Broadway business. Dianne was in the Paris production of the show and Honi knew Héctor Orezzoli and Claudio Segovia, the directors. They had been following him around for the longest, bugging him about doing the show, and he kept saying, "Look, Cholly Atkins is the man! Go get Cholly to do the choreography."

Eventually they saw some footage of Coles and Atkins and they mentioned me at a production meeting. Dianne said, "Cholly Atkins!? Where is he? You've got his phone number? What's he gonna do?" "He's going to do the soft-shoe." She said, "My soft-shoe?" See, Dianne had told them she wasn't going to dance in the New York production. The directors said, "I thought you weren't dancing?" You know how Dianne can give you that look. She said, "Well, maybe I could do one little number."

Immediately she got all excited. Then I get this telephone call. Now keep in mind that I hadn't met the child. She said, "Please, just do this for me." I said, "I don't even know you. I ain't never seen you. You sound pretty good, but I don't know who you are!" She says, "Well, I'm one of your most ardent fans. I've been loving your dancing for a long time." See, now she's going with the flattery thing. Dianne said, "Please, please consider doing this." I told her, "Well, I'll think about it." Mike knew Dianne and everything. He said, "She's a great dancer, man." So they sent me a tape of the Paris show and I picked her out in the chorus.

Finally, I let them talk me into redoing the soft-shoe. I still wasn't too excited about it, but I figured, it's just one little number, a little two-chorus soft-shoe. You can hack it out. Dianne came out to Vegas; Bernard Manners and Ivory Wheeler, the other two dancers, were already here. After we got into rehearsal, I felt better. That first day, they were so elated; we learned about sixteen bars. All they talked about was how much they liked it. That built up my confidence.

Each choreographer for this show was handpicked for his particular style, and individuality was very much a part of what the producers expected from the work. Since Dianne was the assistant choreographer, it was her job to keep a balance between maintaining the commonality of the dance line and allowing for the individuality of the choreographers as well as the individuality of the people performing the choreography. And, believe me, that was a major challenge.

But "Memories of You" was loads of fun. I made new friends, and we all loved each other. It was a wonderful experience. So they didn't have too much difficulty convincing me to redo "After You've Gone." Then I agreed to choreograph "I'm Confessin.'" Rehearsing that piece was disastrous at first because it was hard to understand exactly what Héctor and Claudio wanted. They sent me a tape of the Five Blazers doing a one-man dance in 1929 with Duke Ellington's band and a tape of Josephine Baker dancing. They wanted a combination of the two. I looked at Dianne, "What do you do here?" She said, "Don't ask me."

I couldn't really get the connection there and they couldn't explain it. So I lost a lot of sleep trying to figure that one out. Finally I told them, "Draw me some pictures of the kind of moves you want the guys to do." So they gave me twenty-three story cards with the positions and all. And what they were trying to say was that they wanted the girl to *look* like Josephine Baker, but they wanted the guys dancing around like a one-man dance thing. Once I understood, it worked out fine.

Then they gave me permission to inject a vocal for the dancing boys, which they weren't too cool on at first. I told them, "Look, this will give the number a lift in the center. It's just a matter of another chorus." Héctor said, "No, those boys must not sing. They are a horror!" I said, "But I've worked a lot with people who have no voice quality, but are exceptionally successful. I can make these guys sell the song!" They were still reluctant, but when they heard it, they agreed that it would work. "I'm Confessin'" turned out to be one of the most tender, loving numbers in the show.

The dancers in all three pieces were great. The only problem I had was in "After You've Gone." That was a little bit more energetic than what they had been doing on it. There were a lot of legs and sound and motion with the arms, because it had a lot of shadow stuff in there. What I mean is the dancers looked like silhouettes. We achieved that by using a lot of back lighting and no front lighting. But the producers wanted to also hear it . . . hear good taps, then see good body movement. So combining those two things was a little rough on the guys, physically, until they got it down to where they could master it.

Black and Blue had so many wonderful dancers: Bunny Briggs, Jimmy Slyde, Lon Chaney, Ralph Brown. The other thing that was so great about the show was that it gave a number of black youngsters the kind of exposure to tap that we had growing up. Dianne told me that when Savion went to Paris with the first show, he was more or less a Broadway-style dancer. But while he was there he hung out and jammed with the masters of rhythm tap. She said he lived, breathed, ate, slept tap for six months. That situation just doesn't exist anymore. The young people now can read about it, but to live it is a different kind of thing. So Savion had an incredible experience, a crash course that met every day for half a year.

Then when they came back to New York, the reason for adding the other children was not so much because they needed more people in the show, but because it gave other black kids that exposure. And Dianne was really the one responsible for that because she was the assistant choreographer and the person casting the dancers. For example, when Danny Wooten was hired, some of the powers were in their offices saying, "We don't need another kid!" And Dianne just said, "I like Danny. We'll bring him in." At the audition she could see that he was hungry for this. He just wanted to tap dance. And Héctor was for it, too. His thinking was, "Yeah, bring Danny. Get Danny in here and let him get some experience because this might not happen again."

When we finished straightening out all the kinks, I was tickled to death with the results of my three numbers and real happy for the other choreographers, because their things were very wonderful. Somewhere in there I flew to L.A. for a photo session with them: Fayard Nicholas, Frankie Manning, and Henry LeTang. We got together again when the Tonys were held in '89. That's when Maye and I flew into New York and spent two days with Honi and Maggie.

The award for *Black and Blue* came as a complete surprise to all of the choreographers. I hadn't in a million years even dreamed we'd win "best choreography" when I started out. Right up until the night it was announced, I was skeptical, even though a lot of people were saying that we were front-runners. The other shock was that Héctor and Claudio selected me to make the acceptance speech. Why? I don't know, because I'm not much of a talker.

I guess since the four of us couldn't dance, sing, or talk at the same time, somebody had to do it! So I thought long and hard about what I would say, but one of the things that was uppermost in my mind was a few words of appreciation to Dianne Walker. Really, she should have received a Tony, too. Not only did she work along with us on every number, but after the show started running she was completely in charge of my dances, Frankie's, and Fayard's. During the entire run of two years, she held the choreography together, kept it sharp, and maintained the integrity of the pieces. We were all very grateful to her.

Unfortunately, *Black and Blue* didn't run as long as it should have. This show was an upbeat, exciting production that had people dancing on the way out. It should have set a record on Broadway, because it was just that good. And, boy, the musicians were cooking! Sir Roland Hanna was on piano, Grady Tate on drums, Al McKibbon on bass, Jerome Richardson on alto sax, Claude Williams on violin. There was trombonist Britt Woodman and guitarist Billy Butler. Haywood Henry and Bill Easly, who played clarinet and sax, had also been in the Paris orchestra. The trumpet section included Virgil Jones, Jake Porter, Emery Thompson, and Stephen Furtaldo. Leonard Oxley was the conductor. For the entire run, we had an all-star lineup with great jazz musicians. Some of them were around during the heyday of tap, so they had a true feeling for what Héctor and Claudio wanted.

November of the same year that I got the Tony, I hit the road with New Kids on the Block. Now that was an interesting project. Their manager, Dick Scott, was at Motown with me. We'd worked together a great deal for quite a while. I was surprised that he was managing a white group and so was everybody else. Each time the kids went to a different city to perform, Dick would walk in and all the theater people would stare, "Well, let me see now. How did this happen?"

But he was hired by Maurice Starr, who had been producer and writer for the New Edition and somehow lost control of the group to MCA. So, he went up to Boston and spent about a year putting New Kids together. Personally I think his intention was to get a group of white kids who could do the same type of choreography and music as the New Edition and tour the country with them because the white kids could go places where the New Edition couldn't. And Maurice was able to pull this off because he knew all those kids in Boston. That's where the New Edition was from. He hand-picked the guys for New Kids, trained them, got a record contract and everything with his own money, and he got Dick to manage them because Dick was very knowledgeable. He had been Berry Gordy's right-hand man. He knew how to put a show together and was very articulate— a college grad.

Dick had the best equipment and three big transport trailer trucks that carried everything. There were all kinds of gimmicks, lasers, moving lights; all computerized. Everything that was new, he had it. And they did a great show; made buckets of money. At every concert there were busloads of little children, six, seven, eight, and nine years old. The biggest places could accommodate eighteen or twenty thousand people.

I came on board to put together a short medley of Smokey Robinson tunes because the group was getting ready for a tribute to Smokey. They were singing "Shop Around," "Mickey's Monkey," and one other tune. So Dick called, asked if I was available and when I could get there. I said, "Yesterday!" He said, "Your ticket is in the mail. We'll set up some kind of schedule so you can spend a few hours in each city working with the guys."

They were adorable and they loved Dick. He was almost like a father to them. Especially to the little one, little Joey. When they were on the road, he'd cuddle up next to Dick and go to sleep. They had such a rough schedule. I'd be demonstrating something, and I'd turn around, and maybe a couple of them would be asleep on the floor. They were just that tired because they traveled by bus. They'd finish a concert, check out of the hotel and get right on the bus, get in their bunks, and go to sleep. Then it was on to another location, because these were mostly one-nighters. I always traveled by plane, so I'd meet them in each city.

Everywhere we went Dick would have a rehearsal space all laid out. We'd go in there in the morning, start working, and I'd have it letter perfect—I was driving them, you see. Then one of them would say, "Pops, please, can you stop now?" I said, "Five minutes, okay?" Then it would take another ten minutes to wake them up, "All right, come on, fellas, we've got to get going; we've only got one more hour." We'd stop at two in the afternoon. They'd sleep, eat, then get on the bus and go to the auditorium or wherever they were performing.

Lots of times, they were the opening act. Then I would run by their dressing room. One of them would grab me, "Come on, Pops, show me this. How did we do that today?" See, they knew about my background because Dick had schooled them, so they appreciated this opportunity. It was just hard on them considering the circumstances. But it was a very nice experience and the show with Smokey went over well. He told them, "If I ever need any more Miracles, I'm going to look you guys up."

In April of '92 I worked with a show for the West Coast chapter of the Ladies Who Danced, all black ex-chorus line dancers who performed during the thirties and forties. The program was really a tribute to Duke Ellington. It was like a charity thing, and dancers came in from all over. I had spent a lot of time in different nightclubs working with many of the dancers who showed up. In fact, three or four of the girls were from

back in Ziggy's days. A few of the Copasetics came out . . . Phace
Roberts and LeRoy Myers. I think Buster came that year, too.

Olivette Miller, Bunny Briggs's wife, and Bob Bailey were doing the
master of ceremonies bit. I was the director of the affair. In other words,
I aligned the whole program and set the music, ran rehearsals . . . everything a director would do. The show turned out great; I kept it tight and
sandwiched the right people in between. Ocie Smith sang. Frances
Nealy danced. She was excellent, too. Bunny danced. He and I kibitzed
back and forth about *Black and Blue*.

At one point I called up all the chorus dancers, the Copasetics, and
all the performers. We did the shim sham, then we had a little challenge. I set up a nice big fat finale. At the end there was social dancing
and everybody was visiting. We really had a ball and it brought back a
lot of good memories. You know I always had a special feeling for the
chorus line dancers.

The early nineties was when I started teaching at tap dance festivals on a regular basis. I was very reluctant at first because I hadn't put
my shoes on since *Black and Blue* and it was a chore to try to get back
in shape. Honi had been on my case for years about doing those kinds
of things because, as you know, he was in the forefront of the tap resurgence. He'd say, "Man, you better come on and do this stuff. There's
a whole lot of tap activity. You should be out here with it."

My initial appearance was at the Portland, Oregon dance festival,
which has become an annual thing for me now. Honi and I were there
together in '91 because we were honored as a class act on the closing
night of the performances—and they gave each of us a plaque. We
had a big party afterward with all the instructors, Dianne Walker,
Sarah Petronio, Savion Glover . . . oh, there were quite a few tap
dancers there. It felt great to be back with Honi. During that period
Susan Pollard was working on a documentary called *Honi Coles: The
Class Act of Tap* and we did some interviews together, took photos,
and did quite a lot of shooting that week. I really treasure that footage
of us together.

The people in Portland are some of the nicest I've met in my whole
career . . . Jan and Dick Corbett, Julie Bond, Melissa Hathaway. Di-

anne did a lot to get me into that circle. She even convinced them to offer a vocal choreography class, which turned out to be a big hit. I showed film clips of Gladys and the Pips and other groups and I choreographed something to one of the old Temptations' tunes. Everybody loved it. They were even doing steps in the lobby of the hotel! The next year, when I went back, I taught tap classes, too. Maye went up with me and she had quite a wonderful time. They really rolled out the red carpet for her.

That was right after I went to the University of Colorado, in Boulder, where I taught vocal choreography and tap at the Mile High Tap Summit. I also choreographed a number for the concert. We had three nights of performances scheduled, and since one act had to leave the festival early, Dianne Walker and I staged a piece called "Remnants of the Four Step Brothers" to round out the show. I took some of the dancers out of the classes and we choreographed a dance for the opening. This was a last-minute thing, so Dianne and I whipped it together to help Marda Kirn, who was director of the festival. It worked out real nice for Marda and she was real grateful—sent me all sorts of notices thanking me.

Also, there was another thing that Dianne and I did at an elementary school for troubled kids—those having emotional problems. And they were so happy about the classes. We went over and showed some tapes, and lectured on both tap and vocal choreography. Then we spent about an hour with the kids in the gymnasium doing steps. Matter of fact, the newspapers covered it.

Dianne and I really enjoyed it because the kids got such a kick out of the dancing and they had a chance to poke fun at each other—the ones who were stumbling and couldn't get into the moves, especially the vocal choreography steps. I was supposed to go back and teach a long class, but I never got a chance.

That Colorado engagement . . . well, the main reason it sticks out in my mind is because that's the last time I worked with Honi. On the final night of the concert, he and I were co-emcees. We did some little bits from our old act—comedy things—and took turns introducing the artists. It was well mapped out.

At the time I wasn't really aware that this would be it for Coles and Atkins. We all knew that Honi was recuperating from an operation, but we didn't know how serious it had been. You couldn't always tell what was happening with him because he was a very proud type of guy who didn't like to complain. See, at first, he didn't even want the operation. I called him and told him, "Man, if there's something in there that's got to be cut out, you got to go on and do it."

But it seemed as if he sensed his condition was much worse than it appeared to the doctors. He said, "Man, I'm tired, Chazz, I been fighting this thing and what the hell, give me a little something to make me feel better and just let me go on out of here." I said, "Man, come on with all that old off-the-wall talk. Cooperate with the doctors. It can't be much worse, baby." He said, "Well, I'll think about it." I told him, "I'm gonna stay on you till you do." Mo said, "Oh Lord, I don't need that! I just have to start hanging up on you." I said, "Well, you just do that, because I'm going to stay on your case."

Then in a couple of days Maggie told me that he'd decided to go on with the operation. Afterward, she implied that he was going to be okay, and I talked with him two or three times a week. It seemed like he was getting better. Then he told me he was coming out to Colorado, so I figured he would have a full recovery. I said, "That's great, man. That'll give us a chance to spend a little time together."

At the festival, Honi was very weak, physically, and in talking with him that last day up there, he said the classes had taken a real toll on him. You know that's a mile high up there and the altitude is rough on you. So I thought that was part of the problem because it was hard for me, too. He said he was going to go on home and rest and he thought he wasn't going to make the next festival, but he told me not to mention it to anybody. Both of us were supposed to go to Portland. But after he got back to New York, he said, "I can't make it Chazz, I'm going to lay here and try to get myself together."

Around that time I heard the true results of the operation. Maggie told me that he had cancer, and it was just a matter of time. When I got back from working with the Temps, I messed around the house two or three days; moping around, praying, walking the floor at night.

Maye said, "Why don't you just go on, get a flight and see him while he's still alive." Now, Honi had told Maggie he didn't want anybody to come by. He wanted to just be there with her. And I wanted to respect that. But I'll always be sorry I waited, because when I got there, he wasn't talking or anything. But he grabbed my hand and he really squeezed it a long time.

That was a real trying period because I was losing not only my ex-partner but my best friend. We had been through so much together and I felt that if I had gone in there sooner, I could have talked with him. But I was so sure Honi knew I was there because he had no strength left when he grabbed my hand. He could hardly raise up his arm to do anything. And for him to put that pressure on my hand, it let me know that he knew I was there. Then after a couple of days, he was gone.

When I got back home after the funeral, the Temps were in Japan and the Jays were touring, so Honi's death really hit me hard then because I didn't have any way to shake the thoughts away. Gradually I've gotten around to being able to deal with it. But even now when I'm compiling clips for the festivals and I look at some of these tapes and think back on our partnership, it's hard. Sometimes I can feel real good about our years together and laugh about them, but deep down inside it's still a great loss.

EPILOGUE

Since the Mile High Tap Summit, I've taught at quite a few tap festivals—Chicago, San Francisco, Las Vegas, St. Louis. During the summer of '98, I did a residency at Jacob's Pillow in Lee, Massachusetts. Along with occasional workshops in colleges and universities and various panels on music and dance, I am still involved in my first love, choreographing for vocal groups. All of my main clients have longevity. I've worked with Gladys Knight for thirty-eight years. She doesn't perform with the Pips anymore, but Bubba occasionally does spot appearances in her concerts. I've been with the Temptations for thirty-seven years and the O'Jays for twenty-seven years. And I've loved working with all of them. I always look forward to it.

Whenever the record company puts a new product out on the Jays, we have to go in the studio and rehearse for about eight weeks, and put a whole new show together for that year's tour. Like the Cadillacs and the Pips, the O'Jays can do just about anything I come up with. Plus, they're willing to put in the time that's necessary to set up a dynamic show.

I'm still into directing. That's the main thing I do with Gladys. They say that most choreographers make good directors. But, really, I just love show business. Even though you have some real rough periods, the wonderful times overshadow the terrible ones. Plus you have the opportunity to see things and do things that you probably wouldn't be exposed to ordinarily. All over the world, you get a chance to meet different people and that's been very rewarding. So all in all I'm very happy with my career because it has given me a chance to bring a lot of joy to a lot of people and to cultivate the talents that I recognize in young artists and help them grow. When you see yourself doing that, it brings a real warm feeling to you. "There, I've made a contribution." And it's pretty bad to live a long life and don't contribute nothing.

But I couldn't have done it without Maye. I feel so blessed that we are together and caring for each other. This is a nice little house we've got here. Shoot, we can roll around this place in wheelchairs! Ain't no stairs or nothin' to climb. And we've got plenty of space. So what the heck, we still have a little fun whenever we feel up to it.

The most important thing is to keep as much of our health together as we've got left. Because when you get older, you're going to find that things begin to happen to you just because you're old! It's nothin' that you did to cause that other than *live*! So, you just have to face it. Bunny said Olivette woke up one morning and told him, "I just can't understand this new pain." Without missing a beat, Bunny says, "But baby, you're just old. That's all. You're just *old*, baby."

People are always asking me when I'm going to retire, but like Duke used to say, "Retire to what?" Show business is a great business. It's really like taking a trip. You get ready, you drive on into the garage and get your car checked out. You pull over to the gas tank and they fill it up. And you roll and roll and roll on down the road, stopping here and there. At times you have to refill your tank. Then you keep going and keep moving until eventually you're going to reach your destination. But you don't stop until you just can't do it anymore. And so far, I've been very fortunate. I can't travel as fast as I used to, but I'm still rolling.

So what else was there you wanted to know about?

Groupography

Vocal Groups

Billy Ward and His Dominoes
Blue Magic
Bobby Taylor and the
    Vancouvers
Cadillacs, The
Carino and the Bow Ties
Chairmen of the Board
Chantels, The
Chiffons, The
Cleftones, The
Contours, The
Cookies, The
Creative Source
Crystals, The
Curtis Mayfield and the
    Impressions
D. C. Drive
Delfonics, The
Dells, The
Delta Rhythm Boys, The
Detroit Emeralds, The

Dixie Cups, The
Dramatics, The
Edsels, The
Eighth Day
Elgins, The
Essex
Fifth Dimension, The
First Choice
Five Keys, The
Five Satins, The
Floaters, The
Four Tops, The
Frankie Lymon and the
    Teenagers
Gladys Knight and the Pips
Graham Central Station
Harptones, The
Heartbeats, The
Honey Cone, The
Hundred Proof
Intruders, The

Jones Girls, The
Little Anthony and the Imperials
Love Committee, The
Manhattan Transfer, The
Manhattans, The
Martha and the Vandellas
Marvelettes, The
Smokey Robinson and the
    Miracles
Moments, The
Monitors, The
Moonglows, The
New Birth
New Kids on the Block
New York City
O'Jays, The
Originals, The
Penguins, The
Phil Moore and His Flock
Process and the Doo Rags
Rare Earth
Regals, The
Ron Townsend and Wild Honey
Ruby and the Romantics
Sha Na Na
Shep and the Limelites
Shirelles, The
Solitaires, The
Soul for Real
Spinners, The
Staple Singers, The
Supremes, The
Sweet Inspirations, The
Sylvers, The
Tavares

Three Degrees, The
Turbans, The
Temptations, The
Undisputed Truth, The
Velvelettes, The
Velvets, The
Vibrations, The

Single Artists

Jerry Butler
Gene Chandler
Sammy Davis, Jr.
Betty Everett
Redd Foxx
Aretha Franklin
Marvin Gaye
Robert Guillaume
Major Harris
Gregory Hines
Chuck Jackson
Millie Jackson
Shirley Jones
Gladys Knight
Frankie Lymon
Freda Payne
Ocie Smith
Tammi Terrell
Ron Townsend
Mary Wells
Kim Weston
Dionne Warwick
Mary Wilson
Stevie Wonder
Betty Wright

Glossary

adagio act: female/male dance act popular during the 1930s and '40s; similar to ballroom dance, with well-defined lifts and poses

applejack: a jazz dance step developed in the 1940s; consists of a series of crossovers with a twist of the body; the dancer steps across on the left foot, then steps on the right foot and twists on the left heel; the twist makes the body execute a quarter turn from side to side; performed in four counts; there are many regional variations of the applejack

authentic jazz dance: indigenous American dance derived from African American street dancing with roots in traditional African cultures; its development paralleled, influenced, and was influenced by the evolution of jazz music; adapted for the stage (during its golden age: 1920s, '30s, and '40s) by black chorus lines and professional dance acts who performed to jazz music; moved in a circular pattern from the street to dance halls, nightclubs, and theaters; referred to by some historians as classic jazz dance; kept alive in such contemporary dance forms as vocal choreography, stepping, and hip-hop

black bottom: social-dance step that became popular in the 1920s; dancer touches the floor with the right hand, followed by the left hand, then touches the buttocks with the right hand, followed by the left hand

boogie-woogie: a jazz dance step introduced in the 1930s; dancer digs the ball of the foot into the floor on one and simultaneously pushes the knee and the hip to the side in a half circle on two; this is repeated to the left side; usually preceded by clapping hands and jumping back four times in succession; pattern: jump-clap jump-clap-jump-clap jump-boogie R-L-R-L

bottle dance: novelty dance; bottles are put on stage and performers dance around them

b.s. chorus: a thirty-two–bar tap routine that consists of the time step, cross step, front wing, trenches, and over the top; the first three steps last for six bars each with a two-bar break after each step; the last two steps are four bars each; sometimes referred to as the national anthem of rhythm tap because every dancer is expected to know it and be able to join a group of dancers on stage at any time and perform it unrehearsed

buck dancer: an affectionate term used by black tap dancers of the 1930s and '40s who performed rhythm tap; buck dancing originally referred to flat-footed dancing executed close to the floor

camel walk: a jazz dance step in which the dancer moves forward in a staggering pattern by keeping one leg straight and placing it in front of the other; at the same time the back leg bends; this step alternates from foot to foot; closely resembles the knock-kneed gait of a camel

challenge: competition between two or more dancers; each dancer takes typically four to eight musical bars to display his or her expertise

class act: term used for tap dance acts of the teens, 1920s, '30s, and '40s that were based on precision, elegant dress, detached coolness, flawless execution, and dignity

Coles stroll: a tap dance developed in the fifties by Charles "Honi" Coles as an easy routine for nondancing singers on the *Perry Como Show*; consists of a thirty-two-bar chorus that begins with a simple walk in a circular path; as the walk progresses, it gradually becomes more syncopated by adding tap accents; near the end of the dance, participants move into a straight line, then finish with intricate footwork; also known among rhythm tap dancers as the walk around

cramp roll: tap term; consists of four beats, toe-toe-heel-heel; when performed rapidly, the beats become a roll; used throughout rhythmic combinations

cross step: crossing one leg over the other

drugged: upset or angry about something; "pissed" off; derivative of the expression, "You a real drag, man." Geneva Smitherman defines a "drag" as "a person who is a damper on the fun, a party, or other activity (Geneva Smitherman, *Black Talk: Words and Phrases from the Hood to the Amen Corner* [Boston: Houghton Mifflin, 1994], 100).

eccentric dancer: employs odd physical positions; "catchall for dancers who have their own non-standard movements and sell themselves on their individual styles" (Marshall Stearns and Jean Stearns, *Jazz Dance: The Story of American Vernacular Dance* [New York: Macmillan, 1968], 232).

exotic dancer: a term used in the 1930s and '40s to describe jazz dancers who used choreographed sensual movements and performed in elaborate, skimpy costumes; also referred to as shake dancers

falling off the log: a jazz step in which the dancers lean the upper body to one side, keeping the weight on that side, then cross the opposite leg behind, keeping the weight in the direction that they're going; moving step

flash act: a formal name for jazz dance that uses acrobatic movements

footlights: old vaudeville term for lights right on the front of the stage

gumbeat: to talk; engage in lively conversation

hoofin': another name for tap dancing; affectionate term used to describe dancers who perform close-to-the-floor steps

jazz tap: a combination of jazz movements with rhythm tap; incorporates jazz body movements along with straight tap technique that focuses on skilled use of the feet; has strong visual appeal, even when the sound of the taps cannot be heard

legomania: eccentric steps that involve kicks and twisting of the legs at the knee and the ankle

Lindy hop: a social dance made popular in Harlem's Savoy Ballroom during the late 1920s; also referred to as the jitterbug

modern dance: a term "coined in the early 1930s by *New York Times* critic John Martin to describe the work of a few pioneers—Martha Graham, Doris Humphrey, Charles Weidman and Helen Tamiris—which he linked to the 'modern' music, art and literature of the time. The tag stuck, although this form of dancing really began at the turn of the century and has grown to encompass a multitude of movement styles" (Ellen Jacob, *Dancing* [New York: Variety Arts, 1993], 125).

modern jazz dance: highly stylized form of jazz dance that combines modern, ballet, and classical East Indian movements with jazz steps derived from African American vernacular dance

one-man dance: a routine performed by a group of two or more dancers moving in a line, one behind the other; the synchronized movement of the dancers gives the appearance that one person is dancing

over the back: first Lindy aerial step; partners link arms back to back, the male partner bends over and the female partner rolls over his back into a standing position; developed by Frankie Manning and Freida Washington in the mid-'30s; first introduced at Harlem's Savoy Ballroom

over the top: tap step; "consists of bending forward, springing up, and bringing each leg, in turn, around from the back and across the front of the other leg . . . giving the impression of elaborate and energetic self-tripping" (Stearns and Stearns, *Jazz Dance*, 190).

paddle and roll: tap term; a series of heel and toe movements from one foot to the other

physical drama: using the body kinesthetically to enhance verbal expression while talking or singing; physical use of the hands, eyes, head, etc.

rhythm tap: a highly syncopated style of American tap dance made popular by John Bubbles; Bubbles's unusual accenting increased the dynamic range of tap; he began dropping his heels, dancing four-to-a-bar, and executing turns and combinations that went beyond eight bars (based on the description in Stearns and Stearns, *Jazz Dance*, 214–17) '**round the world:** an eastern black theater circuit of the 1930s and '40s that included New York, Philadelphia, Baltimore, and Washington

'**round the horn:** black nightclub circuit of the 1930s and '40s that included Buffalo, Cleveland, Pittsburgh, Cincinnati, St. Louis, Chicago, and Detroit

scratch dates: short engagements with minimum pay

shim sham shimmy: a jazz/tap dance originated by Leonard Reed and Willie Bryant in 1927 while on tour with the Whitman Sisters Revue; Reed and Bryant initially called this dance Goofus and performed it as a comic finale that was simple and could be learned easily; by 1931, the dance was being performed as the shim sham shimmy at Connie's Inn by an act called the Three Little Words; this dance was also performed nightly by patrons of the Shim Sham Club, a late-night hangout for artists in show business

soft-shoe: evolved from a minstrel dance called the Essence of Old Virginia; steps are executed in a light and delicate manner; usually performed to a medium tempo with easy, relaxed motion

soubrette: a multitalented chorus girl who could sing and dance and was singled out to do specialty numbers in variety shows of the 1920s through the '40s

stair dance: dancing up and down a set of stairs placed on stage; made popular by Bill "Bojangles" Robinson

stride pose: standing with the feet apart; while in motion, the dancer stops suddenly, jumps into the position with the legs apart, then lands with the feet apart and holds that position

strut: a dance with high kicks; derived from the cakewalk

Suzie-Q: comic step introduced in the mid-1930s; hands are clasped together in front of the body; as the body moves to one side, the foot opposite that side crosses over the alternate foot, then the alternate foot steps out and the pattern is repeated

swing dancing: another term for the Lindy hop

trenches: tap term; moving the feet forward and backward in a series of slides with the torso leaning forward; the weight is alternated from one foot to the other; the arms swing in opposition to the feet

truckin': an eccentric step in which the dancer moves forward by scooting from one foot to the other; dancer starts with the foot in a pigeon-toed position, then turns it out with a sweep; repeated on the left foot; while the feet are moving, the right arm is lifted with a bent elbow, the hand is above the head, and the index finger points upward and shakes; a comic step

vernacular dance (U.S.): indigenous North American dance; throughout this book vernacular "refers to dance performed to the rhythms of African American music: dance that makes those rhythms visible. . . . It derives not from the 'academy,' but from the farms and plantations of the South, slave festivals of the North, levees, urban streets, dance halls, theaters, and cabarets. It is constantly changing. The changes, however, always reflect an evolving tradition and a vital process of cultural production" (Jacqui Malone, *Steppin' on the Blues: The Visible Rhythms of African American Dance* [Urbana: University of Illinois Press, 1996], 2).

vocal choreography: a dance genre designed for singers that takes into account such factors as breathing and use of microphones; introduced by Cholly Atkins in 1950s; based primarily on African American chorus-line dancing of the 1920s, '30s, and '40s

wing: a tap step in which one foot scrapes out and up and is then brought back in time to support the weight of the body; used for rhythmic effect; variations include the saw wing, pendulum wing, rolling wing, double wing, scratch wing, and front wing

Selected Bibliography

BOOKS

Balliett, Whitney. *New York Notes: A Journal of Jazz in the Seventies.* Boston: Houghton Mifflin, 1976.

Basie, Count, with Albert Murray. *Good Morning Blues: The Autobiography of Count Basie.* New York: Random House, 1985.

Bethel, Pepsi. *Authentic Jazz Dance: A Retrospective.* New York: The American Authentic Jazz Dance Theater, 1990.

Betrock, Alan. *Girl Groups: The Story of a Sound.* New York: Delilah Books, 1982.

Barnet, Charlie, with Stanley Dance. *Those Swinging Years: The Autobiography of Charlie Barnet.* Baton Rouge: Louisiana State University Press, 1984.

Calloway, Cab, and Bryant Rollins. *Of Minnie the Moocher and Me.* New York: Crowell, 1976.

Chilton, John. *Who's Who of Jazz: Storyville to Swing Street.* New York: Time Life Records, 1978.

Clayton, Buck, with Nancy Miller Elliott. *Buck Clayton's Jazz World.* New York: Oxford University Press, 1986.

Coles, Honi. "The Dance." *The Apollo Theater Story.* New York: Apollo Operations, 1966.

Cooper, Ralph, with Steve Dougherty. *Amateur Night at the Apollo: Ralph Cooper Presents Five Decades of Great Entertainment.* New York: Harper-Collins, 1990.

Dance, Stanley. *The World of Count Basie.* New York: Scribner's, 1980.

———. *The World of Earl Hines.* New York: Scribner's, 1977.

——. *The World of Swing*. New York: Scribner's, 1974.

Dixon-Stowell, Brenda M. "Dancing in the Dark: The Life and Times of Margot Webb in Aframerican Vaudeville of the Swing Era." Ph.D. diss., New York University, 1981.

Early, Gerald. *One Nation Under a Groove: Motown and American Culture*. Hopewell, N.J.: Ecco Press, 1995.

Eberle, Scott, and Joseph A. Grande. *Second Looks: A Pictorial History of Buffalo and Erie County*. Norfolk, Va.: Donning Company, 1987.

Ellington, Duke. *Music Is My Mistress*. Garden City, N.J.: Doubleday, 1973.

Emery, Lynne Fauley. *Black Dance in the United States from 1619 to 1970*. Palo Alto, Calif.: National Press Books, 1972.

Epstein, Daniel Mark. *Nat King Cole*. New York: Farrar, Straus & Giroux, 1999.

Fletcher, Tom. *One Hundred Years of the Negro in Show Business*. New York: Burdge, 1954.

Fong-Torres, Ben. *The Motown Album*. New York: St. Martin's, 1990.

Fox, Ted. *Showtime at the Apollo*. New York: Holt, Rinehart, and Winston, 1983.

Frank, Rusty. *Tap!: The Greatest Tap Dance Stars and Their Stories, 1900–1955*. New York: Morrow, 1990.

Franklin, Aretha, and David Ritz. *Aretha: From These Roots*. New York: Villard, 1999.

George, Nelson. *Where Did Out Love Go?: The Rise and Fall of the Motown Sound*. New York: St. Martin's, 1985.

Gillespie, Dizzy, with Al Fraser. *To Be or Not to Bop: Memoirs of Dizzy Gillespie*. New York: Doubleday, 1979.

Goldblatt, Burt. *Newport Jazz Festival: The Illustrated History*. New York: Dial, 1977.

Gordy, Berry. *To Be Loved: The Music, the Magic, the Memories of Motown*. New York: Warner, 1994.

Green, Stanley. *Broadway Musicals: Show by Show*. Milwaukee: Hal Leonard Corporation, 1996.

——. *Hollywood Musicals: Year by Year*. Milwaukee: Hal Leonard Corporation, 1990.

Groia, Philip. *They All Sang on the Corner*. Port Jefferson: Phillie Dee Enterprises, 1983.

Harnan, Terry. *African Rhythm American Dance: A Biography of Katherine Dunham*. New York: Knopf, 1974.

Hinton, Milt, and David G. Berger. *Bass Line: The Stories and Photographs of Milt Hinton*. Philadelphia: Temple University Press, 1988.

Hirshey, Gerri. *Nowhere to Run: The Story of Soul Music*. New York: Times Books, 1984.

Kitt, Eartha. *I'm Still Here: Confessions of a Sex Kitten*. New York: Barricade Books, 1991.

Knight, Gladys. *Between Each Line of Pain and Glory: My Life Story*. New York: Hyperion, 1997.

Malone, Jacqui. *Steppin' on the Blues: The Visible Rhythms of African American Dance*. Urbana: University of Illinois Press, 1996.

Miller, Norma, with Evette Jensen. *Swingin' at the Savoy: The Memoir of a Jazz Dancer*. Philadelphia: Temple University Press, 1996.

O'Meally, Robert G. *Lady Day: The Many Faces of Billie Holiday*. New York: Arcade, 1991.

Reeves, Martha, and Mark Bego. *Martha Reeves: Confessions of a Motown Diva*. New York: Hyperion, 1994.

Ritz, David. *Divided Soul: The Life of Marvin Gaye*. New York: McGraw-Hill, 1985.

Robinson, Smokey, with David Ritz. *Smokey: Inside My Life*. New York: McGraw-Hill, 1989.

Robinson, Sugar Ray, with Dave Anderson. *Sugar Ray: The Sugar Ray Robinson Story*. New York: Viking, 1970.

Ross, Diana. *Secrets of a Sparrow: Memoirs*. New York: Villard, 1993.

Sampson, Henry T. *Blacks in Blackface: A Source Book on Early Black Musical Shows*. Metuchen, N.J.: Scarecrow Press, 1980.

Seeger, Mike. *Talking Feet*. Berkeley: North Atlantic Books, 1992.

Shaw, Arnold. *The Rockin' 50's*. New York: Hawthorne Books, 1974.

Shook, Karel. *Elements of Classical Ballet Technique*. New York: Dance Horizons, 1977.

Stearns, Marshall, and Jean Stearns. *Jazz Dance: The Story of American Vernacular Dance*. New York: Macmillan, 1968.

Stewart, Rex. *Jazz Masters of the 30s*. New York: Macmillan, 1972.

Taylor, Marc. *A Touch of Classic Soul: Soul Singers of the Early 1970s*. Jamaica, N.Y.: Aloiv Publishing Company, 1996.

Travis, Dempsey J. *An Autobiography of Black Jazz*. Chicago: Urban Research Institute, 1983.

Tyler, Bruce M. *From Harlem to Hollywood: The Struggle for Racial and Cultural Democracy, 1920–1943*. New York: Garland Publishing, 1992.

Walker, Don. *The Motown Story*. New York: Scribner's, 1985.

Warner, Jay. *The Billboard Book of American Singing Groups: A History, 1940–1990*. New York: Billboard Books, 1992.

Wells, Dicky, and Stanley Dance. *The Night People: Reminiscences of a Jazzman*. Boston: Crescendo, 1971.

Williams, Otis, with Patricia Romanowski. *Temptations*. New York: Putnam, 1988.

Willis, Cheryl. "Tap Dance: Memories and Issues of African-American Women Who Performed between 1930 and 1950." Ph.D. diss., Temple University, 1991.

Wilson, Mary, with Patricia Romanowski. *Supreme Faith: Someday We'll Be Together*. New York: HarperCollins, 1990.

Wilson, Mary, with Patricia Romanowski and Ahrgus Juilliard. *Dreamgirl: My Life as a Supreme*. New York: St. Martin's, 1986.

Woll, Allen. *Dictionary of the Black Theater: Broadway, Off-Broadway, and Selected Harlem Theater*. Westport, Conn.: Greenwood Press, 1983.

Work Projects Administration. *New York: A Guide to the Empire State*. New York: Oxford University Press, 1940.

ARTICLES

Balliett, Whitney. "Musical Events." *The New Yorker*, July 21, 1962, 64, 66, 68.

"Black and Blue: Broadway's Red-Hot Revue." *Ebony*, September 1989, 124–26, 128.

Dance, Stanley. "Music to My Ears: Jazz Is a Summer Festival." *Saturday Review*, August 4, 1962, 16, 47.

Doitch, Katie Maria. "Tap Dancing—A Re-Definition." *New Dance* 29 (Summer 1984): 9–11.

Gibbs, Vernon. "Soul, Man." *Crawdaddy* (July 1974): 16–17.

Green, Theophilus. "An Intimate Look at the New Supremes." *Jet*, February 11, 1971, 56–62.

Hepburn, Dave. "Swinging with the Copasetics." *Sepia*, January 1962, 45–49.

Hill, Luther. "The Regal Story." *Flash*, February 14–March 14, 1950, 10–25.

Huber, Melba. "Tap Talk: For Intellectual Rhythmic Superiors." *Dance Pages* (Spring 1992): 18–19.

Jay, Leticia. "The Wonderful Old-Time Hoofers at Newport." *Dance Magazine* (August 1963): 18–19.

Jenkins, Flo. "How the O'Jays Keep It Together." *Right On!* 4, no. 1 (November 1974): 26–27.

Jones, James T., IV. "Soul of the Queen." *Vanity Fair*, March 1994, 56, 58, 60, 64, 66, 68, 70, 73.

Levin, Marj. "Cholly: One of the Great Ones!" *The Detroiter* (September 1973): 26–27, 44.

Malone, Jacqui. "'Let the Punishment Fit the Crime': The Vocal Choreography of Cholly Atkins." *Dance Research Journal* 20, no. 1 (Summer 1988): 11–18.

Masterson, Danielle. "From the Roaring '20s to the Space Age." *Rhythm and Business* 1, no. 4 (June 1987): 16–19, 36.

Morgenstern, Dan. "Newport: 1962." *Jazz Journal* 15, no. 10 (October 1962): 4–7.

Peters, Brock, and Didi Peters. "Tap Dancin': An American Original." *Performing Arts Magazine: Olympic Arts Festival* (June 1–August 12, 1984): KO–17, 18, 19.

Resnikova, Eva. "Black and Blue on Broadway." *New Criterion* 7, no. 8 (April 1989): 60–66.

Silsbee, Kirk. "The Man Who Taught Motown How to Dance." *Los Angeles Reader*, January 20, 1995, 48.

Simpson, Nathaniel. "The O'Jays: Sweeter Today Than Yesterday." *Inside Gossip and Now Magazine*, August 1978, 26–29.

Sommer, Sally. "Feet Talk to Me!: Tap Dance and How It Got That Way." *Dance Magazine* (September 1988): 56–60.

———. "Hearing Dance, Watching Film." *Dance Scope* 14, no. 3 (1980): 52–62.

Stearns, Marshall. "A Night at the Hoofers Club." Newport Jazz Festival Booklet, July 1963.

Stillman, Deanne, "Cholly Atkins, Dancing Machine." *Rolling Stone*, October 20, 1977, 38.

"The Tap Man." *Mojo* 15 (February 1995): 15.

INTERVIEWS

Allen, Johnny. Interview with Jacqui Malone. Detroit, Michigan, April 29, 1996.

Atkins, Cholly. Interviews with Jacqui Malone. Las Vegas, Nevada, and New York, New York, January 25, 1988 through September 30, 1998.

———. Interviews with Marshall Stearns. New York, New York, November 30, 1959, February 27, 1965.

Atkins, Cholly, and Maye Atkinson. Interviews with Jacqui Malone. Las Vegas, Nevada, June 2, 8, 1991; Washington, D.C., April 30, 1994.

Atkins, Cholly, Honi Coles, and Marion Coles. Interview with Jacqui Malone. East Elmhurst, New York, July 17, 1988.

Atkinson, Charles, II. Interview with Jacqui Malone. Buffalo, New York, November 18, 1997.

Atkinson, Evelyn. Interview with Jacqui Malone. Buffalo, New York, November 18, 1997.

Atkinson, Maye. Interview with Jacqui Malone. Las Vegas, Nevada, March 26, 1993.

Bellson, Louis. Interview with Robert O'Meally. San Jose, California, June 8, 1992.

Brown, Buster. Interview with Jacqui Malone. New York, New York, October 31, 1994.

Carroll, Earl. Interview with Jacqui Malone. New York, New York, September 25, 1991.

Coles, Charles "Honi." Interview with Jacqui Malone. East Elmhurst, New York, January 9, 1988.

———. Interview with Effie Mihopoulus. *Salome: A Literary Dance Magazine*, nos. 44–46, 1986: 15–19.

———. Interviews with Marshall Stearns, New York City, November 15, 1960; July 11, 1965; May 1960.

Coles, Marion. Interview with Jacqui Malone. East Elmhurst, New York, October 28, 1994.

Corbett, Jan. Interview with Jacqui Malone. Portland, Oregon, July 15, 1995.

Edwards, Esther Gordy. Interview with Jacqui Malone. Detroit, Michigan, April 29, 1996.

Franklin, Melvin. Interview with Jacqui Malone. Las Vegas, Nevada, June 6, 1991.

Fuqua, Harvey. Interview with Jacqui Malone. Los Angeles, California, April 5, 1996.

Hathaway, Melissa. Interview with Jacqui Malone. Portland, Oregon, July 15, 1995.

Jones, Pauline. Interview with Jacqui Malone. Los Angeles, California, September 27, 1998.

Jordan, Martha. Interview with Jacqui Malone. Las Vegas, Nevada, September 25, 1998.

Knight, Gladys. Interview with Jacqui Malone. Atlantic City, New Jersey, August 3, 1996.

Knight, Merald "Bubba." Interview with Jacqui Malone. Las Vegas, Nevada, June 7, 1991.

Levert, Eddie. Interview with Jacqui Malone. Las Vegas, Nevada, May 31, 1991.

Manning, Frankie. Interview with Robert Crease. New York, New York, July 22–23, 1992. Jazz Oral History Program, Smithsonian Institution.

Miller, Norma. Interview with Ernie Smith. Bolton Landing, New York, September 23–24, 1992. Jazz Oral History Program, Smithsonian Institution.

———. Interview with Jacqui Malone. Las Vegas, Nevada, July 22, 1996.

Moore, Pete. Interview with Jacqui Malone. Las Vegas, Nevada, July 22, 1996.

Murray, Albert. Interview with Jacqui Malone. New York, New York, May 8, 1993.

Myers, LeRoy. Interview with Jacqui Malone. New York, New York, May 10, 1996.

Peyton, Jimmy. Interview with Jacqui Malone. Las Vegas, Nevada, June 4, 1991.

Reed, Leonard. Interviews with Jacqui Malone. Los Angeles, California, April 4, 7, 1996.

Robinson, LaVaughn. Interview with Jacqui Malone. Boulder, Colorado, June 23, 1987.

Stearns, Jean. Interview with Jacqui Malone. Key West, Florida, July 28, 1996.

Strain, Sammy. Interview with Jacqui Malone. Las Vegas, Nevada, May 31, 1991.

Street, Richard. Interview with Jacqui Malone. Las Vegas, Nevada, June 6, 1991.

Tyson, Ron. Interview with Jacqui Malone. Las Vegas, Nevada, June 6, 1991.

Williams, Otis. Interview with Jacqui Malone. Las Vegas, Nevada, June 6, 1991.

Williams, Walter. Interview with Jacqui Malone. Las Vegas, Nevada, June 1, 1991.

Wilson, Mary. Interview with Jacqui Malone. New York, New York, July 24, 1996.

Wood, Bertye Lou. Interview with Jacqui Malone. New York, New York, March 14, 1996.

PANEL PROCEEDINGS

"*Black and Blue*: Cholly Atkins and Dianne Walker." Colorado Dance Festival, University of Colorado, Boulder, Colorado, June 1992.

"Heritage Series." Colorado Dance Festival, University of Colorado, Boulder, Colorado, 6, 7, 8 July 1992.

"From Tap to R & B: Celebrating Choreographer Cholly Atkins." Hirshhorn Museum, Smithsonian Institution, Washington, D.C., April 30, 1994.

"Jazz Talk: Jazz Music in Motion." *Jazz at Lincoln Center*, Stanley Kaplan Penthouse, Lincoln Center, New York, New York, November 8, 1994.

"Just Scratchin' the Surface: How Tap Was Viewed." Colorado Dance Festival, University of Colorado, Boulder, Colorado, June 27, 1987.

"Lady Be Good: Women in Tap." Colorado Dance Festival, University of Colorado, Boulder, Colorado, June 27, 1987.

"Rhythm Business Panel: Living Legends." Colorado Dance Festival, University of Colorado, Boulder, Colorado, July 10, 1992.

"Rhythm Business: Educating the Ear." Colorado Dance Festival, University of Colorado, Boulder, Colorado, June 20, 1987.

"Travellin' Light: The Art of Improvisation." Colorado Dance Festival, University of Colorado, Boulder, Colorado, June 28, 1987.

VIDEO RECORDINGS

Bennett, Stephanie, and Steve Alpert. *Girl Groups*. MGM/UA Home Entertainment Group, 1983.

Blackwood, Christian. *Tapdancin'*. New York: Blackwood Films Release, 1980.

Cranstoun, Bryony. *The Temptations Get Ready*. Picture Music International, UFA Video and Media (UK), 1988.

Cromwell, Art. *Watch Me Move!* Los Angeles: KCET, 1986.

de Passe, Suzanne. *Motown 40: The Music Is Forever*. West Grand Media, 1998.

Gallagher, Dan. *Over the Top to Bebop*. New York: Camera Three, WCBS-TV, 1965.

Glucksman, E. M. *Hi De Ho*. All American News, Inc., Hollywood Select Video, Inc., 1947.

Goldwyn, Samuel. *Strike Me Pink*. New York: HBO Home Video, 1936.

Hancock, Bill. *Jazz Hoofer*. Rhapsody Films, 1986.

Henry, Bob. *Gladys Knight and the Pips*. Bob Henry Productions, Perfection in Performance, and NBC, June 23, 1975.

Horn, David. *Black and Blue*. Japan Satellite Broadcasting, Inc., and Reiss Media Productions, with WNET, 1991.

Kodish, Debora, Barry Dornfeld, and Germaine Ingram. *Plenty of Good Women Dancers*. Philadelphia, Penn.: Philadelphia Folklore Project, 1997.

McCarthy, Peter. *Tapeheads*. Pacific Arts Pictures and National Broadcasting Company, Inc., 1988.

Mann, Ron. *Twist*. Toronto: Sphinx Productions, 1992.

Marshal, Neal, Susan Solomon, and Marty Callner. *Gladys Knight and the Pips and Ray Charles*. Home Box Office/Televisa International Production, Vestron Video, 1984.

Mischer, Don, and Buz Kohan. *Motown 25: Yesterday, Today, Forever*. MGM/UA Home Video, 1983.

Montgomery, Patrick. *Rock and Roll: The Early Days*. RCA/Columbia Pictures Home Video, 1985.

Nierenberg, George T. *About Tap*. Santa Monica, Calif.: Direct Cinema Limited, 1985.

——. *No Maps on My Taps*. Santa Monica, Calif.: Direct Cinema Limited, 1979.

Paige, George. *The Temptations and Four Tops*. MSS, Inc., Fries Home Video, 1989.

Pollard, Susan. *Honi Coles: The Class Act of Tap*. Portland, Oregon: Swenson Company, 1994.

Savin, Lee, and Phil Spector. *That Was Rock: The T.A.M.I./T.N.T. Show*. Media Home Entertainment, 1984.

Selby, Margaret. *Everybody Dance Now*. New York: PBS Great Performances, WNET, 1991.

Index